Praise for Raising Capital For Dummies

"While locating capital has never been a particularly easy proposition, it has become more difficult over the past couple of years. Since the dot-com implosion, it appears more and more early-stage, start-up companies are looking for cash in all the wrong places — with nothing to show for their efforts except a tattered Rolodex and frustrations.

"Fortunately, you now have a new weapon in your arsenal: *Raising Capital For Dummies*. Joe Bartlett and Peter Economy have put together a common-sense guide on how to look for capital in the right places. With the benefit of Bartlett's many years of hands-on experience, *Raising Capital For Dummies* will point you in the right direction. This book is a winner — the sooner you get a copy, the sooner you will get a fair shot at finding and raising the capital you need."

> — Richard Harroch, CEO, Law Commerce, Inc.

"Finally, a book that demystifies venture capital. Joe Bartlett, a legendary venture capital lawyer, offers the first practical and realistic road map to guide entrepreneurs through the maze of financial options and strategic opportunities."

> — Francine Sommers, CEO, Oculus Media, Inc.

"Joe's insights into venture capital financing have been a valuable resource to me for the past twenty years."

> — Andrew Ziolkowski, Managing Director, Forest Street Capital, LLC and SAE Ventures

Raising Capital
FOR
DUMMIES®

Raising Capital
FOR
DUMMIES®

by Joseph W. Bartlett and Peter Economy

Wiley Publishing, Inc.

Best-Selling Books • Digital Downloads • e-Books • Answer Networks • e-Newsletters • Branded Web Sites • e-Learning

Raising Capital For Dummies®

Published by
Wiley Publishing, Inc.
909 Third Avenue
New York, NY 10022
www.wiley.com

Copyright © 2002 by Wiley Publishing, Inc., Indianapolis, Indiana

Published by Wiley Publishing, Inc., Indianapolis, Indiana

Published simultaneously in Canada

For general information on our other products and services or to obtain technical support, please contact our Customer Care Department within the U.S. at 800-762-2974, outside the U.S. at 317-572-3993, or fax 317-572-4002.

Wiley also publishes its books in a variety of electronic formats. Some content that appears in print may not be available in electronic books.

Library of Congress Control Number: 2001092063

ISBN: 0-7645-5353-4

Printed in the United States of America

10 9 8 7 6 5 4 3 2

1B/RX/QX/QS/IN

Wiley Publishing, Inc. is a trademark of Wiley Publishing, Inc.

About the Authors

Joseph Bartlett: Mr. Bartlett is a partner at the New York law firm of Morrison & Foerster, LLP. He is an adjunct professor at New York University School of Law and an expert in (among other things) venture capital. He has published numerous articles and books, including three textbooks about venture capital: *Fundamentals of Venture Capital*, (Aspen, 2000); *Equity Finance: Venture Capital, Buyouts, Restructurings and Reorganizations*, (Aspen 1995, Supps. 1996-1999); *Corporate Restructurings: Reorganizations and Buyouts*, (Wiley 1991; Supps. 1992, 1993); *Venture Capital: Law, Business Strategies and Investment Planning*, (Wiley 1989; Supps. 1990-1994). He also authored *The Law Business: A Tired Monopoly* (Rothman, 1982).

A former undersecretary of commerce, law clerk to Chief Justice Earl Warren and president of the Boston Bar Association, Mr. Bartlett graduated from Stanford Law School, where he was president of the *Law Review*. He's been an acting professor of law at Stanford and an instructor in law at Boston University Law School. He's been profiled in trade publications as one of the leading practitioners in venture capital nationwide and served as counsel, director, and shareholder, with a number of development-stage companies during his 35 years in the venture capital business. Mr. Bartlett is a member of the Council on Foreign Relations, the board of trustees and executive committee of Montefiore Medical Center, and director of Simon Holdings. Mr. Bartlett is admitted to the bar in New York, Massachusetts, and Washington, D.C. (www.vcexperts.com)

Peter Economy: Mr. Economy is associate editor of the Drucker Foundation's award-winning magazine, *Leader to Leader*, and coauthor of *The Complete MBA For Dummies* with Kathleen Allen, *Home-Based Business For Dummies* with Paul and Sarah Edwards, *Managing For Dummies* and *Consulting For Dummies* with Bob Nelson, *Leadership Ensemble: Lessons in Collaborative Management from the World's Only Conductorless Orchestra*, with Harvey Seifter, *Enterprising Nonprofits: A Toolkit for Social Entrepreneurs* with Greg Dees and Jed Emerson, and *At the Helm: Business Lessons for Navigating Rough Waters* with Peter Isler (coauthor of *Sailing For Dummies*). Peter combines his writing experience with more than 15 years of hands-on management experience. He received his bachelor's degree in economics from Stanford University and is pursuing his MBA at the Edinburgh Business School. (www.petereconomy.com)

Dedication

To the intrepid entrepreneurs and businesspeople everywhere who take risks and drive our economy to new heights.

Acknowledgments

We'd like to give our sincere thanks and appreciation to our talented publishing team at Wiley, particularly Mark Butler, Marcia Johnson, Pam Mourouzis, and E. Neil Johnson. We'd also like to thank Pat Boyce, the people at VC Experts, including Ross Barrett, Rich Chinitz and Umut Kolcuoglu, for their help in putting these materials together, Jeffrey Marcus, Bruce Elwood Johnson, Mark Joachim, and Joe's partners and associates at Morrison & Foerster for their technical expertise and contributions, and a very specific and heartfelt thanks to Joe's special assistant, Joan Taylor, for her help in organizing the material.

A special thanks to John Hempill, partner in the Morrison & Foerster, New York office, specializing in corporate finance transactions, for his excellent comments on Chapters 10 and 15. Mr. Hempill has been counsel to issuers, underwriters, and selling shareholders in public offerings, including initial public offerings of new media and Internet-related companies. Mr. Hempill has experience in acquisitions for public and private companies in a variety of industries.

Publisher's Acknowledgments

We're proud of this book; please send us your comments through our Dummies Online Registration Form located at www.dummies.com.

Some of the people who helped bring this book to market include the following:

Acquisitions, Editorial, and Media Development

Project Editor: Marcia L. Johnson

Senior Acquisitions Editor: Mark Butler

Copy Editor: E. Neil Johnson

Acquisitions Coordinator: Lauren Cundiff

Technical Editor: Pat Boyce

Editorial Manager: Pamela Mourouzis

Editorial Assistant: Nivea C. Strickland

Cover Photos: © Stockbyte

Production

Project Coordinator: Dale White

Layout and Graphics: Scott Bristol, Joyce Haughey, LeAndra Johnson, Jackie Nicholas, Barry Offringa, Betty Schulte, Mary J. Virgin

Proofreader: TECHBOOKS Production Services

Indexer: TECHBOOKS Production Services

Publishing and Editorial for Consumer Dummies

Diane Graves Steele, Vice President and Publisher, Consumer Dummies

Joyce Pepple, Acquisitions Director, Consumer Dummies

Kristin A. Cocks, Product Development Director, Consumer Dummies

Michael Spring, Vice President and Publisher, Travel

Suzanne Jannetta, Editorial Director, Travel

Publishing for Technology Dummies

Andy Cummings, Acquisitions Director

Composition Services

Gerry Fahey, Executive Director of Production Services

Debbie Stailey, Director of Composition Services

Contents at a Glance

Cartoons at a Glance

By Rich Tennant

The 5th Wave — By Rich Tennant

" The next time we get an additional round of funding, don't say anything. You're lucky I convinced them 'Ka-Ching, Ka-Ching!' was Swahili for Thank you, Thank you!"

page 259

The 5th Wave — By Rich Tennant

" The SBA called. Based on the quality of our Strategic Development Plan, we might qualify for a low-interest Disaster Loan."

page 205

The 5th Wave — By Rich Tennant

"The investors liked our business plan — particularly the in-depth assessment of our competition, which is who they've decided to invest with."

page 81

The 5th Wave — By Rich Tennant

"So ... how did our first-stage financing go today?"

page 7

Cartoon Information:
Fax: 978-546-7747
E-Mail: richtennant@the5thwave.com
World Wide Web: www.the5thwave.com

Table of Contents

Part II: Second-Stage Financing: Expansion 81

Introduction

Capital — specifically capital in the form of cash — is the lifeblood of any business. New businesses need capital to pay the deposits required to rent office or manufacturing space and to pay newly hired employees, and established businesses need capital to grow, to develop new products and services, and to provide a return to shareholders. Not only that, but owners who've risked their own personal capital to create successful and thriving businesses understandably want to be rewarded, naturally, in the form of cash for their many years of hard work and perseverance.

And if you've been in business for any time at all, you'll know that money truly doesn't grow on trees. Raising capital is no easy task, and it's a task that once started, is never ending. While a million-dollar line of credit with your bank may be sufficient for your needs this year, next year you may need twice that amount. You can never have too much cash and, more often than not, you probably won't have as much as you'd like.

As you browse through this book, keep one thing in mind: An ultimate best way to raise capital for your business doesn't exist. Indeed, you'll soon discover many, many different ways to raise capital, and the ultimate success of each approach for your business depends on a variety of factors, including the nature of your business, total annual revenues, profitability, credit history, your industry, the ability of founders and top executives to create a compelling opportunity for potential investors, and much more. Most successful businesses take a variety of different approaches to raising capital, and they fulfill their needs from more than one source.

This book provides you with the best ideas, concepts, and tools for raising capital — from the tried-and-true to the cutting edge. Apply them, and we're sure that you'll see a noticeable difference in your everyday business dealings — a difference that will make you and your business partners even more successful than you already are.

About This Book

Raising Capital For Dummies is full of useful information and tips that can be used by anyone hoping to raise the money that his or her business needs to grow and thrive. Your current level of financial experience (or lack thereof) doesn't matter. You won't have to have a master's degree in finance, or be a certified public accountant, or even have a rich aunt or uncle to help you out — although that wouldn't be such a bad thing. We'll provide you with an easy-to-understand road map to today's more effective techniques and strategies for raising capital for your business.

The good news is that the information you'll find within the covers of this book is firmly grounded in the *real* world. This book is *not* an abstract collection of theoretical mumbo-jumbo that sounds good but doesn't work when you put it to the test. No, we have culled the *best* information, the *best* strategies, and the *best* techniques — the same ones used in today's more successful businesses. This book is a toolbox full of *solutions* to all your financial questions and problems — all you have to do is put it to work!

And although *Raising Capital For Dummies* is overflowing with useful advice and information, it is presented in a fun, easy-to-access format:

First, this book is a guide to everything that you can possibly need to know about raising capital for your business — whether you're just starting your business and looking for *seed* capital to launch your first product, or your business is well established and you need a shot in the arm to fund a major expansion into a foreign market. What? You've never had to figure out an internal rate of return or net present value before? No problem. We'll show you how. Whatever your question may be, chances are we've already answered it somewhere between these bright yellow covers.

Second, this book is easy to access. What good is all the information in the world if you can't get to it quickly and easily? Have no fear. This book is designed with you, the reader, in mind. Here's how to get to the precise information you seek:

- If you want to find out about a specific area, such as how to find angel investors, or how to get a Small Business Administration (SBA) loan, or what investment bankers can (or can't) do for your business, you can check out the table of contents or the index and quickly flip to the section that covers the answers you're looking for. Faster than you can say "The check's in the mail," you'll have your answer.

- If you want a crash course in raising capital, read this book cover-to-cover. Forget spending lots of money getting your MBA. Forget learning by trial and error. Forget spending countless nights poring over some fly-by-night correspondence course. Everything you need to know about raising capital is right *here*. We mean it.

Third, this book is *fun,* which reflects our strong belief and experience that raising capital doesn't have to be boring. In fact, it can be a great deal of fun.

We'll even help you to maintain a sense of humor in the face of the challenges that all businesspeople face from time to time. That doesn't mean you won't face days when you'll be challenged, but it also doesn't mean you'll face many more days when the satisfaction of landing a big, new source of cash, or tracking down the ideal merger candidate brings you a sense of fulfillment that you never imagined possible.

When your business is a new one, raising capital can be a nerve-wracking proposition, at least until you develop steady streams of revenue and a track record of success. Remember that for even the most successful, well-established businesses, raising capital occasionally can be a hairy experience. Don't worry. Relax. Help is at your fingertips.

And the book is chock-full of our own personal Internet bookmarks for accessing the best business finance resources the Web has to offer. You'll find no filler here — just practical solutions to everyday problems.

Foolish Assumptions

As we wrote this book, we made a few assumptions about you, our readers. For example, we assumed that you're truly motivated to discover some new approaches for raising capital for your business, and that you'll be willing to put these new approaches to work for you. We also assumed that you're willing to take the kinds of measured risks that result in greater rewards and financial returns for your business, and, finally, we assumed that you're ready, willing, and able to make a long-term commitment to raising capital for your business.

How This Book Is Organized

Raising Capital For Dummies is organized into four parts. The chapters within each part cover specific topics in detail. Because we have organized the book this way, it's simple, quick and easy to find the topic that you're looking for. Simply look up your general area of interest, and then find the chapter that concerns your particular needs. Whatever the topic, you can bet that it's covered someplace!

Each part addresses a major area of the hows, whats, and whys of raising capital. Here are summaries of what you'll find in each part:

Part I: First-Stage Financing: Seed Capital and Start-up

The capital needs of start-up businesses are unique, and so are their potential sources of capital. Because start-ups have little or no track record of success, the chance of their being able to attract investments of capital from banks or venture capitalists is far less than businesses with more mileage under their belts. In this part, we look at what it takes to make money, including tapping into personal sources of financing and family and friends. We also consider angel investors and how to approach customers and vendors for financing. Finally, we take a look at the topic of matching services.

Part II: Second-Stage Financing: Expansion

For established businesses that are well past the start-up stage, have established a track record of success, and are looking for capital to finance further growth and expansion, second-stage financing provides many more sources of capital from which to draw. Not only that, but such businesses can command much larger amounts of capital than start-ups looking for first-stage financing. In this part, we explore commercial lenders and placement agents, and the Small Business Administration — a major source of loans and loan guarantees to small businesses. We also consider the oft-overlooked topic of private equity offerings along with the ever-popular topics of venture capital and valuation.

Part III: Third-Stage Financing: Acquisition

When a company's owners have something more in mind than starting or growing their businesses, they want to cash out and to have the opportunity to enjoy the fruits of their labors. That means they must find someone to buy the business, either in part or as a whole. In this part, we explore investment banking, initial public offerings, and mergers — finding out how they can provide the kind of cash that every owner dreams about.

Part IV: The Part of Tens

Here, in a concise and lively set of condensed chapters, you'll find tips that help you quickly raise the capital that your business needs. We'll show you how to avoid those common mistakes that managers make, the best ways to market your products and services, how to improve your cash flow, and much more.

Icons Used in This Book

This icon highlights pointers and processes that will improve your ability to raise capital.

Remembering these nuances of raising capital are intended to help you find, cultivate, and secure sources of funding for your business.

If you don't pay close attention to the advice next to these icons, you wind up paying through the nose.

Although you don't necessarily need to read what's marked with this kind of icon, doing so is a way to gain a better understanding of some of the technical background behind a particular aspect of raising capital.

Where to Go from Here

If you're new to the business of raising capital — perhaps a new entrepreneur, owner, or manager — then you may want to start at the beginning of this book and work your way through to the end. A wealth of information and practical advice awaits you. Simply turn the page and you're on your way!

If you already have plenty of financial experience under your belt, and you're short of time (and what businessperson *isn't* short of time?), then you may want to turn to a particular topic to address a specific need or question. If that's the case, then look in the Table of Contents for a chapter-by-chapter description of all the topics in this book.

Regardless of what course you take through Raising Capital For Dummies, we're sure that you'll enjoy getting there. Please keep one thing in mind: Some material appearing throughout the text about the law and regulations typically are summaries of technical, intricate, and complex concepts and rules that should not be construed as legal advice. Therefore, consulting experienced legal counsel for help may be vital when dealing with these issues.

If you have any specific questions or comments, we'd love to hear from you. Please visit Joe Bartlett at his Web site: www.vcexperts.com or Peter Economy at his Web site: www.petereconomy.com.

Part I
First-Stage Financing: Seed Capital and Start-up

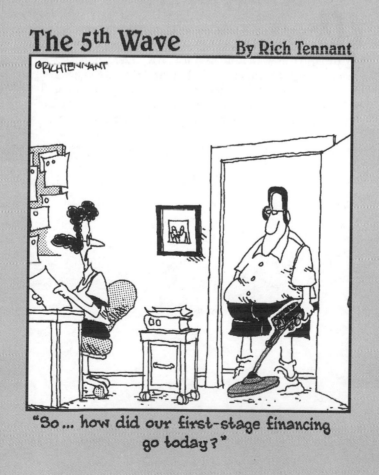

The 5th Wave   By Rich Tennant

"So... how did our first-stage financing go today?"

In this part . . .

*W*e consider the fundamental question of raising capital: Should I consider equity financing, debt financing, or some combination of both? We cover the basics of raising capital for businesses that are in their early stages of growth, including using personal resources, tapping family and friends, finding angel investors, leveraging customers and vendors for your financing needs, and more.

Chapter 1

It Takes Money to Make Money

- -

- -

*T*hat old familiar saying states: "It takes money to make money." Ask any business founder, entrepreneur, or top executive, and chances are that he or she will tell you that statement isn't just a quaint old saying; it's a fundamental truth of doing business today.

No business can operate without the money necessary to pay employees and vendors, and internal sources of cash aren't always enough to keep a business going — especially for start-ups and fast-growing companies that tend to suck up cash far faster than it comes in from sales of company products and services. Sure, all the money in the world isn't always enough to ensure business success — creating a successful business requires hard work, great ideas, dedicated and talented employees, and more than a little bit of luck — but at some point every business needs to raise capital to survive and to thrive.

For most businesses, the four major sources of capital are

- ✔ Founder's or personal investment
- ✔ Internally generated cash
- ✔ Credit granted by vendors (trade credit)
- ✔ Customer advances
- ✔ Cash borrowed from lenders
- ✔ Cash from sale of an ownership stake (equity) in the business

In this chapter, we'll discuss how to assess the financial needs of your company, focusing on the implications for your business of incurring debt versus offering equity. We'll also consider how to put your financial plan into action and discuss a popular method of financing called bootstrapping.

Got Cash? Figuring Out How Much Money You Need

The first step in raising capital is understanding how much capital you need to raise. Do you need $10,000, $100 million, or something in between? Although you don't necessarily have to know this answer down to the last penny, you need to have a pretty good idea of where you need to end up, because the answer has a significant impact on determining what type of financing is appropriate for your needs and where you'll go to get it.

As you begin to get your arms around this magic number, be sure to focus on your long-term and short-term needs. Successful businesses anticipate their future cash needs, make plans, and execute capital acquisition strategies well before they find themselves in a cash crunch. When it comes to figuring out how much money you'll need, keep these three axioms in mind:

✔ As businesses grow, they often go through several *rounds* or stages of financing. These different rounds are often targeted to specific phases of a company's growth (for example, the *seed round* is applicable to start-up companies that are too early in their development to attract the attention of the larger venture capital firms) and, therefore, require different strategies and different networks of potential investors.

✔ Raising capital will be an ongoing issue for your business — you'll never have too much cash. In fact, company growth, acquisitions of other firms, and unforeseen problems can put a very real strain on your company's financial health. Plan for the capital acquisition process to become a way of life for you and your business.

✔ Capital never arrives as quickly as you think it will. It can take some time (from a few months to many, many months) from identifying the need for capital to the time you can actually raise it. Foreseeing your capital needs well in advance through periodic plan updates can avoid delays in getting your financing and growing your business.

Although you'll probably want to prepare full-blown financial documents to determine this number with a reasonable amount of accuracy (essential financial documents are covered later in this section), here's a quick and easy way to get a general idea of how much money you'll need to target in your efforts to raise capital.

1. **Determine your projected sales.**

   How much money do you expect to take in this year? Your projected annual revenues are the starting point for determining how much capital you'll need to raise. You can determine your projected annual revenues by:

- Using your previous year's sales as a baseline and then increasing or decreasing the total by your estimated percentage increase or decrease in sales.

- Asking each one of your managers responsible for sales to provide you with an estimate of revenues for the year, and then totaling the results.

- Selecting a revenue target for the year based on a number that can realistically be achieved.

2. **Calculate your start-up costs.**

   If your business is a new one, you'll need to estimate the one-time costs that can be attributed to start-up operations. Be sure to include the costs of things like:

   - Beginning inventory and supplies.

   - Advertising and promotion related to the start-up of your business.

   - Capital expenditures for furniture, equipment, telephones, computers, fixtures, remodeling, and so forth.

   - Deposits (for example, for building rent) and initial insurance coverage (often, for example, for worker's compensation insurance, the first year has to be paid in advance).

   - Permits, licenses, and related fees.

   - Professional fees including accountants, attorneys, consultants, and others.

   - Unknowns (budget in an extra 25 percent or more to cover unexpected costs).

3. **Tally up your recurring costs.**

   Every business has recurring costs, that is, expenses that are paid on a regular basis. Most of these costs are classified as overhead and include expenditures for:

   - Rent.

   - Utilities.

   - Wages, salaries, and benefits.

   - Phones and Internet access charges.

   - Insurance and taxes.

   - Office supplies.

   - Loan payments.

   - Office equipment leases.

- Additional inventory purchases.

- Ongoing professional fees including accountants, attorneys, consultants, and others.

- Unknowns (budget in an extra 10 percent or more to cover unexpected costs).

Once you've determined the total projected sales, start-up costs (if applicable), and recurring costs, you can easily determine whether you'll be operating at a profit or loss, and how much financing you'll need to reach your goals.

So far, so good. But there's one more thing that the above projections do not consider: your needs for *working capital* — the cash you'll need to maintain your day-to-day operations. It does no good if your sales come in late in the first year. You must have the cash to keep operating until then. To accurately estimate your first year's capital needs, including *working* capital, you need to do a careful monthly cash flow projection — inflow and outflow. Here's how:

✔ Put your start-up expenses in month 0.

✔ Ramp your sales projection over the 12 months as conservatively as you feel you should. Then slip them by the number of days you expect your customers to take to pay you.

✔ Spread your expenses by month according to when you expect to pay them and be sure your inventory estimate ramps consistently with your sales forecast (Remember that you will have to have inventory on hand in advance of your sales).

✔ Next, compute your monthly net cash flow and run a cumulative net cash flow from month 0 to month 12. The first few months will probably show a negative cash flow and the cumulative negative amount will keep growing! At some month (hopefully) you'll start to see a positive cash flow.

✔ Look at the cumulative negative amount at that point on your spreadsheet. That's the *minimum* cash you will need to have to get your business started. This is a minimum only because things seldom happen exactly as you've planned, and especially not in the time frames that you usually expect.

✔ So add to this minimum the amount of "cushion" you estimate you will need for uncertainties. One way to do this is by recalculating your spreadsheet with your sales slipped 2 or 3 months. You really can't control how fast customers will buy and pay for your products! The best and most space-efficient way to express all of this is to show a simple spreadsheet with rows labeled: sales, cash receipts (customer payments), inventory payments, operating expense and purchases payments, net cash flow, cumulative cash flow. Columns will be month 0, 1,

2, and so on, and first year total. Call this "The Plan." Then show a second (worst) case with the sales slipped to calculate the cash needed including the cushion.

Now you know how to calculate your real capital needs, which include the working capital you will need to operate until your business is cash positive. You've also now got a plan that you can use to see if you are on track on a month-to-month basis.

Before you turn to external sources of capital to meet your financing needs, make sure that you first exhaust all possible internal sources, including cutting costs, retaining profit, accelerating the collection of receivables, securing advances from customers, and selling off surplus inventory and fixed assets. Not only will maximizing your internal resources enable you to avoid taking on debt or diluting ownership in your company for as long as possible, it also will reduce the amount that you have to raise when you finally decide to seek capital from outside sources.

Getting Your Financial Ducks in a Row

If you've decided to seek capital — especially if you plan to seek debt financing or promote your business opportunity to outside investors — you need to have the following historical financial documents (for the past three to five years, depending on your lender's requirements) ready to submit along with your loan applications:

- Balance sheets
- Cash flow statements
- Income statements

In addition to historical data, you'll need detailed projections of your business's projected financial activity for up to five years into the future. Specifically, this means forecasted income statements, balance sheets, cash flow statements, and capital expenditure budgets. Year one of the forecast needs to include monthly or quarterly projections, while subsequent years require quarterly or annual projections.

And be sure that your projections are in line with the amount of money that you're requesting from your lenders or investors — significant discrepancies can cast doubt on either your competence or your honesty and neither outcome is seen as a positive enhancement of your ability to raise capital.

Primary sources for start-up capital

In its 2000 annual listing of the 500 fastest-growing small businesses in the United States, *Inc,* magazine (www.inc.com) found that companies on the list utilized three key sources of start-up capital:

✔ Personal assets: 92 percent

✔ Cofounder's personal assets: 36 percent

✔ Assets of friends and family: 33 percent

Venture capital comprised only 4 percent of start-up funds for *Inc.* 500 companies. The median amount of additional financing obtained after start-up was $1,500,000, and, for 83 percent of *Inc.* 500 firms, the primary source of this additional financing was a bank line of credit.

Debt or Equity Financing: That Is the Question

When you get serious about raising capital for your business (and anytime you need cash, it's serious), consider two major avenues:

> ✔ **Debt financing means borrowing money for a fee.** Debt financing is ideal, for example, when you don't want to dilute ownership of your business in exchange for the cash you need. Of course, on the downside, you have to repay the full amount of the debt plus interest at some point in the future. If the debt exceeds your ability to pay it back on schedule, you may be forced to liquidate assets or go into bankruptcy.

> ✔ **Equity financing means selling a piece of your business in exchange for a cash investment.** Equity financing is great if you don't want an obligation to repay a lender, but, on the downside, you have to give up a portion of your ownership in the business. Give up too much ownership, and you may lose control of your business.

So which approach is better for *your* company? The answer to that question varies depending on the goals that you have for your business, the ability of your firm to repay its debt, the amount of money needed, and many other factors. Each approach has its good points and its bad.

 Many companies utilize a combination of both kinds of financing, maintaining a balance between the two. A business with a line of credit, automobile leases, and an assortment of trade credit and short-term loans (all forms of debt financing) may, for example, look to venture capitalists for an infusion of cash to fuel expansion, offer stock options to its employees, or float an initial public offering (IPO) of its stock (equity financing options).

Different flavors of debt financing

A company that doesn't use debt financing at one time or another is rare. You can find plenty of different ways to use debt to fuel your business. Although we cover the various forms of debt financing in great detail in Chapters 2 and 7 (and additional comments sprinkled throughout the book), here are some of the more common types, just to give you a taste of what's available:

- ✔ Short-term commercial loans
- ✔ Long-term commercial loans
- ✔ Home equity loans
- ✔ Working capital lines of credit
- ✔ Leasing
- ✔ Credit cards
- ✔ Accounts receivable financing
- ✔ Inventory financing
- ✔ Corporate bonds
- ✔ Letters of credit

Be careful about the extent to which you use debt financing in your business. Too much debt piled up against your available assets creates an unfavorable *debt-to-equity ratio* (which reflects upon your ability to repay your debt and can provide a clear warning sign to potential lenders — generally a debt-to-equity ratio in excess of 1 is considered bad). Not only that, but putting your company too far in debt overextends your resources, making it more difficult to weather a downturn in sales or unexpected events that impact your business in a negative way.

Different flavors of equity financing

If your company is fast-growing, innovative, and produces terrific products or services, you may find that people aren't interested in just purchasing what you sell, they're also interested in purchasing a piece of your business. Although the make-money-fast days of the recent explosion (and subsequent implosion) of dot-com firms seem to be behind us — taking with them a boom in IPOs — plenty of investors still are looking for good opportunities to put their money to work.

Here are some of the more common ways that you can raise equity capital from investors:

- Angel investors
- Family and friends
- Founder's capital
- Initial public offerings
- Strategic investors
- Strategic partners
- Venture capital

Keep in mind, however, that equity financing is considerably different than debt financing, and in many ways it can be far more intrusive to your business. Here are some of the things you need to consider before committing to an equity financing plan:

- Unlike debt that can be paid off (for example, by getting a new bank), it is very hard to reverse (that is, pay off) an equity investment. The investor will want a lot more money than he put in because of the risk he assumed. So you should generally look at raising equity as an irreversible event. Being cautious is understandable! You'll be living with these investors and their expectations for a long time.

- Equity investors will want to know how, how much, and when they will get their money back. You'll need answers to these questions — that's some of what this book is about. (See Chapters 15 and 16 for more about exit strategies in IPOs and Mergers)

- Don't forget that most start-ups go through several rounds of new equity investors. You can't give away a lot of the equity early on or you'll have too little left for the later rounds — or you'll be faced with losing control of your company in those future rounds (and losing control of your exit strategy, too).

Looking for financing in all the right places

If you look hard enough, you can find the cash that you need to start up your business or fuel its growth almost anywhere. This book covers all these different sources and more in considerable detail.

To give you a taste of what's to come, here are some of the more common sources for business financing:

✓ **Self-funding:**

- Personal savings (See Chapter 2)
- Credit cards (See Chapter 2)
- Trade credit (See Chapter 5)
- Employee stock ownership plans (ESOPs)
- Home-equity loans (See Chapter 7)
- Bartering (See Chapter 5)
- Customers (See Chapter 5)

✓ **Private resources:**

- Angel investors (See Chapter 4)
- Friends and family (See Chapter 3)
- Private equity offering (See Chapter 10)
- Strategic alliances (See Chapter 16)
- Mergers (See Chapter 16)

✓ **Commercial funding:**

- Investment banks (See Chapter 14)
- Commercial banks (See Chapter 7)
- Savings and loan associations (See Chapter 7)
- Credit unions (See Chapter 7)
- Venture capital firms (See Chapter 11)
- Leasing firms (See Chapter 13)

✓ **Government financing programs:**

- Small Business Administration (SBA) loans (See Chapter 9)
- Small Business Investment Companies (SBICs) (See Chapter 9)

Plenty of sources of financing are available to those who seek them. The key is obtaining the kind of financing that is right for your company in an amount sufficient to ensure that you meet your goals. As hard as it may be to believe, one thing is worse than no financing at all: Financing that doesn't meet your needs or that gets you and your business into financial trouble.

Debt financing or equity financing? Some questions to ask

To decide whether debt financing is right for you, first ask these questions:

✔ Will your company's cash flow support repayment of the debt?

✔ Will your company qualify for debt financing?

✔ Will the amount of cash acquired through debt financing be sufficient to meet the company's needs?

✔ Will the additional debt endanger your company's credit rating?

✔ Will your company be able to comply with the loan terms and conditions?

✔ What kinds of collateral or personal guarantees does the lender require?

To decide whether equity financing is right for you, first ask these questions:

✔ Are you willing to lose some amount of control in how the company is operated?

✔ Are current owners willing to dilute their ownership interests?

✔ Is the company attractive to potential investors?

✔ Do the company's financial reporting systems support accurate and timely reporting of financial data?

✔ Are you willing to share in the future profits and equity growth of the company?

✔ Are you willing to share trade secrets and confidential company plans and information with potential investors?

Bootstrapping

Before you run out and begin your search for capital, you may want to consider an approach that many businesses — particularly start-ups and small businesses that may not yet qualify for loans or be able to attract venture capital — have used with more than a little bit of success. It's called *bootstrapping*. It means finding money and resources by any means possible, including begging, borrowing, bartering, sharing, and leasing everything a company needs.

In short, bootstrapping is guerrilla financing.

So, who bootstraps? Many companies do. In fact, some estimates put the total at 75 to 85 percent of all start-up businesses. Three fundamental rules for effective bootstrapping are

✔ **Hire as few employees as possible.** For many companies, employees are the greatest expense. When you add up salary, benefits, overtime, and other employee-related expenses, it doesn't take long for any budget to feel the pinch. Bootstrappers avoid this pinch by hiring (and paying) as few employees as possible.

✔ **Lease, share, and barter everything you can.** No, you don't have to pay cash for everything that you need for your business to run. Many companies share facilities, equipment, and even employees with one another to spread out their respective costs. An increasing number of firms also have discovered the wonderful world of *bartering,* the trading of goods and services to other companies in exchange for the goods and services that are needed. See Chapter 5 for an in-depth discussion of bartering.

✔ **Use other people's money.** Why use your own money when someone else will let you use his or hers? We're not talking about getting a loan, we're talking about convincing a vendor to allow you to pay 30 or 60 or even 90 days after you receive your goods from them. Or, on the other hand, obtaining payment from your customers before you deliver their goods or services. In each case, you have an opportunity to use someone else's funds to your advantage — for a while, at least.

Bridgepath.com: Bootstrapping their way to success

When Bridgepath.com — the first competitor-to-competitor Internet exchange for permanent and temporary staffing firms — was formed in San Francisco in 1997, the founders decided to turn to bootstrapping to finance their company's start-up. Bridgepath.com's approach may not be for everyone, but it worked for the founders. The result? Bridgepath.com (www.bridgepath.com) was able to raise almost $1 million in venture capital after a year of bootstrapping.

The company's bootstrapping techniques included

✔ Bartering with vendors in exchange for services. The company's accountant, for example, accepted help with designing and implementing a Web site in lieu of cash payment.

✔ Negotiating with four different long-distance telephone companies until striking the best deal possible, saving thousands of dollars for the company.

✔ Asking employees to bring in spare furniture to furnish their offices, and utilizing abandoned furniture. The result? The cost of furnishing each of the company's offices was kept to $50 or less.

✔ Convincing vendors to accept delayed payment for goods and services provided to the company.

✔ Paying employees lower than average wages in exchange for stock options.

Some of the more common approaches to bootstrapping are

- Seeking funds from friends and family.
- Getting a home-equity loan.
- Offering equity to employees and vendors in lieu of salary or cash payments.
- Bartering for goods and services.
- Tapping your credit cards.
- Convincing vendors to accept extended payments.
- Starting your business part time while working a full-time job.
- Getting an extra job.
- Working from home or in your garage.
- Sharing offices with another company.
- Encouraging customer financing (deposits and early payments).
- Looking for angel investors.
- Pooling founders' savings.

Although the need for bootstrapping tends to go away as a business grows and becomes more established — and therefore becomes more attractive to conventional lenders and investors — any company, no matter how big or how small, can benefit by applying bootstrapping techniques in its day-to-day financial activities. One of the greatest dangers as businesses become more established is the growth of *overhead* — the costs of facilities, administrative personnel, equipment, utilities, office supplies, furniture, and so forth — at a rate far faster than the growth of a company's sales. This is a recipe for poor profits, sluggish growth, and loss of competitive edge. Bootstrapping can help keep your company lean and mean while keeping overhead in check and profits high.

Choosing a path

Personal and business factors drive your capital needs, and you'll need to recognize this in a very personal way. If, for example, you are in a manufactured product business, you will need more capital than someone starting a professional services business. The fact that you need more capital means that you will have devote more of your time dealing with the issues surrounding the quest for capital.

Starting from scratch

Starting a business from nothing is the dream of many people, but it is, without a doubt, one of the most difficult things you can do. The rewards — mental and financial — can be tremendous, but ask anyone who's already been down this path, and he or she will tell you that it's anything but easy. According to small business Web site AllBusiness.com (www.allbusiness.com), the majority of successful entrepreneurs start with small sums of money, often $5,000 or less. In fact, the average start-up cost for companies listed on the most recent *Inc.* 500 list of fast-growing small businesses was only $25,000, and roughly half of those businesses were started at home.

AllBusiness.com cites five ways to start a thriving business without spending a lot of cash:

- **Keep your day job — for now.** You may be able to start your business by working on it during weekends and evenings. That way, you can afford to experiment with different versions of your business until you find one that seems likely to succeed. Also, it's far easier to get some of your initial credit set up when you are still employed with a steady income. Ideally, you can get your business on track and accrue a healthy backlog of orders before you quit your job.

- **Work part-time.** Try shifting from full-time to part-time work when you start your business. Such a move makes the most sense in the early stages of your new venture, when you need to devote more time to finding customers and delivering products and services to them.

- **Go from two incomes to one income for a time.** If your spouse is employed, his or her income (and benefits such as medical insurance) may cover basic living costs long enough for you to start your firm. This may mean creating a new spending plan for your family, but adhering to new budget guidelines for a few months is a small price to pay for long-term success.

- **Turn your employer into a client.** You may be able to start your new business as a consultant or supplier to your old firm.

- **Get creative about financing.** You may be the best source of financing for your new business. For one thing, you won't charge yourself interest. So begin your search for start-up cash by rummaging around in your personal treasury. Be wary of tapping into retirement accounts; you probably can't afford to risk those funds. Instead, design a budget that boosts your savings rate and sets that money aside in an account for your new business.

If you need money right away, you also can consider borrowing money from family members and friends. But don't borrow more than you're willing and able to repay over time in the event that your business doesn't work out. Alternatively, some family members or friends may be willing to risk their money in exchange for an equity stake in your business.

Credit cards are a tempting — but expensive — source of starting capital. If you resort to them for cash, your business plan needs to include a specific schedule for paying back that money within a year or so.

If you are a very private person — and you would prefer not to have other people meddling in your finances — you should first go down a path of bootstrapping, moving towards slow and conservative growth using bank lines of credit. As your business gets larger (and your capital needs increase), you might consider a subsequent private placement of equity, and then a sale of your company through a merger.

If, on the other hand, you are *not* concerned about privacy *and* want to grow as fast as possible, you should go the venture capital path to an initial public offering (IPO). Conversely, the professional services start-up may well be able to grow rapidly without raising equity capital — an equity event — to the consternation of the founder who wants to find a rationale to make his investment liquid.

Things quickly get more complex when you consider a founder who wants to grow to an IPO as soon as possible, but who is an inveterate recluse. The mismatch between personal inclinations (behavior), personal goals, business model needs, and financing realities is one of the most important issues for a company and its founder. There are ways to handle almost every mismatch, and proper planning can overcome almost any obstacle.

Luck can account for a few good financing outcomes, but far more positive results have occurred when a goal, strategy, and plan were in place. If you want to sell as an exit strategy, for example, then first think about who would want to buy you and why. Then make your company irresistible to them. Much of this does not require calculations, just common sense and back-of-the-envelope calculations.

Chapter 2

Tapping into Your Personal Resources

● ●

In This Chapter

▶ Mining your savings account for start-up costs

▶ Launching your business with credit cards

▶ Taking advantage of home equity

▶ Thinking about using your retirement funds

● ●

*1*f you're an entrepreneur seeking capital for a new company, or you're looking for a quick way to raise some cash without filling out a bunch of forms and providing page after page of financial statements and projections to obtain a bank loan or wining and dining an endless stream of potential angel investors, you've come to the right place. See Chapter 4 for more on angel investors.

The very first thing that many people think of when it comes to raising capital is tapping their own resources — savings accounts, retirement plans, home equity, credit cards, and more. Why? Because it's quick and easy.

But before you empty your bank accounts, max out your credit cards, and raid your retirement funds, keep one thing in mind: The majority of start-up businesses fail within five years after they're started. When you put your own money into your business, you're putting your own personal financial well-being — and the well-being of your family, pets, and other dependents — at risk as well.

In this chapter, we take a look at using the financial resources already at your disposal to your advantage while minimizing your personal risk in doing so. These resources include personal savings, credit cards, home equity, and retirement funds.

Taking a Dip (into Your Savings)

A major source of funds for entrepreneurs and owners of start-up businesses has traditionally been the entrepreneur or owner himself or herself. You surely have heard more than a few stories of entrepreneurs who scrimped and saved until they had a large enough nest egg to strike out on their own.

Even if you decide to approach a bank for a loan, you'll likely find that the lender wants you to put a significant amount of money down — perhaps up to 20 percent or 30 percent of the total loan value. Where is this money going to come from? From your own savings.

But while self-funding has steadily declined as the preferred method of raising capital (according to a 2000 study cited in the next section, only 19 percent of small-business entrepreneurs used self-funding as a source of capital for their businesses), it still plays a significant role in the vast world of raising capital.

So what are some of the good things about using your own cash to finance your business?

- ✔ No strings are attached to your own money — *you* decide how and when you will use the cash for your business, and you remain fully in control of your business.

- ✔ You have no complicated forms to fill out and no bankers or investors to schmooze.

- ✔ Your money is readily available to you.

Of course, using your own money to finance your business isn't always a good idea. Here are a few of the not-so-good things to consider about this financing option:

- ✔ There are no guarantees of business success — you can lose your entire savings if you're not careful.

- ✔ You lose out on interest income on your savings.

- ✔ Your cash may earn a higher return if invested elsewhere, say, in the stock market.

Whenever you decide to borrow money from your personal savings to raise capital for your business, be sure to fully document these transactions in writing. Set up a business bank account and place your funds in it. When investing your own funds in your business, it's important to be able to track them for tax purposes and to be able to monitor their usage.

Why use credit cards?

For most of us, pulling out a credit card to pay for purchases — at the grocery store, the gas station, in a department store — is an almost everyday occurrence. Credit cards are convenient; they can be used almost anyplace — including ordering items over the phone or online — without having to stop by the bank to pick up enough cash for the day's shopping. Similarly, there are a variety of reasons why businesses use credit cards. Here are the most common:

- ✔ **Convenience:** 86 percent
- ✔ **Most are widely accepted at places we do business:** 36 percent
- ✔ **Consolidation of monthly billing statements:** 35 percent
- ✔ **Reward/airline miles:** 28 percent
- ✔ **Competitive interest rates:** 9 percent
- ✔ **Other:** 13 percent

Credit Cards: Not Just for Breakfast Anymore

Although *self-financing* — paying a business's start-up cost from personal savings or other personally owned cash resources — was traditionally the primary source of capital for new businesses, that no longer is the case. According to a recent study on small business financing conducted by National Small Business United, only 19 percent of entrepreneurs were self-financed (defined for the purposes of the study as including the use of personal funds and home equity loans).

The most common source of capital for small businesses? Credit cards. Approximately 50 percent of small-business owners surveyed said that they had used credit cards within the previous 12 months to finance expenses, while only 43 percent of small-business owners said that they had used bank loans within the previous 12 months to finance expenses.

According to the National Small Business United study, the most popular business uses for credit cards include the following:

- ✔ **Travel and entertainment expenses:** 69 percent
- ✔ **Day-to-day expenses:** 64 percent
- ✔ **Large capital outlays:** 46 percent
- ✔ **Inventory/items for resale:** 34 percent
- ✔ **Other:** 6 percent

If you have access to credit cards, they can be an excellent source of capital for your business. When starting up a new venture, consider setting up one or two personal cards that will be used only for the new business. This keeps the records straight, it's easy to do, and the limits will be high as long as you still have a job when you apply for the cards. Pick cards with low introductory rates — preferably for at least six months.

And while some cards — Visa, MasterCard, and the like — have preset spending limits, others, such as certain cards offered by American Express, do not. If you've ever hit a spending limit while in the middle of a business trip to Europe, you can appreciate the sheer beauty of a card with no preset limit.

Turning Your Home into an ATM

If you own your home, you may be sitting on a gold mine. Depending on how long you've owned your home, how much you paid for it, how the housing prices in your area have fared, and how much equity you've built up over the years, you may be able to pull a significant sum of money out of it in the form of a home equity loan or line of credit.

Home equity loans offer two key advantages that have made them particularly popular:

- ✔ The interest paid on home equity loans is generally tax deductible, even for individuals and nonbusiness entities.

- ✔ Interest rates for home equity loans are generally far lower (from a few points, to ten or more) than credit cards, and somewhat lower (a point or more) than unsecured personal and business loans and lines of credit.

Understanding how home equity loans work

Exactly how do home equity loans work? When a lender grants a loan on the equity in your home, it does so only after determining how much your home is worth and the amount of money you still owe on your mortgage loan. Let's say you bought your home a few years ago for $100,000, putting $10,000 down and taking out a mortgage loan for the remaining $90,000. Further, let's assume that the value of your home has risen to $125,000, and you have paid your mortgage loan down to $85,000. The difference between the current value of your home and the amount of money required to pay off your mortgage loan is your equity, in this case $40,000 ($125,000 – $85,000).

But while you may have $40,000 of equity, a lender will usually grant you a home equity loan for only a portion of that total. When you apply for a home equity loan, the lender will loan you up to a certain percentage of the equity you have in your home, perhaps 85 or 90 percent. In this example, that works out to a loan of $34,000 (at 85 percent) or $36,000 (at 90 percent).

Two major types of home equity loans exist:

✔ **Term equity loan:** A term equity loan provides you with a lump sum of money to use as you see fit. You make equal payments to the lender on a monthly basis for a fixed period (most often 15 years) at a set interest rate. Variable-rate equity loans are also available, with interest rates that change periodically depending on predetermined interest rate benchmarks.

✔ **Home equity line of credit:** Like a credit card, a home equity line of credit enables you to draw any sum of money out of your home equity account up to a predetermined cap and to pay it back over time — in part or in whole. In this way, you can use your credit again and again as you repay it. Home equity lines of credit are most commonly established with variable interest rates, which change periodically depending on predetermined interest rate benchmarks. Any outstanding loan balance will need to be paid back to the lender if the loan is terminated, most often when the house is sold.

Financing your business with a home equity loan

Home equity loans generally bear higher interest rates than a first mortgage, but the rates are usually far lower than those on credit cards, and you have up to 15 years to pay back the loans. This arrangement makes home equity loans a great way of obtaining the capital you need for your business.

The key danger with home equity loans — and the main reason banks love to make them — is that you pledge your home as security in the event of loan default. If you fail to make your loan payments, you'll be forced to give up your home. This is something most people would prefer not to have to deal with.

There's Gold in That Retirement Fund

In this section, we're getting close to the end of the road when it comes to using your own sources of financing to fund your business. There are a few other unlikely sources of cash, such as cashing in a life insurance policy or printing your own money (just joking about that one!).

What if your personal savings, your credit cards, and your home equity won't provide you with the cash you need? What if your credit isn't so hot, or lenders aren't exactly falling all over themselves to give you the loan you seek for some other reason? What if you have no chance of attracting an angel investor or floating an IPO? What then?

If you have a retirement fund, a 401(k), an Individual Retirement Account (IRA), or some other form of retirement or pension, you may be in business. Not only do you have a good chance of pulling together the capital you need for your business, but you may be able to do so fairly quickly and easily.

Many employers offer retirement plans to their employees. The most popular of these plans are known as 401(k) plans. A 401(k) plan enables you to make contributions from your pretax earnings to your own retirement account. In many cases, the investor's employer matches his or her contributions, and many plans allow the investor to direct where the investment goes — into a specific stock mutual fund or other formal investment program.

With a 401(k), you have two options for obtaining the capital you seek.

Withdrawing cash from your 401 (k)

In the first option, you can simply withdraw the cash you want in the form of an early withdrawal. There are a couple of problems with this approach, however:

- ✔ When you withdraw the funds, you may incur — subject to your age — an early withdrawal penalty (10 percent of the total amount of money withdrawn), and the money will be considered taxable income in the tax year you withdraw it.

- ✔ The funds you withdraw will no longer earn you money as an investment, with interest compounding over time. There is no guarantee, of course, that the investment into which you sink this money (your business) will experience a comparable rate of return.

Using your 401 (k) to get a loan

In the second option, you can obtain a loan against your 401(k) account. This approach is generally preferred to an early withdrawal because you aren't required to pay the 10 percent penalty, nor are the funds counted as taxable income. You do, however, have to pay interest on the loan, just as you would on any other loan. And one more thing: if you quit your job to start your new business, you may or may not be able to keep your 401(k) account (and your loan) active with your old employer. Be sure you're familiar with your company's policies on 401(k)s *before* you quit, not after! Here are some key guidelines for 401(k) loans:

- ✔ The interest rate on 401(k) loans is usually fairly low — perhaps just a bit over the prime rate (the interest rate charged to their very best and most creditworthy customers).

- ✔ You must repay the loan in full within five years. Repayments are generally made through payroll deductions.

- ✔ Loans are limited to 50 percent of the total value of the 401(k) investment account balance, up to a maximum loan of $50,000.

- ✔ Termination from your firm — whether you quit or are fired — may mean that you'll have to repay the loan immediately (some plans do allow you to continue the loan as long as you continue to make payments — check with your employer to be sure). If you fail to do so, the loan will be treated as an early withdrawal, you'll be required to pay the 10 percent penalty, and the funds will be considered taxable income.

While this section focused on 401(k) retirement plans, there are many other forms of retirement and pension plans in use by businesses today. Some of these other retirement and pension plans may have similar provisions as 401(k)s, allowing you to take early withdrawals or loans. Check with your plan administrator to find out what your options are.

For many businesspeople, 401(k) retirement plans are a source of capital that makes sense. It's your money, after all — why not put it to work for you now rather than later? If you're seriously considering putting the money in your account to work now, keep these things in mind:

- ✔ In most cases, you won't be able to make a phone call and have the cash from your retirement account an hour or two later. It may take several weeks for your plan administrator to process your request and cut you a check. So the sooner you need the cash, the sooner you need to initiate your request.

- ✔ If you decide to make an early withdrawal from your tax-deferred retirement plan [IRA or 401(k)], you're going to pay a fairly hefty penalty for the privilege. Any distributions before you turn 59½ are subject to a 10 percent early withdrawal penalty, as well as counted as taxable income. This may be a very high price for you to pay to obtain capital for your business. But if it's all you have and you're determined to make your business a success, it may be your best shot.

As we mentioned at the beginning of this chapter, tapping into your personal resources is a time-honored approach to raising capital, especially for start-up enterprises. If you have the funds available and you can afford to lose them, then by all means dive right in. But if the loss of these personal funds would cause you to lose your home, throw your family's life into disarray, and send you to the poorhouse, you'd best search for alternative sources of capital.

Chapter 3

The Rolodex Round: Family and Friends

- -

In This Chapter

▶ Figuring out who to ask

▶ Making your pitch

▶ Staying out of legal trouble

- -

*W*hen a business is first getting started, the potential sources of capital are few and far between. Your own resources are a logical first place to look — Chapter 2 tells you how to tap into your savings, your credit, and so on. What we talk about in this chapter are ways of raising money *after* your own resources are tapped out and *before* you're ready for the angel round when you seek capital from wealthy individuals (see Chapter 4).

What to do? Well, you go to your Rolodex and start figuring out how to navigate your way through the friends and family, or *2Fs round.* (Some cynics refer to this round as the *3Fs round* — friends, family, and fools.)

Pounding That Rolodex

Before we get down to the nitty-gritty of the friends-and-family round, make sure that you understand who your friends are. The circle may be wider than you think. When you're looking for start-up money, it pays to be diligent and far-reaching in your initial efforts, but you can start with the folks closest to home.

Family

Blood is thicker than water. The most obvious source for friends-and-family round capital is your immediate family, particularly your parents and grandparents.

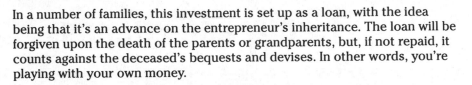

In a number of families, this investment is set up as a loan, with the idea being that it's an advance on the entrepreneur's inheritance. The loan will be forgiven upon the death of the parents or grandparents, but, if not repaid, it counts against the deceased's bequests and devises. In other words, you're playing with your own money.

Be respectful of your siblings' feelings when you're getting money from your parents. If you aren't respectful, you may cause a family feud.

Friends

Aside from family members, most people have their closest and longest-lasting relationships with their friends. As such, friends often are with us through thick and thin, and they are your partners, advisors, and confidants in much of what life brings your way. For an entrepreneur seeking start-up capital, or for established businesspeople looking to garner widespread interest and participation in an investment opportunity, friends are a natural choice.

Be careful, however, when you decide to mix friendship and business. Many friendships have been ruined when the needs of the business became more important than the friendship between the parties, or because of petty jealousies or conflicts arising as a result of the business relationship. If you really cherish your friendship — and you're concerned that your friendship might be harmed by introducing your business into it — you may be better off to avoid raising capital from your friends.

Here's a typical example of a device that you can use to diversify risks on both sides of the equation, particularly when dealing with friends: An entrepreneur puts a very high percentage of her assets into her own company, say, $200,000 or $300,000 of her $1 million nest egg. She wants to invest another $100,000, but that number pushes her pretty close to the choking point; she's becoming pretty illiquid in the portfolio she plans to use for emergencies and/or retirement. One way to be creative is making an arrangement with a friend who also is entrepreneurially driven. The entrepreneur invests $100,000 in her friend's company and, in return, he invests $100,000 in the entrepreneur's business. That way you indirectly make an investment in your own company, but you've also significantly diversified the risk.

Teammates

Rugby, anyone? We're talking about postgraduate teams here. Although it isn't for everybody, we've been playing club rugby for the past umpteen years and developed a number of close friendships. The rugby motto is taken from Shakespeare's *Henry V:* "For he to-day that sheds his blood with me shall be my brother."

Your teammates on any amateur sports team may range from unemployed actors to plutocrats. In fact, one of our teammates from years past runs one of the largest financial institutions in New York City. Nothing is like spending 80 minutes in the scrum with someone to get a line on his strengths and weaknesses. That information is useful when you go for the kill in terms of raising capital.

Fellow members of organizations

Make sure that your friends-and-family round includes organizations of which you are a member. As de Tocqueville remarked, the United States is built on voluntary associations. For example, some of the premiere American life insurance companies started as benevolent organizations of individuals and families in a given geographical location or specific line of work. The founders pooled their resources to help the members through occasional catastrophes — burial societies are one example.

Make sure that you understand all the organizations that you and your family belong to.

School ties

Some alumni associations have small seed funds designed for providing graduates with very early stage capital. In recent years, this form of giving has become a favorite pastime for rich alumni, particularly those who made their money through venture-capital-backed enterprises. They put up some seed capital, cut the university in for a portion (or all) of the investment, and make capital available to graduates — potentially a win-win situation for all involved.

Also, don't neglect your high school and college reunions. Seek out the individual who was the biggest "go-getter" when you were in school together and try to coordinate your reunion plans with him or her. You may be surprised how your classmates turned out — just as they may be surprised how *you* turned out!

The power of family and friends

One recent trend is for contributions to a given institution or society (including some of a religious nature) to be mandated for soft loans and grants to members of the society who want to become entrepreneurs. The arrangements entered into by a particular immigrant group — the Korean grocers in New York City — exemplify this paradigm.

The seed capital for the ubiquitous and highly successful Korean groceries comes not from the state or from Santa Claus, but rather, once the successful members of this close-knit group are launched in the U.S., they've willingly made loans and investments available to enable newly arrived members of the group to get their start in what has become a network of highly successful, hardworking businesspeople. Obviously, the eligibility specifications are narrow in this case, but a number of others have used the model with the idea of substituting self-help for charity.

Fellow business travelers

If, as entrepreneurs often do, you fly coast to coast, you will find yourself sitting next to a total stranger for six or eight hours — with about 2 inches separating you. If you're looking for capital, our advice is to strike up a conversation. No fooling, folks. Any number of enterprising people have been able to either raise money directly or develop contacts provided by a seatmate with whom they've been trapped on an extended airline trip. You can start with the usual: cursing the airline. After you've become blood brothers in that regard, you can start talking about your proposition.

Professional contacts

Submitting an *over-the-transom* (unsolicited) plan to a venture firm is not likely to get you very far. Most venture firms make their investment decisions on the basis of plans that they helped develop or that sources they know and respect forwarded to them. The trick, therefore, is obtaining an introduction.

If you don't have access to a placement agent (a professional hired to find investors for your opportunity — See Chapter 8 for more on placement agents), consider employing your professional associates — that is, your law or accounting firm. A savvy partner can showcase your opportunity to his or her associates — many of whom may be interested in a piece of the action — and sometimes they invest themselves (the lawyers, anyway).

Understanding What Goes into the Exchange

So, what does a family and friends deal look like? In reality, no one single model exists for investments made by family and friends, and company owners historically used a variety of different investment vehicles. As in other kinds of financing, however, family and friends investments break down into to major categories:

- **Debt financing.** In some cases, investments by family and friends are made as straight loans of cash to a company's owners. The debt is paid back to the investors by way of regular payments (often monthly) with interest added to compensate the investors for the risk they bear in making the investment. Debt financing confers no ownership stake (equity) to the investors — the owners retain full control of the company.

- **Equity financing.** In other cases, investments by family and friends are made through the purchase of securities such as stock. In this way, investors become part owners of the company — proportionate to the amount of money that they invest — and the original owners give up some amount of control over the company.

Regardless of the many different investment alternatives available, the family and friends round is likely to be a straight common stock issuance. There isn't enough money to construct an elaborate securities structure, including a convertible preferred. Accordingly, the notion is that everybody is generally *pari passu* — holders of a single class of common stock.

One of the worst things you can do in the early stages of your company's existence is to give out stock promiscuously. By the time you have finished the journey from embryo to IPO, you'll find yourself personally owning only a trivial percentage of the company. You may have created a $100 million company, but if *your* percentage is down in the 1 percent or 2 percent range when you sell, you'll find that you've been working like a slave at a substandard wage for no reason. Given enormous opportunity costs, your outcome would have been better had you taken up basket weaving as a profession.

Making Your Pitch

If, like so many people, you're averse to rejection, you're going to have to get over it. Raising seed capital is hard. One of our most successful clients used to say that he had to get used to receiving two orders from potential investors: "Get out and stay out." This business is not for the faint of heart or the shy and retiring; energy, persistence, and a thick hide are desirable even when (or perhaps particularly when) you're approaching friends and family. In this section, we'll give you some tips that help ensure that you get more yeses than noes when you ask for capital.

Being candid: It's refreshing

Nothing can offend a friends-and-family investor more than a pitch that sounds like one of those pesky recorded announcements that seem to plague our telephones right as we sit down to dinner. We think that you get more takers when you're candid about the risks your company is likely to encounter and modest in your claims about potential rewards.

Everyone says that his or her forecasts are conservative so don't even bother using that word. We prefer to say something to this effect: "Look, this is a very high-risk proposition, and the chances of success are way less than 100 percent, and maybe even less than 50 percent. We think we can sell this company for a price that will return to you 3 or 4 times your investment, but a lot of things have to go right."

If only because a candid pitch stands out from all the other drivel that investors hear these days, you may be pleasantly surprised.

Going to the end of the line

No conscientious owner wants his or her investors to get stuck holding the bag when a good investment goes bad, but that is especially true of the class of investors that comprises your family and friends. Giving assurances to friends-and-family investors may be a good idea such that if things don't go well, you'll use your best efforts (these are not ordinarily binding promises) to make good on their investments before taking anything out of the deal for yourself.

Suppose, for example, that your friends and family invest $1 million in your company with a premoney valuation based entirely on your sweat equity of $2 million. Assuming that you really mean to see it through, nothing is wrong with assuring your friends and family that, in the event of an indifferent or disappointing result (say, the company is sold for $1.5 million), their cash investments will be paid out of the proceeds before you take out your hoped-for $2 million. In other words, you'll pay them back before you take any money yourself.

Finding strength in numbers

One way to pitch to any investor class, whether it's angels, friends and family, or venture capitalists, is sponsoring a private function such as a breakfast in your office or at another friendly venue. Invite eight or ten people to attend — including friends, family, and potential angel investors (see Chapter 4 for more about angel investors). You'll be surprised at how the investors are encouraged by the presence of others in the community, plus the give and take during a question and answer (Q&A) period; you can reserve your one-on-one pitches for breakout sessions after the event. Remember: Events are most useful when they're scheduled with advance planning and thought, even at the friends-and-family level.

Keeping It Fair and Legal

Raising capital from friends and family poses difficulties that go beyond the purely economic. Let us count the ways:

- ✔ You aren't necessarily dealing with so-called accredited investors. This heightens your responsibility to tread carefully from a legal standpoint, to make adequate disclosures, and to ensure that your friends and family understand the risks of their investment in your business.

- ✔ You are legally responsible for soliciting only the amount of cash that, given the generally high risk of early-stage investments, the friend or family member can afford to lose.

In other words, you need legal advice, even if only family members are involved. Otherwise, you may wind up with financing that doesn't pass muster under federal (and perhaps state) securities laws.

You won't necessarily go to jail if you violate these laws. As a matter of fact, a jail sentence, absent fraud, is unlikely. However, an offering that can't be defended as exempt may prove to be an embarrassment and a hindrance to later financings — and it may give the investors a chance, if the company is a bust, to sue you for their money back. In short, you're subject to the securities laws from the day you start selling securities (and the definition of what constitutes a security is very broad).

The fact that your investors are close relatives does not constitute an official and legal exemption. Play by the rules.

Valuing your business fairly

To repeat: The trick to success when raising capital from family and friends is avoiding the risk of losing lifelong friendships and family relationships. Believe us, ruining these relationships simply isn't worth it. You must bend over backward not only to be fair but also to give every appearance of fairness. At the outset, be sure that you assign a reasonable value to your idea or plan, one that you can, if necessary, easily back up with hard data.

When you're asking your friends and family to invest because they're your friends and family, the underlying assumption is that, absent that special relationship, they would not be investors. If you bowl them over with a highly aggressive valuation — one that is extremely optimistic at best — two things can happen:

- ✔ The company is such a howling success that everybody makes out like a bandit.
- ✔ More in accordance with the odds, the company won't reach expected levels, and some level of disappointment will set in. If that disappointment is fueled by the notion that friends and family were taken advantage of, then the founder faces the worst-case scenario: loss of not only cash but also valuable relationships.

Making the valuation fair is the trick. That's no mean feat because, at the early stages of a company's existence, the question of what is fair is subjective.

One of the answers, then, is using next-round pricing. The investment in which friends and family participate is a bridge loan, convertible into equity at the next-round price and usually at a discount of, say, 20 percent from that price. If, at the angel or Series A stage, the company is priced premoney at $3 million, then the 2Fs investment is priced at $2.6 million. That way, you take a potential bone of contention off the table. Someone else is doing the pricing; neither you nor your dear relative is fixing that number, so Thanksgiving dinner will be much more pleasant. For more information on this approach, see the Q&A discussion in Chapter 4.

Managing expectations

Next, you should pay close attention to a psychological imperative. When you raise money from friends and family, no matter how long and hard you describe the deal as a high-risk, *equity* investment, the likelihood is that they will expect you to give them their money back if things don't work out. They may not say it, and it may be the farthest thing from your mind, but that's what happens in real life.

If it saves you money, it's as good as cash

You're going to need professional services to get your company off the ground. If you don't have cash to pay lawyers, accountants, and such, bartering may be your best option.

If your publishing venture is dependent on advertising revenue, you talk with your vendors about free advertising for their firms. If you're building a site, you talk about a prominent position on your home page, telling the world what a good job your vendors have done for you and your company. If you're a content provider, you acquire content by swapping: "Any original content that my company originates will be available to you; in turn, we can pick and choose from your content to attract visitors to our site."

But keep in mind that when you get free advice, it may be of the highest quality, or it may be worth what you're paying for it — nothing. In fact, if you wind up with casual, offhand (and therefore negligent) advice, you may be worse off than when you started. We don't say this to talk you out of mooching services wherever possible. You do what you have to do in this life. We do say, however, to be cautious.

In-kind contributions (nonmonetary factors that help you run your business) are another substitute for cash. Your college roommate may be highly successful with a significant income, running, say, her own firm. Your first instinct will be to hit your old pal up for cash. That's your primary need. However, dollars to donuts she has a husband, she has kids on the way, and she is putting every spare dime she can find into a trust fund for the specter of gazillion-dollar college tuition. Despite your friendship, cash is the wrong thing to ask her for. But that doesn't mean she can't help you out.

Maybe your successful college roommate has established her business in a suite of offices with some expansion space. Ask her if you can camp out in a spare office during the early stages of your company's existence. You will agree to get out anytime that she tells you to hit the road and to pay your own phone bill. But you'll tap into her receptionist, and you'll fix the system so that someone answers the phone by giving your name and your company's name, as if you had a freestanding office. You have a mail drop, use of the fax machines (which you pay for, of course), e-mail, and all the other accoutrements of a real live office. You'll be surprised how much easier it is to mooch contributions in kind versus that scarcest of resources — cash.

If you aren't prepared to give the money back, or at least do your best in the course of your lifetime to get it back to your friends and family, you may find yourself putting that most valuable commodity — their friendship — at risk. At the very least, if the deal doesn't work out as you planned (and the majority of them don't, we're sorry to say), be prepared to see that every available dollar goes to recoup the investments of the friends and family before you take out one personal dollar.

You'd better be ready to pay yourself no more than survival wages while your friends-and-family capital is at risk. Nothing ruins a relationship faster than a justified suspicion that *your* compensation was anything approaching lavish during the period you're using *their* capital to get going.

Raising money is serious business. You need to pay the same respect in the friends-and-family round that you would to investors in the professional round. First and foremost: put your understandings in writing. Use a placement memorandum, a disciplined approach, an elevator summary — all the professional tools. Otherwise, you're simply asking them to loan you money and you're risking the very real possibility that they may misunderstand the investment they're making, or the promised returns, or both. Putting your understandings in writing not only gives your family and friends the respect they are due, but it also helps you avoid confusion and contentious debates down the road. A good lawyer also can help. This is investment capital you're talking about, after all, not a $20 loan that will be repaid next week.

Giving special consideration to family and friends

Constructing an elaborate set of agreements that confer special rights on friends and family is not customary, for good economic reasons. Not enough money is around to have the lawyers negotiate, say, a convertible preferred stock deal with all the usual bells and whistles. Generating capital is the idea, not sucking it up in concessions granted to your investors. That being the case, what special consideration should you give family and friends? Well, no one right answer to that question will apply in every situation, but a couple of suggestions are definitely in order.

- ✔ Obligate your company to give frequent reports, as often as quarterly, to all your investors. Nothing is more annoying to a private equity investor than sending a check to an early-stage company and then hearing nothing further until the entrepreneur either hits a home run or strikes out. Be sure to require that unaudited financial statements and other pertinent information (how the company is doing against plan, for example) are sent to investors periodically and on time.

- ✔ Your investor's circumstances may change, and the investment may no longer be appropriate for him or her or (perish the thought) for his or her estate. Set up a mechanism, sometimes referred to as a buy-sell agreement, whereby the individual investor and/or his legal representative (the executor of the estate, for example) have the right to *put* (sell) the investment back to the company when a death or other significant change (such as a disability or bankruptcy) is involved. The company may have a right to *call* (buy the investment back) as well. The call is, in fact, generic in the typical case — in the form of a restriction on transfer. In the case of an investor's death, the company usually has a first call on the stock, and then other investors are given a chance at any left over stock.

Buy-sell agreements are relatively simple. They set up a system for appraising the investment's fair value as of the time the purchase or sale is exercised and they create a mechanism to carry out the transaction. Because these are long-term, highly illiquid investments, particularly in the early stage, you need to anticipate the *worst case* — that circumstances will change so significantly that separation is called for.

A buy-sell agreement usually enables the company to pay off the agreed-upon amount over time because the company may not be in possession of enough cash to make a lump-sum payment. An interest-bearing note secured by the stock being *put to* or *called by* the company is a typical instrument.

For ease of reference, and without pretending that such is the final word on the subject, we include a draft of a buy-sell agreement that contains a reporting requirement at the end of this chapter.

Sample Buy-Sell Agreement

(**WARNING:** *This sample copy is provided for purposes of illustration only. The provisions of this agreement are highly complex and technical, and may vary depending on controlling law; you should consult your own lawyer rather than use this sample unadvised in an actual transaction.*)

SHAREHOLDERS AGREEMENT, dated as of February __, 20__, by and among _____, Inc., a Delaware corporation (the "Company"), _____ of St. Louis, Missouri (the "Investor"), and _____ and _____ (collectively the "Founders," the Investor and the Founders sometimes hereinafter collectively referred to herein as the "Shareholders" or individually as the "Shareholder").

[PREAMBLE]

The Investor is purchasing 50,000 shares (the "Shares") of the Company's Common Stock, $.001 par value per share (the "Common Stock") pursuant to that certain Subscription Agreement of the same date herewith between the Company and the Investor (the "Subscription Agreement"), and the Founders hold a total of 880,000 shares of Common Stock in equal (440,000 each) proportions; and one of the conditions to the closing of the Subscription Agreement is the execution and delivery of this Agreement.

NOW, THEREFORE, in consideration of the mutual covenants and agreements contained herein and other good and valuable consideration, the receipt and sufficiency of which are hereby acknowledged, the parties hereto agree as follows:

Right of Co-Sale

1.1 If any Founder proposes to sell any Shares ("Co-Sale Shares") of Common Stock to a party or affiliated group (the "Transferee") in a transaction or series of related transactions involving the sale of more than [50,000] such Shares or resulting in the

Transferee for the first time controlling the power to vote more than 50% of the total votes for nominees to the Company's board of directors, such Founder shall first give reasonable notice in reasonable detail to the Investor in sufficient time to allow the Investor to participate in the sale on the same terms and conditions as such Founder. To the extent any prospective purchaser(s) refuses to purchase Shares or other securities from the Investor exercising its rights of co-sale hereunder, the Founder shall not sell to such prospective purchaser or purchasers any Shares unless and until, simultaneously with such sale, the Founder shall purchase the offered shares or other securities from the Investor. Notwithstanding the foregoing, the provisions of this Section shall not apply to (i) any pledge of Co-Sale Shares made pursuant to a bona fide loan transaction that creates a mere security interest; (ii) any transfer to the ancestors, descendants, or spouse or to trusts for the benefit of such persons of a Founder; or (iii) any bona fide gift; provided that (A) the transferring Founder shall inform the Investor of such pledge, transfer or gift prior to effecting it and (B) the pledgee, transferee, or donee shall furnish the Investor with a written agreement to be bound by and comply with all provisions of Section 1. Such transferred Co-Sale Shares will remain "Co-Sale Shares" hereunder, and such pledgee, transferee, or donee shall be treated as a "Founder" for purposes of this Agreement.

Reports

2.1 The Company agrees that, as long as the Investor holds any Shares of Common Stock, the Company will furnish such Investor, within 45 days after the end of each fiscal quarter and within 90 days after the end of each fiscal year, unaudited financial statements. The obligations of the Company under this Section shall terminate upon the earlier of: (i) an initial public offering of the Company's Common Stock, (ii) the closing of a merger or consolidation in which the Company does not survive; (iii) the closing of a sale of all, or substantially all, of the Company's assets; or (iv) the closing of a transaction constituting a change of control of the Company whereby a nonaffiliate of the Company acquires more than 50% of the Company's Common Stock. The Investor hereby agrees to keep such information confidential, will not disclose it to any third parties except to its affiliates, beneficial owners and its and their respective advisors, and will disclose it to its employees only on a need-to-know basis, except as necessary for the Investor to enforce its rights under this Agreement, or pursuant to a subpoena or otherwise pursuant to any legal process or as otherwise required by law.

Put Right

3.1 In the event of one or more of the following events or conditions: The filing of a petition in bankruptcy by or against the Investor; an adjudication that the Investor is an insane or incompetent person; any assignment by the Investor for the benefit of his or her creditors; any transfer, award, or confirmation of any such Shares to the Shareholder's spouse pursuant to a decree of divorce, dissolution, or separate maintenance, or pursuant to a property settlement or separation agreement; or any testamentary or other similar disposition of any interest in such Shares upon the Investor's death;

3.2 Within thirty (30) days after the occurrence of an event described above, the Investor or his trustee in bankruptcy, personal representative, guardian, executor, or administrator (as appropriate) (the "Seller") may, at his or her option, give notice to the Secretary of such event, specifying the date of such event, describing in reasonable detail the nature of the event, the number of Shares affected, and the price per Share offered by the Seller, which shall be the fair value of the same in the opinion of the Seller; the Company, hereby obligated to purchase the offered Shares, shall within 15 days accept such offer at the price offered or notify the Seller it elects to establish the fair value per Share (the "Purchase Price") in accordance with the following procedure.

3.3 If Seller and the Company are unable to resolve any disagreement with respect to the Purchase Price within ten (10) business days following receipt by Seller of the notice referred to above, the disagreement shall be submitted for resolution to a nationally recognized accounting firm mutually agreed to by the parties or, if no agreement is reached, selected by [Big Five Accounting Firm] (the "Evaluator"). The Evaluator shall act as an arbitrator to determine and resolve such dispute, based solely on presentations by the Company and Seller and not by independent review. The Evaluator's resolution shall be made within thirty (30) days of the submission of the dispute, shall be in accordance with this Agreement, shall be set forth in a written statement delivered to Seller and the Company, and shall be final, binding and conclusive.

3.4 The Company and Seller shall each pay one-half of the fees and expenses of the Evaluator in resolving any disagreements as provided herein.

3.5 Within two (2) business days after the Purchase Price is finally determined, the Company shall pay to Seller by wire transfer of immediately available funds to such account as Seller shall designate in writing, the amount of the Purchase Price per Share times the number of Shares offered. If the Company is unable to pay such Purchase Price at that time, the Company may elect to pay such Purchase Price in three installments by delivering a promissory note (the "Note"), secured by the Shares, paying interest at the then existing prime rate charged by [Large National Bank] and payable one-third upon the date specified in this Section 3.4 and one-third, principal and accrued interest, on each of the succeeding anniversaries.

Miscellaneous

4.1 Duration of Agreement. The rights and obligations of the Company and the Investor under this Agreement shall terminate on the earliest to occur of the following: (a) immediately prior to the consummation of the first underwritten public offering by the Company pursuant to an effective registration statement under the Securities Act of 1933 of any of its equity securities for its own account in which the aggregate gross proceeds to the Company equal or exceed $5,000,000, or when the Company first becomes subject to the periodic reporting requirements of Section 12(g) or 15(d) of the 1934 Act, whichever event shall first occur, (b) immediately prior to the consummation of the sale of all, or substantially all, of the Company's assets or capital stock or a merger, consolidation, reorganization or other business combination of the Company which results in the transfer of more than 50% of the voting securities of the Company, or (c) the tenth anniversary hereof

4.2 Legend. Each certificate representing Shares of Common Stock and Common Stock shall bear the following legend, until such time as the Shares of Common Stock and Common Stock represented thereby are no longer subject to the provisions hereof:

"The sale, transfer, or assignment of the securities represented by this certificate are subject to the terms and conditions of a certain Shareholders Agreement dated [Month, Day, Year] among the Company and holders of its outstanding capital stock. Copies of such Agreement may be obtained at no cost by written request made by the holder of record of this certificate to the Secretary of the Company."

4.3 Severability; Governing Law. If any provisions of this Agreement shall be determined to be illegal or unenforceable by any court of law, the remaining provisions shall be severable and enforceable in accordance with their terms. This Agreement shall be governed by, and construed in accordance with, the internal laws of the State of New York.

4.4 It is acknowledged that it will be impossible to measure the damages that would be suffered by the nonbreaching party if any party fails to comply with the provisions of this Agreement and that in the event of any such failure, the nonbreaching parties will not have an adequate remedy at law. The nonbreaching parties shall, therefore, be entitled to obtain specific performance of the breaching party's obligations hereunder and to obtain immediate injunctive relief. The breaching party shall not urge, as a defense to any proceeding for such specific performance or injunctive relief, that the nonbreaching parties have an adequate remedy at law.

4.5 If any action at law or in equity is necessary to enforce or interpret the terms of this Agreement, the prevailing party shall be entitled to reasonable attorneys' fees, costs and necessary disbursements in addition to any other relief to which such party may be entitled.

4.6 Binding Effect. This Agreement shall be binding upon and inure to the benefit of the parties hereto and their respective permitted successors and assignees, legal representatives and heirs. Nothing in this Agreement, express or implied, is intended to confer upon any party other than the parties hereto or their respective successors and assigns any rights, remedies, obligations, or liabilities under or by reason of this Agreement, except as expressly provided in this Agreement. The administrator, executor or legal representative of the Investor shall have the right to execute and deliver all documents and perform all acts necessary to exercise and perform the rights and obligations of the Investor under the terms of this Agreement.

4.7 Counterparts. This Agreement may be executed in one or more counterparts, each of which shall be deemed to be an original, but all of which taken together shall constitute one and the same instrument.

4.8 Notices. All notices to be given or otherwise made to any party to this Agreement shall be deemed to be sufficient if contained in a written instrument, delivered by hand in person, or by express overnight courier service, or by electronic facsimile transmission (with a copy sent by first-class mail, postage prepaid), or by registered or certified mail, return receipt requested, postage prepaid, addressed to such party at the address set forth herein or at such other address as may hereafter be designated in writing by the addressee to the addresser listing all parties. All such notices shall, when mailed or telegraphed, be effective when received or when attempted delivery is refused.

IN WITNESS WHEREOF, the Company, the Investor, and the Founders have executed this agreement in counterparts as of the date first above specified.

_____, Inc.

By: _____, President

By: _____, Investor

By: _____, Founder

By: _____, Founder

Chapter 4

Angel Investors

• •

• •

*A*t some point in the life of every successful business, there comes a time when it becomes especially hard to get the capital necessary to maintain growth and profitability. It's when the business is too large for the relatively small investments of family and friends to make much difference any longer, but too small to attract the interest of venture capitalists or investment banks — or even commercial banks, for that matter. When this time comes, it may sometimes seem like the only thing that can save the business is an angel sent from heaven.

Actually, angels do exist, but they aren't sent from heaven. These angels are actually angel investors, and they have saved many businesses from failure by providing them with the capital they needed just when they needed it. An *angel investor* is a high-net-worth individual (as opposed to a professionally managed venture capital firm — see Chapter 11) who's willing to make a private equity investment in an emerging-growth company. An angel is not necessarily a professional investor. He or she may be dealing with inherited money, capital acquired in real estate or oil, excess cash from a high-tech IPO, or funds from a number of other sources.

The only qualifications for being an angel are the following:

✔ **Possession of sufficient capital.** Although no strict definition of *sufficient capital* exists, the price of admission is certainly more than a few hundred or a few thousand dollars. A minimum of $10,000 in cash available for investments may not be far off the mark.

✔ **The willingness to devote — or, actually, to wager — a portion of personal capital to high-risk, potentially high-reward investments.** For every investment opportunity that makes investors rich, there are many more that fail to break even.

✔ **"Accredited" status.** *Accredited status* means that the angel is wealthy enough (in terms of assets and/or income) to absorb the high risk of investing in illiquid equity securities (securities that cannot be readily bought and sold on the open market). Regulation D put into effect by the Securities & Exchange Commission sets out the accredited investor test, presumably to protect the public from falling into traps by investing in securities that are riskier than the investor's apparent ability to absorb such financial risks would suggest. Roughly speaking, accredited investors must meet the following criteria:

- Minimum net worth (with spouse) of $1 million

- Minimum income of $200,000 a year ($300,000 for a married couple) for the preceding two years, coupled with an expectation to match that income in the current year

Although individuals have always invested in emerging-growth companies, the rise of angel investing in the last decade or so has been remarkable and has given an enormous boost to the amount of capital available to businesses in the United States. According to the Small Business Administration, more than 250,000 active angel investors in the U.S. are investing at least $20 billion in more than 30,000 small companies each year. That's a lot of money going to a lot of businesses.

In this chapter, you can find out everything you need to know about angel investors — who they are, what they do, and how to find them. We also explain which kinds of deals angel investors typically find attractive. Finally, we take a look at what a typical angel deal looks like.

Angels: Getting to Know You

Angel investing has become an increasingly popular source of capital for businesses — and an important first step on the way to more formal sources of capital, such as venture funding or an IPO. Here are some of the reasons:

✔ Most angels expect a lower rate of return on their investments than venture capital and other professional firms do. (A desire to double their investment in three years is not out of the ordinary for many angels, whereas VCs and other firms might expect returns that compound at more than 30 percent.)

✔ Angel funding can often be obtained much more quickly than venture capital.

✔ Angel investors are often less aggressive in their demands for ownership and control of the business than venture capital firms are.

| ✔ The process of *due diligence* (where the investor checks out a potential investment) is less rigorous than in more formal funding situations.

For these reasons and others, finding an angel investor is often the strategy of choice for young and high-growth businesses that are looking for cash infusions in the range of $100,000 to $1 million — too small to land on the radar screens of venture capital firms and investment banks — but that do not yet have the track record to get this kind of money in the form of a bank loan or line of credit.

As much press as angel investors get these days, you'd think that they're falling all over themselves looking for places to park their money. That is not quite the case. First of all, the universe of people with enough extra money to invest in fairly risky ventures is relatively small. Second, the recent dot-com meltdown has made many potential angels wary of investing in relatively risky start-ups and high-growth companies. That being the case, it pays to understand where you're most likely to find angel investors and what kinds of investments they look for.

Understanding where angels come from

A rise in income and a robust stock market have created enormous wealth, at least for the top tier of U.S. taxpayers. That wealth has enabled individuals to set aside a portion of their capital for what are called *alternative investments* — investments other than securities and rated debt, including early-stage companies.

Angels have played an increasingly significant role in this sector because there are more of them, and they have more money than in prior periods — the wealth factor academics frequently cite. Personal wealth has a good deal to do with entrepreneurship. Data show that rising residential real estate prices stimulate the venture economy, as entrepreneurs and angels put their newfound wealth to work by borrowing against the value of their residences and putting the capital in emerging-growth opportunities.

Also, the celebrated wins in venture capital have drawn more players to the game. Reading about the sensational good fortune experienced by the early shareholders in Microsoft, Cisco, Intel, and the like has encouraged others to play. During the past 10 to 20 years, many major business successes have become angels — they are still fairly young, they aren't ready to retire yet, and they want to keep their fingers in the entrepreneurial pie. Of course, this happy picture has been spoiled somewhat by the dot-com meltdown, but as the economy begins perking back up, angels will be back in force.

Finally, early-stage opportunities have pulled in angel capital because professionally managed venture capital has largely deserted the early-stage sector, preferring to go after bigger fish.

The dearth of venture capital for brand-new ventures opens up an opportunity for angel capital — nature abhors a vacuum. Angels, by and large, are not competing with professionally managed funds. That doesn't necessarily mean that angels get good deals (a point we talk about later in this chapter), but they do have the advantage of avoiding competitive auctions with prices spiking upward because of bidding from venture capitalists with more money than they know what to do with.

Does your angel measure up?

Just as the number of angel investors has been increasing during the past several years, so too has the average size of angel investments. A decade ago, the average investment size was in the range of $48,000 to $60,000. Today, that range has grown to an average investment size of $145,000. And even when angels pool their money and invest in syndicates, the size of the average start-up deal is only about $600,000, raised from six to eight angel investors. The size of the investment often depends on the type of angel involved. (We explain the various types of angels in the following section.) First-timers like to put their toes in the water slowly; serial angels are semiprofessionals — and they're much more willing to invest larger sums of money in their chosen companies.

A Who's Who of Angels

Other than "having a high net worth," no one-size-fits-all description of an angel investor exists. The levels of experience and particular interests of angel investors vary widely. But certain overall classifications can be useful if you're hoping to match your capital needs with the right kind of investor.

Wondering what kind of angel is right for your kind of investment opportunity? Here's a guide to the many different types of angels:

✔ **Serial angels** are perhaps the most productive angel type in the sense that these angels often add significant value to the companies in which they invest. A serial angel has done it before — he or she has put money on the table for an investment in an early-stage opportunity, cashed out (or "harvested," as they say) the investment, and then put the profits into the next opportunity.

A subset of serial angels (also known as *celebrity angels*) consists of former entrepreneurs — people like Netscape's Jim Clark and Microsoft's Paul Allen. Although their fortunes take them way beyond typical angels, entrepreneurs who have built major companies and sold them usually retain their appetite for the game.

✔ *Tire kickers* are the opposite of serial angels. They lack a genuine commitment to angel investing — at least at present — but they're using the process as a means of educating themselves.

✔ *Trailblazer angels* are experienced investors, typically partners in investment banks and venture capital firms. Although their firms may not trouble themselves with any deal worth less than $50 million (the breakpoint for the VCs these days is a round of more than $8 million, which means a premoney valuation between $12 and $20 million), the individual partners, usually with the blessing of their employers, are often interested in incubating deals that show exceptional promise, with an eye on keeping a link to the company until it reaches adolescence and becomes a desirable client for the angels' host organization.

Some venture capital firms and investment banks have rules against this practice because conflicts of interest can get tricky. For example, the VC firm and individual partners may invest in the same enterprise but at different price levels. However, many banks and firms encourage angel investing as a way to keep the pipeline flowing.

These angels are often the most desirable because of the so-called chaperone rule, which states that the odds of a start-up company succeeding are significantly enhanced when the company has a *chaperone* from the get-go, an experienced guide on the trip from the embryo to the IPO.

✔ *Retired angels* ("the Godfathers") are a common phenomenon. A number of business executives have been able to generate enough personal capital to enable them to quit their jobs and "retire." As a group, they are vigorous, in full possession of their faculties, sometimes young (in their late 40s or early 50s), and perfectly capable of keeping up in the so-called rat race.

Often restless and looking for something to do — charitable and other pro bono activities soak up only a portion of their energy — many naturally turn to angel investing, but with a distinct point of view. They aren't looking to become passive investors; they're looking to add their skills and experience to the companies in which they invest, often serving on their boards and, in most cases, at least as advisors.

✔ **Socially responsible angels** are investors who are interested in *double-bottom-line investing* — that is, doing well by doing good. Many of these individuals can be contacted through the Community Development Venture Capital Alliance, a prestigious nonprofit organization based in New York (www.cdvca.org).

✔ **Angel syndicates** are groups who episodically invest together, joining their capital for more influence in more material deals. The best-known syndicate, the Band of Angels in Palo Alto, California, has 120 members, averages $600,000 per investment, and has invested close to $50 million total. Syndicates such as the Band of Angels have helped legitimize this particular form of collective investing.

Within the various categories of angels, angel investors have earned a variety of nicknames. These nicknames, coined by Robert J. Gaston in his book, *Finding Private Venture Capital for Your Firm: A Complete Guide* (John Wiley & Sons, 1989), tend to indicate more precisely the motivation that drives the angels to invest their hard-earned money in often-risky ventures:

- **Daddy Warbucks:** Because these are the wealthiest angels — comprising about 39 percent of all angel deals and investing 68 percent of all angel funds — they are perhaps the most important angels of all. If you're a smart seeker of angel investment funds, you'll direct much of your search efforts toward locating a Daddy Warbucks.

- **Cousin Randy:** These angels typically invest only in business opportunities presented by their own relatives — if you're not related to Cousin Randy, chances are that he (or she) isn't going to write you a check anytime soon.

- **Dr. Kildare:** These angels tend to be doctors, lawyers, and accountants. If they hear about your opportunity, it's likely to have been through their professional colleagues — other doctors, lawyers, and accountants.

The typical angel

Unfortunately, you can't identify angel investors simply by looking at their nametags or by sizing up the cars they drive. Angels are male or female, they're young and they're retired, and they come from all walks of life. The majority of angel investors do, however, share some general characteristics. According to studies on the topic:

- Angels are predominantly male (around 97 percent).

- The average age of an angel is 48 to 50.

- Anywhere from 80 percent to 94 percent of angels have college degrees, of which 42 percent to 56 percent have graduate educations.

- Around 87 percent of business angel investors have moderate to substantial general business experience.

- Angel investors tend to invest locally, often no more than an hour or so from their homes or offices.

Angels are significantly more entrepreneurial than venture capitalists, with 75 percent to 83 percent having operational start-up experience, compared with only about a third of venture capitalists. One study found that the average number of entrepreneurial investments made by business angels during the last five years was 2.45, while two West Coast studies claim that angels typically make two or three investments every three years.

Around 75 percent of angels claim that their principal source of wealth is their own past business, while the remaining 25 percent earned it from quoted investments. The size of angel investments ranges as follows: 20 percent of less than $25,000; 40 percent of $25,000 to $99,000; 25 percent of $100,000 to $250,000; and 15 percent of more than $250,000.

How an angel puts a value on your company

Valuation — putting a value on a business — is a difficult task even for professionals. The task is that much more daunting for nonprofessional investors, a subset of the investment universe that includes most angels. The more sophisticated angels have wrestled with the issue and come up with a solution: *next-round pricing.* This methodology may be best illuminated in question-and-answer format.

Q: How do you value a start-up in the angel round when there are no revenues, customers, nor complete management teams . . . just a concept and some intellectual property?

A: Increasingly, the answer is that you don't. You value the company for the purposes of allocating percentage interests for a given amount of money on the basis of the next round, the so-called Series A round.

Q: Why postpone the valuation?

A: First, it's very hard for angels, particularly angels who are not routinely involved in the venture capital business, to come to an intelligent estimate of valuation when so many factors are yet to be known or realized. Secondly, angels are often friends and family (the angel round is sometimes called the friends-and-family round), and there's a natural reluctance to drive a hard bargain with a relative, a former college roommate, or the best man at your wedding.

Q: Why is the price per share in the Series A round more accurate?

A: It isn't necessarily more accurate. However, odds are that it may be because it has been negotiated with professionals — the venture capitalists. Moreover, the company has shown progress in the interim, at least presumably, and because the VCs are professionals, the awkwardness of negotiating with one's father-in-law doesn't exist.

Q: Is the price the same for the angel and the Series A round? Isn't that a bit unfair to the angels?

A: Yes, it is. Therefore, the price is not the same. Ordinarily, the price per share of the angel round is stated as a price that's discounted, say, 20 percent to 30 percent from the price in the Series A round. The reason for that is to reward the early — and highest-risk — money.

Q: What happens if there is no Series A round?

A: There is a default option — a penalty price, in effect. The start-up is given the opportunity to give the angels their money back, which is usually impossible, or issue shares at a low valuation (at below market prices), meaning maximum dilution to the existing shareholders.

Q: If you use this methodology, what kind of security do the angels get?

A: It's ordinarily styled as a bridge loan, convertible into common stock, or sometimes convertible into preferred stock at the same price or — in the case of preferred stock — entailing the same conversion price as the VCs pay in the Series A round.

Q: If the angel round is convertible into preferred stock, who holds the common stock of the company?

A: The founders and the employees, and maybe some friends and family.

The Outer Limits of Angel Deals

The good news is that angels have a clear field in the early-stage sector. The bad news is that the market is extraordinarily inefficient. First and foremost, no clearinghouse of information exists on the size, shape, and pricing of deals on the one hand and on the location and contact information of angels on the other. In fact, with some significant exceptions that we discuss later in this chapter, if an entrepreneur wanting to attract angel capital were to take out an ad in the *Wall Street Journal* or otherwise promote his or his concept publicly, that method could be deemed illegal and enforcement action could be taken.

An SEC rule forbids "general advertising and general solicitation" for investors in privately held companies. (Start-ups, by definition, are privately owned.) As a consequence, angel access to interesting deals has been hit-or-miss.

To find angel investors, you usually engage in what is euphemistically called networking — going to industry events and rubbing elbows with the other participants with the hope that some of them will be looking for investments, mining professional relationships (asking your lawyer and/or accountant for leads, for example), and exhausting your Rolodex.

Local business associations are the most common way to get plugged in, but the networking process takes a lot of time — usually more time than is available after you've started operations. It's best to establish your Rolodex well *before* you start operations — having your angels lined up first is even better. You alone may not be able to devote enough time to the process, and your management team may need to help. In addition, understand that getting capital from angels is not like withdrawing cash from an ATM — if you're putting together an angel round with multiple angels, getting the capital you need can take 6 to 12 months.

The dirty shame, of course, is that, because of market inefficiency, square pegs are unable to find square holes very effectively or frequently. You may have an extremely interesting and attractive proposal, but if you fail to bump up against an angel or two, your concept can starve in its infancy.

On the other side of the coin, a ready, willing, and able angel may wind up with nothing but second-rate deals to review because there is no reliable way to tap into a superior deal stream. The nature of the beast is that a lot of bad deals get funded and a lot of good deals do not.

In recent years, a number of activists have tried to lessen the market's inefficiencies, but none of them — to date, anyway — has been significantly successful. The marketplace is inefficient, and the players simply have to get used to it. Entrepreneurs looking for angels must be extraordinarily creative in figuring out ways to get their executive summaries around within the limits of the law. If you don't make the effort, you don't have a fair chance of reaping the rewards.

What You Can Expect from Your Friendly, Local Angel

Although entrepreneurs have all sorts of expectations from their angels (some of which are realistic, and some of which are anything but), there are realities respecting the items angels will actually deliver. The key things that angels provide to entrepreneurs include

- Capital
- Leads to other angels
- Good advice

Angels can get you the capital you need

First and foremost, angels provide companies — particularly relatively new and high-growth enterprises — with the capital they need to expand, to conduct research and development, or to bring a new product or service to market. As we mentioned in the introduction to this chapter, more than 250,000 active angel investors in the United States are investing some $20 billion in more than 30,000 small companies each year.

If you're an entrepreneur looking for capital, one of the first places you should look is the angel investor market.

Angels can introduce you to other angels

Angels also provide leads to other angels who write checks. One of the first questions any investor asks when viewing an early-stage opportunity is, "Who else is in?" If a well-known angel in a particular community has made an investment, that fact alone often has magnetic power. The lead angel's investment is as well-known as "the Good Housekeeping Seal of Approval" — and for obvious reasons. A potential investor will think, "Well, if it's good enough for so-and-so, it's good enough for me; so-and-so knows this business backward and forward."

Angels make great advisors

The third thing angels provide to entrepreneurs is good advice on a number of topics. For example:

✔ Who are the best lawyers and accountants in town?

✔ How do you put together a budget intelligently?

✔ How do you forecast?

✔ What is the best marketing strategy for my company's products?

Many of the issues have been the focus of the angel's professional concern for years. You can run all these items by a group of angels, each one contributing in different ways. And the price of the advice is usually right — it's free. Because the angel has a stake in the game, his or her counsel is more valuable than the advice you would ordinarily receive at that price. You pay for the advice by selling stock to the angels, presumably at a favorable price per share.

The 411 on Angels: Where to Find Them

After reading this chapter, you may have decided that finding an angel investor to provide the capital you need for your business is now your number-one priority. If so, that's great — there are a lot of angels out there providing a lot of cash to a lot of businesses.

Yet, that brings you to the $64,000 question (or, more accurately, the $500,000 or $1 million question): Where do you go to find an angel? We thought you'd never ask! Here are a few of the very *best* places to start your search.

Networking

One of the best ways to find an angel is networking with as many people as you can, telling them about your business opportunity and your search for investors. You never know who may be interested in throwing a little money your way: your lawyer, your accountant, your doctor, a friend of a friend, a rich aunt — they all may be looking for a place to invest their cash. The more people you talk to about your opportunity, the greater the chances that an angel will appear.

That means getting out of your office and setting aside time to socialize with others. Playing golf is a time-honored way of mixing business with pleasure — countless deals have been struck on the links. If your college alumni group has a chapter in your area, you can join it and start attending functions. Becoming active in local business associations, such as the Association for Corporate Growth or the Chamber of Commerce, or in a national service organization, such as the Lion's Club, Rotary, or Jaycees, is a great way to meet potential angels.

The more people you tell about your opportunity, the better your chance of finding the capital you need.

Lists

There are a variety of sources for finding an angel in your neighborhood (none of which is complete). Perhaps the best-known angel network is a quasi-government facility called the Access to Capital Electronic Network (Ace-Net), which matches angels and entrepreneurs. Contact Ace-Net on the Web at www.ace-net.sr.unh.edu. There you can find the names and addresses of the network's affiliates throughout the United States. See also the discussion of Ace-Net in Chapter 6.

The MIT Enterprise Forum is a facility that invites entrepreneurs to present business plans. It isn't an angel network per se, but it's a way to reach angel investors. You can find it on the Web at http://web.mit.edu/entforum/www/index.html. The forum has chapters from California, the District of Columbia, Massachusetts, New Hampshire, New York, Oregon, Pennsylvania, Texas, and Washington.

Robert J. Robinson and Mark Van Osnabrugge's book, *Angel Investing: Matching Start-up Funds with Start-up Companies — A Guide for Entrepreneurs, Individual Investors, and Venture Capitalists* (Jossey-Bass, 2000) contains a list of associations with their addresses and contact information. This list extends for 72 pages and is definitely worth consulting. It features mainly not-for-profit and civic economic development organizations. It isn't a list of all the angel clubs in the country; as a matter of fact, it isn't particularly useful if you're looking for an informal angel club that meets, say, for a Thursday breakfast once a month in the offices of a local law firm or investment bank. These meetings take place in various cities; the New York New Media Association plays host to a typical angel affair once a month (see www.NYNMA.org). And VC Experts (www.vcexperts.com) is a source of information on angel clubs in selected other cities. See Chapter 6 for a discussion of angel clubs.

Venture capital clubs

One often-tried gambit for raising cash from angels is to make a presentation at a forum organized by a venture capital club. Venture capital clubs consist of an organizer and a mailing list of individuals and entities in a given region that have demonstrated interest in venture capital. More than 100 such groups are in the United States; they meet monthly over breakfast or lunch. The most important part of a typical meeting is the "Five-Minute (or 60-Second) Forum," in which anyone can speak about his or her venture or interest (finding a job, for example) for a limit of one to five minutes. The purported purpose of attending these meetings is making contacts and not necessarily finding offers of funding.

Venture capital clubs, sometimes called dating services, are not to be confused with the trade association to which most professional managers belong, the National Venture Capital Association, membership in which is limited to venture capital organizations, corporate financiers, and individual capitalists. Although there tend to be more people looking for capital at these club meetings than there are offering it, more than a few entrepreneurs have gotten the angel financing they needed by becoming active members of venture capital clubs.

The Internet

The Internet is fast becoming an excellent resource for finding angels or groups of angels who are interested in investing in all kinds of different businesses. Although it may never be an adequate substitute for the old-fashioned face-to-face interaction that meeting angels in social situations provides, no search for angel investors would be complete without checking the Internet — for information about angel investing and to meet potential angel investors.

Here's a selection of Web sites to help jump-start your search:

- ✓ **Garage Technology Ventures:** www.garage.com
- ✓ **Private Equity Network:** www.nvst.com/pnvHome.asp
- ✓ **National Venture Capital Association:** www.nvca.org

Rather than enumerate the vast universe of online resources here, we have devoted an entire chapter — Chapter 6 — to the topic. Be sure to check it out!

Chapter 5

Customers and Vendors

*B*elieve it or not, vendors (the companies you buy from) and customers (the folks you sell to) are often happy to provide financing to companies just like yours, either directly or indirectly. In fact, many vendors have integrated financial incentives into their marketing strategies as a way of building their businesses, and they depend on this financing to attract new customers and retain current ones. And guess what? You're not limited only to your vendors — your customers can become a source of financing, too, simply by agreeing to certain methods of payment that get you your money before you significantly expend resources on their orders or projects.

That being the case, why not take advantage of these opportunities?

In this chapter, we examine different kinds of financing available from vendors through something called trade credit, and we consider the benefits of financing provided by so-called vendor/lenders and by a seemingly unlikely source: your own clients and customers. Finally, we take a look at the wonderful world of bartering and how it's changing the way companies around the world do business.

The Ins and Outs of Trade Credit

How would you like to get 30 days of credit without filling out a stack of detailed loan forms at your bank and without pledging all your assets (and perhaps even your first-born child) as collateral? Sounds good, doesn't it?

And then, what if this credit were provided to your company absolutely free? That's an offer that no one can refuse. And it's an offer that many companies make to their customers when they agree to bill them for products delivered or services rendered — and giving their customers 30 days to pay their bills — instead of requiring them to pay immediately. This practice, known as *trade credit,* is a powerful form of financing, and if you take advantage of it, it can generate tremendous cash flow opportunities for your business.

Businesses offer trade credit in many different forms. Here are a few of the most common ones:

- A delay in payment on purchases of goods or services
- Sales on consignment where you pay your vendors only after the item is sold
- Financial incentives to purchase certain products, including rebates, funds for cooperative advertising, shelving fees, and more.

The advantages of trade credit for you, the purchaser of a company's products, are readily apparent:

- You possess the product or service for several weeks before you have to pay for it — perhaps even reselling it before you pay your vendor.
- It's unlikely that you'll be required to make any sort of down payment or pay interest.
- Many companies are more than willing to offer trade credit.

Vendors benefit as well. By offering trade credit, they increase their sales and potentially capture more market share. All in all, it's a win-win situation for vendors and customers alike.

Getting trade credit isn't always quite as easy as snapping your fingers — you may have to fill out a brief application. Your vendor then may check your credit references to ensure that you have a stable history of repaying your financial obligations on time. Here are some of the elements of a typical agreement for trade credit:

- The name of your company and anyone authorized to execute the agreement for you
- A promise that all the information you provide is true and complete
- A pledge to live up to the terms of the agreement
- A statement asserting that if any information you provide proves to be false, the agreement is violated and you may be found in default
- A clause spelling out that you are responsible for any costs — for collection, legal fees, and so on — associated with your violation of the agreement

Getting your foot in the door

Of course, there's a bit more to establishing trade credit than simply filling out an application. If your business is relatively new, don't expect companies to fall all over themselves sending you their products without you first paying for them. Because trade credit actually is a short-term loan to your business, companies offering trade credit to you will first want to be assured that you're a good risk.

That being said, a right way and a wrong way exist for establishing your first trade credit. The steps that follow show you the right way.

1. **Establish limited credit.**

   An equipment lease from a manufacturer such as for a copier is often one of the easiest first credits to establish for later use as a reference. Your landlord is another reference. Your bank is the third. Treat these references as if they were gold and establish a good payment track record. Then pick two or three of your important vendors and meet with them personally. Do whatever is necessary to get them to start extending you some form of credit with the aim of using them as your references for future credit applications — almost every credit application requires credit references. You may not get the best terms on these first trade credits, but once you establish them along with the initial three, you'll be on your way.

2. **Be prepared to provide financial statements to prospective creditors.**

   The format of your financial statements need to focus on your balance sheet and cash flow. Be prepared to discuss the stability of your sales and customers!

3. **Be prepared to make personal guarantees of payment.**

   Before you have credit references or for very large credits, you may have to make personal guarantees that ensure repayment of the debt in the event your company defaults. Before you sign any personal guarantees, be sure that you are fully willing and able to financially withstand the potential consequences of doing so.

4. **Once credit is established, review your company's credit report.**

   Errors or material omissions on your credit report often can hurt your credit. Correct them ASAP. Keep a semiannual tickler on your calendar to review your report regularly.

Do you know your credit score?

Just as individuals have credit ratings maintained by the big three consumer credit bureaus, Equifax, Trans Union, and Experian, so too do businesses.

When it comes to rating business credit, however, Dun and Bradstreet (D&B) — with its database that includes more than 55 million businesses around the world — is clearly the 2,000-pound gorilla, and it is a company to which you need to pay close attention.

So, why worry about credit ratings and companies like Dun & Bradstreet? Because before they grant you trade credit, your vendors are going to want to be sure that your business is a good credit risk. One of the best ways of doing so is checking your credit rating with an independent credit-rating service such as Dun & Bradstreet.

While D&B offers a variety of informative business reports to its clients, of immediate interest is one report in particular — the Credit Scoring Report. It tells your vendors whether they should consider offering you trade credit. Here are the key elements of the D&B Credit Scoring Report:

- ✔ **Credit score class.** This score is D&B's assessment of your company's payment habits, ranked on a scale of 0 to 5. A rating of 1 indicates a company that is at low risk of an account becoming delinquent within the next 12 months, a rating of 5 indicates a company with a high risk of an account becoming delinquent within the next 12 months. Note that a score of 0 indicates bankruptcy or a location that is out of business.

- ✔ **Credit score percentile.** This score is an indication of how your company ranks against all other businesses in D&B's database. A ranking of 1 is the highest risk; a ranking of 100 is the lowest risk.

- ✔ **Commercial credit score.** This rating predicts the likelihood of an account becoming severely delinquent within the next 12 months. Based on a scale of from 101 to 660 (with 101 the highest risk and 660 the lowest risk), each 40-point increase or decrease indicates a doubling or halving of risk.

- ✔ **Average high credit and highest credit.** This number gives your vendors an indication of the extent to which you have been granted credit in the past.

- ✔ **PAYDEX score.** This score provides your vendors with an instant overview of how your firm pays its bills, and how quickly you're likely to pay them in the future. A score of 100 is tops — you consistently pay early — and a score of 20 is at the bottom, indicating slow payments made up to 120 days late.

Making sure that your D&B reports are as good as they can possibly be clearly is in your best interest. A good report can make a tremendous difference in the willingness of vendors to extend trade credit to your firm. You can improve your ratings by:

- ✔ **Always paying your bills on time.** By avoiding late payments, you'll improve your credit scores. Paying your bills early improves your credit scores even more (although doing so may have a negative impact on your cash flow).

✔ **Heading off problems before they become problems.** If for some reason you can't make a payment on time, contact your vendor to let them know ahead of time. Explain your problem and work out a revised payment schedule. Doing so not only saves your vendor from a nasty surprise, but you may also head off a negative credit report as well.

✔ **Periodically check your credit scoring report.** Keep close tabs on your own credit scores to determine where you're weaknesses are. If, for example, your PAYDEX score indicates that you consistently pay slowly to 90 days, work on improving the speed of your payments.

Vendor/lenders: The Joys of Financial Incentives

Your vendors and suppliers want your business. In fact, some of them are so eager to get your business that they're willing to extend you 30 days of credit without charge. This short-term loan — commonly known as trade credit — is a terrific deal for any business that can get it.

As great as trade credit is, some vendors have that deal beat. Not only will they give you 30 days to pay their invoices, but they'll set you up with special financing deals to buy their products, too. In particularly competitive markets — think office copiers and telecommunications equipment and services — manufacturers almost literally fall over one another in their zeal to offer potential customers extremely attractive financial incentives to buy their products, including

✔ Low or no down payments

✔ Super-low interest rates

✔ Extended payment plans

✔ Substantial discounts from list price

Many manufacturers of equipment, vehicles, durable goods, and other relatively expensive items offer special financing deals, either through third-party financing or through a captive financial-services subsidiary. General Motors, for example, offers financing — including loans, leases, and other financial instruments — through its General Motors Acceptance Corporation subsidiary. Knowing that these special deals exist — and then seeking them out whenever possible — can give your finances a real boost.

More tricks of the trade

You can take advantage of a variety of lesser-known, but highly effective ways of using vendors financially. Savvy business owners and managers make it a point to take advantage of as many of these opportunities as possible.

✔ **Goods for inventories or resale:** Consignment can work well in certain retail situations. If, for example, you're selling a product that uses another product (in other words, your software that works with certain hardware), the hardware vendor has many programs for getting you loaner or evaluation units for free (or very low cost), and often offers better than 30-day terms on resale items. You can also set up *JIT* (Just-In-Time) or *drop shipment* ordering programs to minimize your inventory investment. Long-term (or exclusive) supply contracts with key vendors also open doors to good financing options. These can go under various names such as OEM Agreements, Reseller Agreements, Partner Agreements, and so forth.

✔ **Facilities:** Building lease agreements (especially for retail) can often be structured as a base rent plus a percentage of sales (or similar variable). This approach can initially reduce monthly payments until your sales ramp up (or down). In areas like Silicon Valley, reducing your rent or lease costs by offering stock or warrants in your company isn't unusual. Of course you can always renegotiate your lease to a longer term or at a different rate. Landlords often offer free months of rent for such arrangements because they want to keep their rental rate up, and in return, you won't have to pay rent for a few months.

✔ **Deposits:** Deposits are real cash drains to be avoided whenever possible. In their place, use some other form of collateral in lieu of cash. If you have a bank line of credit, work with your bank to use a *standby letter of credit* in lieu of cash deposits. Ask whether your vendor will accept a security agreement (maybe requiring a UCC filing as well) for some asset you have that he can sell if you failed to pay.

✔ **Equipment and software:** Look into *lease to buy arrangements* that enable you to conserve your cash. More software is being offered on a rental basis, so that outlays can be minimized for those sometimes costly purchases.

✔ **Services:** Service providers offer a wide range of deals such as *level billing,* which can effectively stretch out your payments more than 30 days. For any completion type of contracted services (such as professional services), be sure to minimize the initial payment and maximize the payment due on completion.

✔ **Labor:** Rather than hiring employees, you can use temporary help services to stretch out your payroll from weekly or biweekly to a 30-day pay.

✔ **Key suppliers:** When you have one or two sole-source suppliers, you may be able to pay them in stock or convince them to invest if they think your business is important to their strategy or success. Doing so can help put them on your team and may lead to an exit strategy (such as merger) at later date.

Before you run out and apply for a loan from a bank or other financial institution for a piece of needed equipment, check to see what kind of financing and other incentives your vendors will offer you to buy or lease from them. Depending on how much they want your business, you may be glad you did.

Getting Your Customers to Finance Your Company

Believe it or not, your customers and clients are another ready source of cash and other forms of capital. Don't believe us? Well, here's how:

- ✔ **Bill in advance.** Many businesses require their customers to put down a deposit, pay a retainer, or provide some other form of advance payment as a normal part of doing business. This practice is common with construction companies, law firms, and consultants, for example. It can be a common practice for your business if you can convince your customers and clients that it makes sense for them to agree to it. Sure, this may be a tough sell if you've never billed your customers in advance before — you'll have to couch your pitch in terms of how advance payment also will benefit them — but the rewards are well worth the effort you'll expend getting them.

  Deposits, advance billings, retainers, and the like are really forms of customer financing because you're paid before you do any work. Advance billing is a sweet deal when you can get it — your accountant (and your cash flow) will be extremely happy with the infusion of cash.

- ✔ **Bill your clients early and often.** Some companies that provide products or services over long periods agree to bill their clients at the end of the delivery cycles. Doing so is a mistake. Providing an invoice as often as you can — weekly probably wouldn't be too often from your perspective, would it? — during the course of a long delivery cycle is much better for you.

  The point is that the sooner you're paid for products and services that you deliver to your customers, the better able you are to take advantage of not having to pay your own vendor invoices for a full 30 days — in essence providing you with a cash float. The key is collecting fast and paying slowly (but on time!). Successfully managed, this float can have a terrifically positive effect on your company's cash flow.

- ✔ **Require payment on delivery.** Many businesses require payment on delivery of a product or service. When was the last time that you bought, say, dinner at a nice restaurant and then asked them to bill you?

That isn't how it works — you must pay the restaurant cash or give your server your credit card before you leave. Otherwise, you'll be washing dishes in the back.

Although requiring customers to pay on delivery of a product or service may not generate much in the way of customer financing — it may buy you a few days at most — it definitely prevents a situation where you're waiting (and waiting . . .) for payment to arrive days, weeks, or even months after you delivered the goods or services.

✔ **Outright investment.** Occasionally, a customer looks at a company that it does business with and likes what it sees — so much so that the customer decides to invest money in a product, a process, or the company itself.

Customers investing in companies they do business with is not uncommon, especially in high-tech industries, where companies are always on the lookout for new technologies that can give them an edge over competition. Many even have divisions whose primary job is identifying and investing in interesting customer technologies. Prepare for this possibility by having an open mind for that sort of investment and by dropping hints to your customers that you would welcome partnerships.

Although having your customers pay you for your products and at the same time having them provide you with financing may seem like a dream, it happens much more often than you might think. Take a close look at how your company asks customers to pay for the products and services they buy. Every dollar you can swing into some form of advance or accelerated payment is a dollar of financing that you're getting for free from your customers.

Barter: Who Needs Money?

Barter — exchange of a product or service for another product or service rather than a cash payment — has been around for a long time. Before humans invented the idea of money, they traded things of value to obtain things of value. If someone had a nice mastodon hide gathering dust in her cave, for example, she could trade it to one of her neighbors for several baskets of fish or perhaps some bone tools.

Bartering has come a long way since those ancient times, and nowhere is this more the case than in business. According to industry statistics, in North America alone, more than $7.5 billion in sales are transacted each year by the commercial barter industry, comprising more than 300,000 businesses. The number of firms involved in bartering is expected to quadruple to 1.2 million by 2008.

You're in good company if you barter

If you think that bartering is limited to marginal businesses or mom-and-pop operations, you're wrong. Big business has discovered the benefits of bartering in a big way. Here are but a few deals from www.barterasia.com:

- Textron Inc. traded $455 million worth of milling supplies to Poland for copper and brass.

- Coca-Cola has traded its products for everything from Korean toothpick frills to Bulgarian forklifts to penetrate foreign markets.

- General Motors barters in more than 30 countries. For example, the company traded locomotives for tea in Sri Lanka and then sold the tea for cash to English tea dealers.

- McDonnell Douglas bartered DC-9s and DC-10s to Yugoslavia for crystal glassware, cutting tools, leather coats, and canned hams. The company sold the hams to its employees.

- PepsiCo trades syrup and technology for Russian vodka.

- Ford traded cars, trucks, and vans to the Winter Olympics for promotional rights.

- Occidental Petroleum built a chemical plant and provided materials in exchange for $20 billion worth of ammonia from Russia.

In the world of business, three primary flavors of barter exist:

- **Small business exchanges:** These barter exchanges bring small-store owners and small retailers together to trade among themselves to avoid having to pay cash for needed supplies and services. Approximately 400 small business exchanges exist in the United States today. You can find them through a search of the Internet or by contacting one of the barter associations listed at the end of this chapter.

- **Corporate barter:** Corporations barter a wide variety of products and services to liquidate excess inventory, utilize idle capacity, expand sales, and penetrate new markets while increasing cash flow and conserving precious working capital.

- **Countertrade:** Countertrade occurs when large multinational companies (think IBM) are required by countries with weak currencies or by law to take partial payments in the form of goods rather than cash.

An increasing number of businesses are making barter an important part of the way they do business. You can, too.

The good news about bartering

Although bartering goods and services does not generate cash (and therefore is not a source of capital per se), it does enable companies to conserve their cash — spending it only when and where they absolutely need to do so. It's no wonder, then, that the catchphrase of companies that have integrated bartering into their financial planning is, "Think trade first!"

Bartering offers a number of financial advantages to those companies that do it. Bartering:

✔ **Improves cash flow:** When you can avoid spending money for goods and services that you need to run your business — resulting in a decreased flow of cash out of your company — you're improving your cash flow.

Remember, however, that every business needs cash to function. Trying to run a 100 percent barter business wouldn't be practical — you must have cash available to pay employee salaries and pay vendors who aren't in the mood to accept whatever you have to barter. (For example, good luck trying to get your local electric utility to accept printed circuit boards in lieu of cash when it comes time to pay your electricity bill or to get your employees to split 10,000 pounds of goose down in lieu of paychecks!)

✔ **Frees up cash for other uses:** Bartering enables you to conserve cash, freeing it up for other uses. If, for example, you need to purchase photocopiers and personal computers, and you're able to barter some of your own goods or services for the photocopiers, you'll have more cash available to purchase the personal computers you need. You then have several options available: Either buy more computers, buy better computers, or simply redirect the cash savings to another purpose.

✔ **Converts excess inventory:** Finding yourself stuck with excess inventory is not difficult. All it takes is an unexpected downturn in the economy, a change in buyer preferences, or an unseasonable change in the weather, and your shelves can be chock full of product that's going nowhere fast. Bartering can help you convert this excess inventory into something that your company really needs while putting your inventory to productive use.

These reasons alone compel many companies to make barter a part of their financial mix. By reducing the need for cash, bartering can reduce your need to secure financing from outside sources — creating a healthier bottom line for your company.

Bartering dos and don'ts

If you're convinced that bartering is the thing for you and you want join the party, be sure that you do it the right way. Companies that are used to cutting a check to pay for their purchases need to know that bartering is a different way of doing business, and doing it right means you need to keep these things in mind:

✔ **Consider joining a barter exchange.** Sure, you can go it alone when it comes to lining up barter deals — and this may be the way to go if you're a really big player and you already have a partner lined up — but exchanges offer many advantages for companies that participate in them. Not only do you have a much greater variety of products and services to choose from, but you also have a much greater chance of finding a company that wants what you have to offer. Participants often earn "trade dollars" when they sell their products or services through a barter exchange, and they're free to use those trade dollars to purchase goods and services from other participants. To find a barter exchange, do a search on the Internet or contact one of the barter associations listed at the end of this chapter.

✔ **Pay your taxes.** In the United States, a barter transaction is the same as a cash transaction as far as the Internal Revenue Service is concerned, and the fair market values of the items traded are classified as taxable income. When you participate in a barter exchange, your transactions are reported to the IRS on Form 1099-B.

✔ **Set aside no more than 15 percent of your total annual sales in barter.** Bartering is particularly useful for liquidating surplus inventory and unproductive assets (such as those obsolete computers sitting in the back of your warehouse) and for utilizing excess capacity. As long as a transaction's incremental revenue (the value brought into your company) exceeds its incremental cost (the value of the items you barter away in trade), conducting a barter transaction makes sense.

If you're new to bartering, the best thing to do is to start small. Join an exchange and try some easy transactions just to get the hang of things. As you get more comfortable with how bartering works, increase the value of your deals until you're at a level that makes sense for your company. You'll be a seasoned pro before you know it!

Is barter for you?

Barter can work for any company, and many of the world's largest companies make barter an integral part of their financial strategies. If it's good enough for Coca-Cola, General Motors, Xerox, Pitney-Bowes, Ford, Mitsubishi, and about 65 percent of the rest of the Fortune 500, according to industry statistics, we bet it's good enough for you.

Before you launch your bartering program, take a moment to answer yes or no to the following questions. The more yes answers, the more positive an impact you can expect bartering to have on your company's financial picture.

✔ Do you have excess capacity or inventory?

✔ Is your cash flow tight?

✔ Are your customers' cash flows tight?

✔ Are your goods and services suited only to companies in a particular industry?

✔ Do you regularly run promotional discounts or other similar activities?

✔ Do other businesses in your industry regularly engage in bartering?

✔ Do your products or services appeal to a broad customer base?

✔ Does your inventory or service have a long shelf life?

✔ Are referrals and word-of-mouth primary marketing methods for your company?

✔ Have you lost valuable customers because they couldn't afford your products or services?

And one more thing to consider: Companies — particularly telecommunications firms — of late have been on the receiving end of much bad press about how they've misused barter to pump up their earnings. Some companies have, for example, swapped — in a barter — time on their various systems and booked the revenues. This type of accounting is considered overly aggressive and may land you in hot water if you engage in it.

If you're still not sure whether bartering is right for you, contact one of the following associations of professional barterers — they'll be happy to connect you with someone who can help.

✔ **International Reciprocal Trade Association**
175 West Jackson Blvd., Suite 625
Chicago, Illinois 60604
312-461-0236
www.irta.com

✔ **National Association of Trade Exchanges**
24600 Center Ridge Road, Suite 480
Westlake, Ohio 44145
440-835-3654
www.nate.org

Chapter 6

Matching Services

● ●

In This Chapter
▶ Understanding online and offline matching services
▶ Exploring the future of matching services

● ●

*E*ver since the first business crawled out of the primordial ooze millions of years ago, entrepreneurs have faced the difficult task of locating the capital they need to operate and expand their businesses. This difficulty is further compounded by the fact that most entrepreneurs already have their hands full running their businesses — dealing with employees, suppliers, customers, and clients — and may not have any idea of where even to begin their search for capital, much less how to acquire it, once they find the correct forum.

For a young or small business without much of a track record, matching services — putting you together with angel investors, venture capitalists, and other potential investors — can be just the ticket for finding needed capital. If you've ever experienced a dating service — you know, where you put together a profile that details your likes, dislikes, and personal attributes (or lack thereof), and the service sets up dates with potential loves of your life — then you already know what a matching service is.

Understanding How Matching Services Work

A matching service brings people looking for capital together with people looking for opportunities in which to invest their capital. Such organizations are more effectively used when you're looking for *early money* — capital for a relatively new or high-growth enterprise. They provide you with an opportunity to put information about your company out there for all to see, hoping to attract someone who'd like to throw some cash your way.

A matching service differs from hiring a placement agent (discussed in detail in Chapter 8) because most matching services are fairly passive, relying for the most part on chance encounters between companies and potential investors. Placement agents, on the other hand, actively and aggressively seek out potential sources of capital and then do everything they can to convince them to invest in the business that employs them.

Entrepreneurs are the classic little guys, a couple of techies inventing a new process in their garage or lab and attempting to exploit it commercially. Investors, however, traditionally have been the big guys — pools of capital managed by professionals, capital furnished by rich families (the Rockefellers, the Phipps, the Whitneys, the Watsons), and, increasingly, institutional investors (insurance companies, university endowment funds, and, more important, pension funds).

Through the years various experiments were aimed at enabling little investors to share in the handsome returns that were being captured by the members of the elite venture capital club. In this chapter, we take a quick look at the kinds of matching services that worked (and didn't work) in the recent past, the more promising matching services available today, and the future of matching services. You can also discover an extremely comprehensive listing of online matching services, along with charts describing the offerings of a variety of matching services, online and offline.

The Tried and True: Offline Matchmaking Services

Since time immemorial, matchmakers played a necessary role in putting people who need capital together with those who have it. Traditionally, matchmaking was accomplished in-person — offline — on a personal, one-to-one basis. And, although the Internet has introduced a new element by automating the capital matching process and providing much larger forums in which to work, it isn't likely that offline matching will be replaced by it anytime soon.

Getting to know you

As prevalent as online matching services are, you still can hook up with a matching service in person. On-site services generally play host to monthly or quarterly events — often referred to as "Danish and diligence" — designed to bring investors and entrepreneurs together, usually over breakfast, lunch, or dinner. Online services, on the other hand, are global in nature, while on-site matching services typically are local.

Similarly, the sponsoring organization typically entices some 30 or 40 potential angels to, oh, say, a breakfast, at which two or three entrepreneurs present their business plans. The sponsors generally conduct some due diligence and screening of initially submitted business plans, but they don't put themselves in a position of recommending any particular investment. Instead, they serve as mediums of exchange.

Presenters generally are asked to schedule a due diligence meeting at some subsequent date, usually at the entrepreneur's offices, where angels, intrigued with the possibilities, can meet and engage in a thorough investigation of the business involved.

Some of these matching services levy a variety of charges on the angels and the entrepreneurs, and others do not. If the organization charges for its services, it may include

- A fee paid by the angels to attend
- A fee levied on the entrepreneur to have the company's business plan considered
- A fee levied on entrepreneurs whose plans are selected for presentation
- A success fee, expressed in cash and/or warrants in the company assessed against companies that successfully complete a financing by reason, in whole or in part, of the occasion.

One more thing to keep in mind — especially if you're trying to land some inexpensive capital: Online matching services are much more likely to charge fees than their offline counterparts. How much they charge varies considerably from firm to firm, so be sure to shop around.

Danish and diligence

Here is a partial list of the breakfast-club type meetings (including, in some cases, the types of investors that they attract) that occur around the U.S.

- New York City: New York New Media Association
- Boston: The Common Angels
- Morristown, New Jersey: Venture Association of New Jersey, Private Investors Forum

- Austin, Texas: The Angel Posse
- Palo Alto, California: The Band of Angels
- Portland, Maine: Maine Investors Exchange (MIX)
- Santa Fe, New Mexico: Gathering of Angels

Face time

In addition to the Danish and diligence events — also sometimes referred to as Open Forums — a variety of other face-to-face opportunities match angels and entrepreneurs. These events usually don't necessarily distinguish between angel and institutional investors, but rather they're focused on giving entrepreneurs an opportunity to showcase their plans to any interested party, including not only investors but also consultants, perhaps customers, and potential joint venture partners. In other words, they're networking events such as:

- Venture fairs
- Venture capital clubs that feature so-called 60-second presentations
- Industry conferences
- Seminars
- Trade association meetings
- Quasi-social gatherings epitomized by Cyberpubs and Cybersuds get-togethers.

In addition, newsletters list deals for one and all; some of them are online. *The Private Equity Review* (www.nvst.com) is a prominent example, as is *Alley Cat News* (www.alleycatnews.com). Trade shows host booths where entrepreneurs also can present themselves.

The Internet to the Rescue?

The Internet promises to open new vistas in the bargain-demolishing old and inefficient ways of doing business that historically have excluded little guys from seeking capital. Its charms were, therefore, apparent to those who had been appalled at the inefficiency of the private markets at the early stage. The result has been a spurt in the number of so-called matching services.

The more prominent matching services are, as one can imagine, the ones that use the Internet as their medium of exchange, either in whole or in part. Unfortunately, no authoritative list of matching services exists. A couple of lists, one developed by us and one found in *Angel Financing* magazine, are set forth at the end of this chapter. However, a good deal of flux in this sector of the business means that such lists constantly are subject to change. Yet, they provide an overall sampling of the online group that still will be fairly accurate by the time you read it.

What online matching services can do for you

A variety of matching services currently offer their services online. More are springing up (and more are disappearing, for that matter) with each passing day. But, before discovering who all these services are, and how to contact them to get your piece of the capital pie, first take a look at what online matching services can do for you.

Garage Technology Ventures (www.garage.com) — founded by Guy Kawasaki of Apple Computer fame — is perhaps the most well-known of this crop of online matching services. The services it offers to the companies that it works with are quite extensive, and they're indicative of the kinds of services that other online matching services offer. They provide

- **Access to capital.** Garage Technology Ventures matches mostly angel investors with high-tech start-ups looking for initial financing in the range of $2 million to $5 million.

- **Strategic and operational guidance.** Garage Technology Ventures helps companies refine their business plans and recruit talented executives and technical help. Garage Technology Ventures also provides referrals to experienced professional advisors such as lawyers and accountants.

- **Training in making effective pitches.** Garage Technology Ventures teaches its clients how to make effective pitches to potential investors, and how best to communicate their investment opportunities.

- **Marketing and public relations advice.** Garage Technology Ventures works closely with its clients to create effective marketing strategies and comprehensive public relations campaigns — the kind that attract investors and their capital.

- **Forums.** Garage Technology Ventures sponsors forums at which companies and investors can meet offline — face-to-face — to get to know one another and trade information about business opportunities. Events such as showcase breakfasts enable member companies to pitch their businesses to a variety of venture capital, corporate, and angel investors.

Keep in mind that each online matching service varies in the services that it offers to firms seeking capital and in the clients that it serves. Before you settle on one particular matching service, be sure to check out several to see which can best meet your needs.

ACE-Net: Matching service pioneer

One of the earliest matching services, ACE-Net (www.ace-net.org) is affiliated with the Small Business Administration. The brainchild of Alan Patricof and his partner, Pat Cloherty, ACE-Net is an acronym for Angel Capital Electronic Network and is a government-sponsored matching service that was established in 1996. ACE-Net is affiliated with 36 local networking organizations, many of which are in university or state-supported entrepreneurial development centers. The Small Business Administration sponsored the initiative, which is maintained by the Center for Venture Research at the University of New Hampshire. As of early 2001, approximately 36 investors and 300 entrepreneurs were participating in the ACE-Net system.

A number of variations on the AceNet theme are providing similar services. Some examples include:

- ✔ The New York New Media Association (www.nynma.org) conducts one- or two-day events at which as many as 20 to 30 companies present, often to audiences numbering in the hundreds.

- ✔ The Massachusetts Software Development Council (www.swcouncil.org) plays host to a similar colloquium.

- ✔ Investment banks, such as Hambrecht & Quist and Alex Brown, sponsor marathons at which a number of companies — usually the bank's clients — present. In the latter case, the presenters may already be public companies seeking capital, and private firms that have not yet gone public.

Indeed, a cottage industry has sprung up based on such events. The trick is finding out who's going to present at, say, the H&Q medical conference and then buying that company's stock immediately before the presentation. Buyers are likely to benefit based on the theory that the stock normally enjoys an upward price spike, simply because of the good news — and it is almost always good news — that the company gives out at the conference.

The good news (and bad) about online matching

Just like almost everything else in life and in business, the world of online matching services has its good and bad points. Be sure to give serious consideration to both before you dive in.

- ✔ **Good news:** The good news, of course, is obvious. If the matching service model works, either as it currently is formulated or as it morphs with a changing economy, based on practical experience, the activity at this critical stage in the emerging growth/entrepreneurial sector will necessarily increase and, it is hoped, prosper. Good deals will get done, bad deals will lose their allure, and the economy of this country will be significantly advantaged.

✔ **Bad news:** Several of the services that came into being on the theory of matching angels with entrepreneurs have, either by accident or design, climbed up the food chain, so to speak, and are posting deals that are now more VC-versus-angel oriented.

✔ **Really bad news:** The competitive risk of posting one's business plan online is another problem area. It may be — despite diligent efforts to preserve confidentiality — that the audience for your business plan is comprised of would-be competitors or customers and vendors who want to learn something more about your company than you want to discharge.

As we've indicated, some matching services, that is, those that haven't registered as broker/dealers under the 1934 Act, are in for a surprise if they elect to charge success or placement fees. By the time this material is published, an expected SEC enforcement action may well have been initiated, and it won't be long, we predict, before unregistered sites must either close down or suspend operations (at least the fee generation portion thereof) until the necessary licenses have been obtained. And if you've affiliated with such a matching service, not only are you likely lose the financing you seek, but you may well lose any fees you've paid. That isn't exactly our idea of a win-win opportunity.

Matching venture capital services

Increasingly, some matching services mimic the venture capital industry — segueing from early- to later-stage investments. Garage Technology Ventures, for example, suggests that the majority of the investors favoring the deals on its site are institutions. OffroadCapital.com, an online matching service that went out of business in 2001, had a threshold that was well above the traditional angel sector. Such sites resemble investment and merchant banks, much like Wit Capital, doing conventional private equity financings of institutional caliber but using the Internet as the medium for propagating the opportunity.

These organizations typically are registered as broker/dealers under the Securities &

Exchange Act of 1934, and they charge fees that mimic those of conventional mainstream placement agents — with the added element, in many cases, of a fee charged to the investor and to the company. Moreover, in those instances where the matching service admits entrepreneurs of less-than-institutional grade (institutional grade in this case meaning companies that are ripe for a Series A round of venture capital investment), the screening is rigorous. Garage Technology Ventures screens literally thousands of deals for each one it agrees to post, a result of the fact that its intake mechanism (the Internet) is so broad-based.

The SEC speaks: How can an Internet posting be a private offering?

When the Internet is involved, the issue is slippery. The slipperiness stems from the ancient legal rule that to qualify as a private offering, the placement must entail neither general advertising nor general solicitation. Obviously, any transaction posted on the Internet involves general solicitation — solicitation of the entire wired world, in fact. Realizing this and reacting to a series of industry proposals, the SEC has adapted some of its pre-existing doctrine.

✔ First, all investors must be prequalified by the matching service by filling out a questionnaire confirming, among other things, that he or she is *accredited* (see Chapter 4 for an explanation of an accredited investor).

✔ Second, any online posting must be password-protected so that only specified individuals have access to the deals. That mitigates, at least to some extent, the inherent element of general solicitation.

✔ Finally, angels admitted with the appropriate password to the magic circle must not invest for a period of 30 days in any posted deal.

If the letter and the spirit of these rules are followed, then a matching service can use online technology to spread the word, so to speak.

The danger, of course, is that promoters addicted to *sharp practices* (or so-called penny stock fraud), boiler rooms, and bucket shops will use the Internet not only to push questionable publicly traded securities but also private offerings. If that turns into a widespread problem, then you can expect action from the SEC. For the moment, however, if the rules are followed, online matching services are protected from any allegation that they're engaging in offerings that need to be publicly registered.

Looking into the Future

When venture capitalists get together over a couple of beers and feel like lampooning the kind of business model that has cost investors untold millions through the years, they usually start with a leadoff sentence like: "Such-and-Such Research company predicts an $X billion [trillion] market for Internet widgets in the next five years." The sendup then features a dewy-eyed entrepreneur contending, with great conviction, "Assuming our company captures only a small fraction of that market, simple arithmetic shows that it will be a billion-dollar company." The veterans then break out in knowing guffaws.

You can't take the research results of any old firm that thinks it has a lock on what the future holds for any other company to the bank. Time and time again, the sure thing turns out to be anything but that, and the company flying low under the analyst's radar becomes the overnight darling of investors.

Having made that perhaps overly cynical point, what do we think is in fact going to happen? The answer is in our view is, it depends. Nevertheless, we think

✔ That the angel-sector market eventually has to become more efficient than it is today. It certainly couldn't get much worse.

✔ That matching services will have a good deal to do with creating those efficiencies, but we also expect a consolidation among existing services as business models undergo metamorphoses on the bases of hard experiences.

✔ The surviving matching services will be the ones that are able, in the final analysis, to point to a competitive track record.

But, as always, the proof of the pudding is in the eating. The ultimate success of winners and plight of losers will not be keyed on the volume of deals or eyeballs to the site but rather on the good old-fashioned criteria: Who made money and how much? While the future of online matching services remains to be fully realized, Tables 6-1 and 6-2 show you where they are today.

Table 6-1	Fees and Parameters			
Company	*Deal range*	*Investor fee*	*Entrepreneur fee*	*Geographical market*
ACENet	$250k-$5M	$450	$450	U.S.
EarlyBird Capital	$3M - $10M	$0	$0	Communities
Direct Stock Market	$5M - $20M	N/A	Yes	U.S.
Garage	$2M - $15M	Waived	No	U.S. primarily
MeVC.com	N/A	N/A	N/A	Publicly traded
NVST	All	$0	$0	US
SinoBit	$250k-$3M	Yes	$0	China
University Angels	All	$0	$199	Communities
Vcapital	$5M - $50M	N/A	N/A	U.S.

Table 6-2		Company Services Offered to Clients			
Company	Library / Education	Community / Discussion	Financial analysis tools	News	Broker / Dealer
ACENet	Limited	No	No	No	No
EarlyBird Capital	No	Yes	No	Yes	Yes
Direct Stock Market	Yes	No	No	No	Yes
Garage	No	No	No	Yes	Yes
MeVC. com	Yes	No	No	No	No
NVST	Yes	No	No	No	No
SinoBit	No	Yes	No	No	N/A
University Angels	No	Yes	No	Yes	No
Vcapital	Yes	No	No	No	Yes

Links to online matching services

If you want to find the best online matching services, then it wouldn't hurt for you to have a guide helping to show you the way. You can do an online search using your favorite search engine (try plugging in the keywords "online matching service"), or you can try any of these sites:

✔ America's Business Funding Directory (www.businessfinance.com)

✔ Capital Key Advisors (www.capitalkey.com)

✔ Dealflow (www.dealflow.com)

✔ Environmental Capital Network (www.ecn-capital.com)

✔ Garage Technology Ventures (www.garage.com)

✔ MoneyHunt (www.moneyhunter.com)

✔ MyPrivates.com (www.myprivates.com)

✔ NVST.com (www.nvst.com/pnvHome.asp)

✔ vfinance.com (www.vfinance.com)

✔ Venturescape (www.venturescape.com)

Part II

Second-Stage Financing: Expansion

The 5th Wave
By Rich Tennant

"The investors liked our business plan — particularly the in-depth assessment of our competition, which is who they've decided to invest with."

In this part . . .

A growing business needs plenty of capital to take care of current needs while fueling future needs that fast are arriving. This requires a serious approach to raising capital, an approach that is broadly based and ongoing. Here, we take a look at how to work with commercial lenders and placement agents, and we explore a particularly important financial resource for many small businesses: the Small Business Administration. We discover private equity offerings, venture capital, valuation, and more.

Chapter 7

Commercial Lenders

· ·

· ·

Few businesses are able to operate strictly on a cash basis, running their day-to-day operations, paying employees, purchasing inventory, and so forth without occasionally taking on debt to provide the funds they need to cover cash shortfalls or to allow for expansion. Every industry and business has its up cycles and its down cycles, and loans provide a ready source of cash to help businesses get through those inevitable down cycles.

Loans are one of the most popular ways for businesses to obtain financing. As an indication of loan activity in the United States, the Small Business Administration alone holds a portfolio of some $45 billion in loans and loan guarantees (where the SBA agrees to cover losses to the lender in the event of default by the borrower). Without these loans, one thing is certain: Fewer small businesses would be in business today, and many more people would be looking for jobs (see Chapter 9 for more information on the Small Business Administration).

In this chapter, we take a look at the many different kinds and sources of loan financing and how to improve your company's chances of qualifying for a loan. We also discuss how to apply for a business loan.

A Loan for Every Occasion

One of the first things most businesses do when seeking capital is to apply for a loan. Few businesses have never received loans from financial institutions at one time or another in their existence. The most common loan types include

✔ **A microloan** sponsored by the Small Business Administration

✔ **A line of credit** from a commercial bank

✔ **A long-term equipment loan** from a large manufacturer's captive financing company

In short, a loan is simply borrowed money that must be repaid to the person or business that provides it. How that money is repaid — and the requirements to which the borrower must adhere to obtain the loan and remain in the lender's good graces — is what makes one loan different from another.

Attention: important lending terms ahead!

The world of commercial lending is chock-full of unique terminology. Not only will knowledge of the meaning of this jargon make you more comfortable when you're talking to potential lenders, it also will help you be much better able to effectively analyze whether a loan will be advantageous to you. Here are some key lending terms for you to become familiar with before you dive into the lending pool:

✔ **Term:** The length of time the borrower has to repay the debt. In the case of a five-year loan, for example, the borrower is expected to repay the debt in full by the end of the five-year loan term.

✔ **Short-term loan:** A loan with a term of less than one year.

✔ **Long-term loan:** A loan with a term of one year or more.

✔ **Principal:** The amount borrowed.

✔ **Interest:** The fee paid currently or added to the loan amount — most often expressed in percentage terms as an interest rate — to pay the lender for providing and servicing the loan. Generally, the higher the risk, the higher the interest rate.

✔ **Collateral:** Something of value (a specific asset) that the borrower pledges to the lender in exchange for a loan. When a borrower takes a mortgage loan to buy a house, for example, the house is pledged as collateral for the loan. If the borrower defaults and discontinues making loan payments, the collateral is forfeited to the lender, who is then free to dispose of it as he or she wants.

✔ **Down payment:** The amount of cash paid by the borrower at loan inception to obtain a loan. The down payment reduces the loan amount, most often by a fixed percentage such as 5 or 10 percent.

✔ **Payments:** The incremental repayments of a loan from the borrower to the lender. Payments usually fall into two categories:

- *Regular payments:* Most often occurring on a monthy basis, where each payment repays a portion of the principal plus a charge for interest.

- *Balloon payment:* No regular payments are made, but the entire loan amount plus interest is due at the end of the loan term.

✔ **Asset-based financing:** A loan that requires the borrower to pledge its most valuable assets — including things such as equipment and receivables — in the event of default.

✔ **Compensating balance:** This is an amount of money that a lender requires a borrower to put on deposit with the lending institution as a condition of the loan.

✔ **Clean up period:** A specified period during the course of a loan (most often a line of credit) in which the borrower is required to pay off the loan, proving that the borrower is not overly dependent on the loan.

✔ **UCC 1:** A document that evidences a lender's security interest in a borrower's personal property.

✔ **Personal guarantee:** Sometimes a bank won't agree to make a business loan unless the company's owner agrees to guarantee the loan personally. If the company defaults on the loan and is unable to pay the debt, the lender has the right to pursue repayment directly from the owner's personal assets.

As a start-up, you may not be able to avoid personal guarantees, but you can reach an understanding with your banker about what has to be done to eliminate them in the future. Of course the quality of your personal finances affects the use of a personal guarantee, but more important, they will affect your ability to get a loan at all.

✔ **Secured loan:** A loan for which the borrower has pledged collateral that is generally considered less risky than an unsecured loan. Be sure to offer your *least valuable assets* as security whenever possible, saving your best for last (in other words, try to finance your inventories before your receivables, if you can). Keep the security narrow — to one class of (or even specific) assets if you possibly can. Using the firm's total assets as security precludes other financing options.

✔ **Unsecured loan:** A loan for which no collateral is pledged. Generally considered riskier than a secured loan, with higher interest rates as a result. It is almost impossible for a business to obtain an unsecured loan, although owners may be able to obtain unsecured personal loans depending on their own situation.

Different kinds of loans

In the world of finance, an incredible variety of loan types exist along with an almost infinite universe of different loan terms and conditions. There is no one "right" answer when it comes to which kind of loan is best. Depending on what stage your business is in — and your unique capital needs — one kind of loan may be better than another at any given time. All of these kinds of loans are available from commercial banks and a variety of other lending institutions.

- **Business loan:** A standard business loan is a loan of a specific amount of money — say, $1 million — for a fixed period of time. Because they are unsecured, such loans are difficult for new or small businesses to obtain (unless such loans are guaranteed by the Small Business Administration) and can be hard for even mid-sized and large businesses to acquire unless they can demonstrate strong financials to potential lenders.

- **Line of credit:** Perhaps the most common type of loan made to businesses, a line of credit works much like a credit card. The lender agrees to provide a certain amount of credit, and the borrower can draw from the line of credit in any amount up to the credit limit whenever he or she wants to. Payment can be made in part or in full, with a minimum monthly payment required based on the amount of money borrowed against the line for that month. However, you'll rarely get this common form of credit without security.

- **Receivables financing:** Receivables financing is a short-term loan made against a company's accounts receivable. The loan's intent is to provide cash that bridges the period from the sale of a product to a customer to the receipt of payment from the customer for that product. By pledging its receivables as collateral, the borrower agrees in the case of loan default to forfeit future customer payments until the loan is repaid. This type of asset-based lending is common today. You can usually get 75 to 90 percent of "qualified" receivables unless you have poor credit-risk customers.

- **Inventory financing:** Inventory financing is a short-term loan made against a company's inventory. It provides a bridge from the time a company buys the raw materials to produce a product to the time the finished product is sold to a customer. The company's inventory is pledged as collateral for the loan. This kind of financing is relatively hard to arrange and depends heavily on the nature of your inventory. Hard components (such as computers) that can be easily sold if you default are the easiest to finance.

- **Equipment loans and mortgages:** These loans — specifically to purchase equipment, buildings, and other high-priced items — are common, especially if you have other credit set up with your bank. Such loans can, however, be set up separately from your current bank, and this is one good way of establishing a second source of bank credit.

Entrepreneurs and owners of business start-ups commonly tap into other sources of loan financing, including personal loans, home equity lines of credit, and credit cards (for more information on these and other financing alternatives, be sure to check out Chapter 2). When it comes to raising capital, borrowers and lenders definitely have no lack of creativity.

Doctor Livingstone, 1 Presume? Exploring Sources of Loans

Many potential sources of loans exist — from commercial banks to insurance companies to the government. But understand that many lenders are quite conservative about lending their money to early-stage businesses, making the proposition more difficult than you might prefer. Start-up ventures often find that getting a loan from most of these institutions (except through the Small Business Administration, which specializes in loans to small enterprises) is difficult because they prefer to lend money to well-established businesses with proven track records of growth and strong financials.

Selecting a source for a loan ostensibly depends on how you plan to use the loan proceeds:

- ✔ How much you plan to borrow
- ✔ The size and age of your business
- ✔ Your business's financial history and stability

Approaching potential lenders with whom you already have relationships first is a good idea. The bank that handles your deposits or payroll is a good example. The better a financial institution knows your business, the better your chances are for obtaining the loan that you need.

Certain financial institutions are interested only in working with companies that are of a specific size or larger, while others offer a wide variety of loan programs serving a broad range of clients. Bank of America, for example (and many other large banks, for that matter), has a unit that specifically serves and provides unique products to small businesses, while another group within the bank targets mid-sized and larger ($500 million or more in sales per year) companies.

In any case, be sure to do your homework and target potential lenders that are likely to be interested in providing the loan you seek.

Commercial banks

A *commercial bank* is a profit-making institution that accepts cash and other forms of monetary deposits and provides a variety of services to its depositors, including savings and checking accounts, mortgages, and business and student loans. *Wholesale banks* are commercial banks that specialize in servicing business customers.

According to the Federal Deposit Insurance Corporation (FDIC), there are currently more than 8,000 commercial banks in the United States holding a bit more than $6 trillion in assets. Big names in the commercial banking industry include Citibank, Fleet National Bank, Wells Fargo Bank, Bank One, and First USA Bank.

Commercial banks are your best target by far — they offer a wide range of business services and credits, and some deal only with businesses.

Savings institutions

Savings institutions include *savings and loan associations* — federally chartered banks that accept deposits in interest-bearing accounts and provide mortgage loans — and *savings banks,* which are like savings and loan associations but are chartered by the states in which they do business. Savings institutions generally offer the same kinds of products as commercial banks do, including savings and checking accounts and home and other loans.

According to the FDIC, there are currently more than 1,500 savings institutions in the United States, controlling approximately $1.2 trillion. Big names in the savings industry include Alliance Bancorp, Downey Financial, Virginia Capital Bankshares, GSB Financial, and FirstFed Financial.

Overall, savings institutions are a good option for your real estate financing needs, but not so good for general business needs.

Credit unions

Credit unions are not-for-profit "members-only" financial cooperatives with members sharing a common affiliation, such as working for the same company, belonging to the same union, or being members of a specific branch of the armed forces. Credit unions accept deposits and provide a variety of financial services, including savings and checking accounts, credit cards, and more. "Profits" from operations are returned to credit union members in the form of dividends on savings, lower loan rates than commercial banks offer, and lower service fees.

According to the National Credit Union Administration (NCUA), there are currently more than 10,000 credit unions in the United States controlling more than $470 billion in assets. Some of the largest credit unions include Pentagon Federal Credit Union, Boeing Employees' Credit Union, Orange County Teachers Federal Credit Union, American Airlines Federal Credit Union, and GTE Federal Credit Union. You may want to consider your own affiliations and join a credit union if you're eligible.

Credit unions are personal finance oriented but may handle very small business needs or equipment loans.

Finance companies

A *finance company* is a business that specializes in making loans to individuals and businesses. While some finance companies do not limit the use of funds received under their loans, other finance companies — particularly captive finance companies (finance companies that finance only products manufactured by their parent companies) of manufacturers that loan money to help customers buy the company's products [for example, GE Capital and General Motors Acceptance Corporation (GMAC)] — do limit how loan proceeds are used.

In general, finance companies charge higher interest rates than banks, savings institutions, and credit unions, because they are willing to make loans to higher-risk borrowers. Captive finance companies often offer special rates on the products their parent companies produce, and they're definitely worth a look when you have specific equipment needs.

Familiar finance companies include Advanta, LendingTree.com, Household International, NOVUS Financial, and AmeriCredit Corporation.

Finance companies are a good source for term loans and poor credit risks. Beware of them, however, and be sure to check them out with some of their borrowers because they can have tough terms.

Small Business Administration (SBA)

Although the Small Business Administration (SBA) doesn't do much direct lending itself, it guarantees millions of dollars in business loans to small businesses every year. These loans, processed through commercial banks and other approved private-sector lenders, are available in amounts from a couple of thousand dollars up to $2 million.

The top ten commercial banks

When you need a really *big* loan, why not target a really *big* commerical bank? Here's a list of the top ten commercial banks by total assets as of December 31, 2000:

1. Bank of America, National Association: $584.3 billion

2. Citibank, National Association: $382.1 billion

3. The Chase Manhattan Bank: $377.1 billion

4. First Union National Bank: $231.8 billion

5. Morgan Guaranty Trust Company of New York: $185.8 billion

6. Fleet National Bank: $166.3 billion

7. Wells Fargo Bank, National Association: $115.5 billion

8. Bank One, National Association: $101.2 billion

9. Suntrust Bank: $99.5 billion

10. U.S. Bank, National Association: $82.0 billion

SBA loans are good when you are looking for long-term debt money, but you can expect to tie up all of your assets as security for it. Then, if you need more credit (for example, when your receivables grow faster than you expect) in a couple of years, you will have no place to go for it except to do an entirely new deal with your SBA lender, or somehow pay off your loan and start from scratch.

For detailed information about SBA loans, take a look at Chapter 9.

Qualifying for a Loan

Although obtaining loans from banks is particularly difficult for start-up businesses, well-established businesses are welcome, and they make up a large portion of most banks' loan portfolios. Even a business that's been around for years, however, must qualify for the loan it wants; that is, it must meet the bank's criteria before the bank is willing to grant credit. In this section, you'll find out the best approaches for businesses — particularly new businesses — to establish credit.

The standard rule that banks and other financial institutions use to judge the creditworthiness of a company (or an individual, for that matter) is known as the five Cs:

✔ **Capacity:** Will your business have the financial wherewithal to make loan payments — in full and on time — as required by your agreement with the bank? Will your cash flow support the additional burden of debt on your business? If the answers to these questions are no, you aren't going to get the loan.

To turn a no into a yes, figure out how to increase your company's revenues while lowering expenses. Even better, get your financial house in order *before* you apply for the loan.

✔ **Capital:** Capital represents the ratio of your company's debt to assets or equity. A company with a high debt load versus equity or assets will have a hard time getting a loan from most banking institutions; a low debt load is attractive. Improve your chances of getting the loan you want by minimizing the amount of debt your business carries and maximizing equity and owners' investments in the business.

✔ **Character:** Are you personally a good credit risk? Do you have a history of meeting your own financial obligations, including repaying loans on time and avoiding defaults or bankruptcies? If your own credit is shaky, a lender will surmise that your character is less than sterling. If that is the case, do whatever you can to repair your credit before applying for a loan.

Obtain a credit report from one of the major credit reporting agencies (Equifax at 800-685-1111, Experian at 800-682-7654, or Trans Union at 316-636-6100) and take action on any problems that show up.

✔ **Collateral:** What kind of property can your company pledge to the loan in case of default? In many cases, lenders may require that you pledge assets or property to secure your loan. Your ability to pledge sufficient collateral greatly enhances your chances of getting the loan you seek.

✔ **Conditions:** Conditions include the health and growth potential of the markets within which you operate and the demographics of the typical buyers of your products and services. Although you can do little to influence or control the behavior of your markets or your customers, you can define exactly which markets and customers you plan to target.

Before applying for a loan, review these five Cs and honestly assess how your company measures up. Can you improve in certain areas? Can you make changes in your current financial picture to make your company more attractive to potential lenders? If you take charge of your own financial destiny, there's no reason why you can't get the loan you want for your business.

Eight Steps to Getting the Loan You Want

Whether you're the owner of a start-up technology company or the CFO of a Fortune 500 firm, the process of obtaining a business loan is much the same. Here's an eight-step process for obtaining the loan you want:

1. **Get your personal finances in the best shape that you can.**

2. **Find out which banks in your community handle your industry best.**

   If possible, find out what their preferred loan types are and their general lending policies and practices.

3. **Set up a meeting with the bank(s) to discuss your business needs, such as deposits, payroll, payables, and financing. Confirm your understanding of their lending practices and get their commitment to consider a secured loan for your company if you give them your deposits and other business.**

   Unless you or your company has millions in net worth, don't waste your time on trying to get unsecured debt.

4. **Choose the bank (and banker) that you would prefer to deal with — for a long time — but don't burn your bridges with your other contacts!**

   You will want to keep them interested as well for later competition. Put a tickler on your calendar to go to lunch again with them in the next six to nine months.

5. **Set up your checking, payroll, and payables accounts with your new bank.**

   Be sure everything is running smoothly for a couple of months. Be sure your accounting system can stand up to outside review by the bank!

6. **Prepare your bank-oriented business plan and meet with your banker to verbally request the type of credit that you want (and that fits their practices).**

   A *bank-oriented* business plan is light on marketing text and technical data and heavy on financial data — especially projected cash flows and details on your assets. Include current and accurate financial statements hot off your accounting system. Remember: the scariest thing to a banker is that you will grow too fast for your capital base — slow and steady is good to a banker! Have a savvy friend review your package before you sit down with your banker.

7. **Do not expect him to jump on your deal.**

   He will need to dig into certain areas, go to his "committee", and kick your tires. Invite him to see your operations and meet your accountant and attorney.

8. Sign your loan agreement.

With a bit of luck, you'll negotiate and sign your deal within 4 to 8 weeks.

Most businesses have been turned down more than once or twice for loans. If you're turned down for a loan, figure out exactly why — don't be shy about asking your loan representative to detail the exact reasons why your business was not a suitable candidate for the requested loan. Then take the time to plan and implement changes to your business that will make it more attractive to lenders. This may mean doing anything from decreasing long-term debt to improving profitability to simply being in business for another year or two.

The Equal Credit Opportunity Act

If your business is located in the United States, the law offers a number of protections to ensure that potential lenders do not discriminate against your company. The Equal Credit Opportunity Act (ECOA) prohibits creditors from denying you a loan based on reasons that have nothing to do with your creditworthiness, including race, religion, and national origin.

According to the ECOA:

✔ You cannot be denied business credit on the basis of your race, religion, national origin, sex, marital status, or age — or that of your customers. For example, if you request a loan to open a store, a creditor can't deny your application based on your race or your customers' race.

✔ If your application for business credit is rejected, you can find out why. You must submit a written request for the reasons within 60 days of the denial. The creditor must give you the specific reasons in writing within 30 days of your request. If you don't agree with the reasons, consider discussing your concerns with the lender; you may be able to resolve the issues.

✔ If your business is small (less than $1 million in gross revenues), the lender must keep records of your credit application for one year after telling you of its credit decision. If your business grosses more than $1 million, the lender has to keep your records on file for only 60 days after denying you credit. If you ask that your records be kept longer, however, or if you ask for a written statement of the reasons for denial, the lender must keep your file for a year. If you don't ask about the reasons for denial within 60 days, the law permits the creditor to destroy your records. Note that these records could be important for any legal action you consider against a lender.

You have the right to sue a creditor that doesn't comply with the law. Understand, however, that filing a suit won't get you much credit — in the short term, at least. If you have a complaint about a government lender, public utility company, small loan and finance company, travel and expense credit card company, or other non-bank creditor, you may want to file a complaint with your friendly, local office of the Federal Trade Commission (www.ftc.gov).

Requesting a loan *before* you need it is a good idea. Not only will your financial position be stronger, but you'll also be less desperate to close a deal. This puts you in a better frame of mind, making you appear less eager, and gives you an advantage in negotiating the best loan conditions. And most loans don't happen overnight. It may take weeks or even months for a loan to fund after you start the process.

Chapter 8

Placement Agents

· ·

· ·

The function of a placement agent is, as the name implies, to place securities — that is, to raise funds for a company that's in the market for capital. The engagement of a placement agent is an interactive process. The agent helps the company and its management sell a security, but it doesn't do so in a vacuum. Most placement agents, for example, ask the company for a list of likely prospects. That list needs to be prepared with care and imagination — not just slapped together by someone who's more interested in beating the rush-hour traffic than in finding the best placement firm for the job.

Many businesses — unless they go public with an IPO — must find the capital they seek through private sources. That is where a placement agent enters the picture. A good placement agent can get you the cash your business needs on financial terms that work for your company. A bad placement agent can be the source of a long-term organizational headache not unlike the eruption of Krakatoa in 1883.

One thing to keep in mind, however, as you read this chapter: Placement agents for rounds of financing projected at $5 million or less are few, far between, and often unreliable. The reason: The fee, given the time and work involved, isn't viewed as sufficiently lucrative.

In this chapter, you find out all you need to know about placement agents — from what they are to who they are and where to find them. We take a close look at how placement agents make their money and how much you can expect to pay for their services (and believe us, you *will* pay). Finally, we arm you with tools that you need to protect yourself from unscrupulous placement agents, and we discuss what to do when you find yourself in a bad situation that's quickly getting worse.

A Who's Who of Placement Agents

Entrepreneurs trying to raise equity capital privately face an almost unlimited variety of private-placement options and alternatives. But private-placement opportunities can be hard to track down for someone who isn't plugged into the system on a full-time basis. One of the best ways to canvass all the alternatives is to use a *placement agent* — an experienced individual or firm that has knowledge of the capital markets and can guide a company to the most likely sources of investment capital.

If you were going fishing on a river that you never had seen before and were interested in catching fish — which beats the heck out of *not* catching fish — the best way to do it would be to hire an experienced guide. A fishing guide's job is to take you and your bait to the place where the fish are biting and to help you attract those fish to your hook. This fishing analogy is not all that different from the role that a placement agent plays in securing capital for a business. The assumption is that some individual or firm will be attracted to the investment proposition. But if you throw your bait any old place in the river, you might catch a fish, or you might not. You can, however, hire an experienced guide who will take you to the likeliest spot, and you can cast your fly where the guide tells you. The guide doesn't catch the fish for you — at least if you're a real fisherman — but, if any good, he or she will increase your chances of bringing your quarry into the net. A good placement agent can do the same for *your* company.

We again must stress that it's hard to persuade a legitimate private-placement agent to render much in the way of services to a firm in the concept or garage stage.

The sections that follow present some basic facts about the different levels of placement agents available to the broad range of firms seeking capital.

The first tier: The crème de la crème

As in most business enterprises, the investment-banking sector is divided into tiers. At the top are the crème de la crème: Goldman Sachs, Morgan Stanley, Credit Suisse First Boston, and other multinational firms often referred to as *bulge-bracket* investment banks. These banks act as placement agents by handling major public and private offerings; they also engage in an advisory capacity for mergers and acquisitions (very lucrative), and, in some cases, retail brokerage, and they trade securities for their own accounts.

SEC Rule 144A: Why it isn't for you

In addition to their role as placement agents in public offerings, major-league investment banks act as agents in the sale of securities in *private* offerings — offerings to institutional investors. Such transactions can closely resemble public offerings.

A specific SEC rule, Rule 144A, enables companies to access a quasi-public market (assuming that all purchasers are institutional buyers managing more than $100 million in OPM (other peoples' money) by using methods that a layperson would say entail an offering to the public. For companies looking for capital in the early stages of their development, however, public offerings and Rule 144A transactions are of only academic interest. The only way for emerging growth companies to raise equity capital is to attempt a conventional private placement, meaning a placement of securities to a limited number of investors in an offering that does not involve what the SEC calls "general advertising" and "general solicitation." That means the market is, as it has been historically, highly inefficient. If you can't advertise the product you're selling — in this case, stock in your company — you must figure out some other way to get the word out. And legal restrictions surrounding a private offering mean that the methods ordinarily employed are best described as hit-or-miss.

These companies have billions of dollars in capital, offices around the world, and partners who take home high six-figure (and often much more) compensation each year. Increasingly, they're allying with other financial institutions, primarily commercial banks. The focus of their activity is in New York and London, but their representatives travel in every conceivable market to find and service customers. Many are publicly owned; a few, such as Bear Stearns, are still private.

For most entrepreneurs, first-tier firms are not an option. Although these top firms are capable of raising billions of dollars for financial institutions, their services generally are not available to entrepreneurs seeking early stage capital. Occasionally, individual partners may be angel investors on their own time and with their own money (see Chapter 4), but that doesn't mean that the bank itself is likely to sign up as a placement agent.

Bulge-bracket firms often sponsor the organizational ally of private equity funds — venture capital — and buy out and participate in their management. One of the oldest is the alliance between Sprout Capital and Donaldson, Lufkin, & Jenrette (now being merged into Credit Suisse First Boston). However, in early stage financing (an angel round, for example), soliciting the likes of Sprout Capital is not a productive use of your time.

Here's a checklist of the kinds of deals that first-tier placement agents handle:

- ✔ Established firms with strong track records
- ✔ Funding minimums of $25 million
- ✔ Institutional investors as the target audience

The second tier: Early stage experts

Below the bulge-bracket firms are a group of firms that once acted as placement agents for early stage financings but have shifted their efforts to the big leagues. These firms, starting with Hambrecht & Quist (which is now owned by Chase Manhattan Bank), grew up in the venture capital/high-tech arena. They include the likes of Robertson Stephens, Alex Brown, and SG Cowen — upstarts that began as so-called *boutiques,* specializing in high-tech and usually located on one coast or the other. These firms are, by definition, interested in new ideas and new technology. However, they by and large have graduated to spheres beyond the angel round.

In terms of raising private equity for emerging growth companies, they set their sights on financings at or above the $15 million (plus or minus) level, which ordinarily implies a good deal of maturity for the issuer (the company seeking capital) in terms of customers, revenues, and net earnings. Moreover, many of these firms have been acquired by major financial institutions — for example, Alex Brown by Bankers Trust and then by Deutsche Bank — and are therefore opting for major-league rankings, all of which takes them above and beyond the seed and early stage financing sectors.

Here are a few things to remember about second-tier placement agents:

- ✔ They deal with emerging growth companies.
- ✔ They work with funding minimums of $15 million (more or less).
- ✔ They focus on companies with breakthrough products.
- ✔ They're technologically sophisticated.
- ✔ They're becoming as elitist as the bulge-bracket firms.

The third tier: Regional investment banks

At the next level is a group of regional investment banks — Dain Rauscher, U.S. Bancorp Piper Jaffray, Adams, Harkness & Hill, Robinson-Humphrey, Friedman Billings Ramsey, and First Albany, to name just a few East Coast and Midwest members. The regionals may act as placement agents at a relatively early stage, but, again, with prosperity, many have moved to what you might call a better neighborhood. In other words, they have a high cutoff in the level of financing and the maturity of the issuers they're willing to consider.

The regionals enjoy one critical element in the fundraising process when you think of angel investors: They almost always have a *retail brokerage capacity* — a slew of retail brokers residing throughout the region who are in contact with potential customers. However, not many retail brokers are willing to introduce a high-risk opportunity to a valuable customer. In the event of failure, the broker could lose the customer. And the commission on a $2 million or $3 million private placement is usually not enough to light up a big broker's eyes.

In many instances, retail brokerage networks are not so much interested in "writing tickets," as it's called, as they are in introducing customers with assets to the financial institution employing them — *asset gathering*. The economics of the business being what it is — particularly on the brokerage side because commissions have shrunk — growing the amount of assets under management (where an annual fee can be charged for little work) is a higher priority than struggling through an early stage financing. Don't overlook retail brokers and investment banks, however. If the deal is attractive enough, retail brokers cover a lot of ground.

Here's a checklist of things to remember about third-tier placement agents:

- ✔ They work with local companies.
- ✔ They have funding minimums of $5 million (more or less).
- ✔ They understand the local markets.
- ✔ They can be as picky as the major-leaguers.

The fourth tier: Boutiques

The fourth tier is composed of so-called boutiques. A typical boutique is a collection of experienced investment bankers who have left their major-league firms to strike out on their own, usually in a loose alliance with other individuals of like persuasion.

Boutiques attempt to do all the interesting things that their former employers did. With prominent exceptions, they like to be involved in advisory work for mergers and acquisitions work, and often consider themselves advisors rather than bankers. They don't ordinarily maintain true brokerage functions, and they don't write tickets, nor are they members of the New York Stock Exchange.

Need to find a placement agent? Look here!

Finding placement agents is a tough assign-ment. The ultimate resource is *The Corporate Finance Sourcebook,* published by National Register Publishing, owned by the Lexis-Nexis Group. The *Sourcebook* is published annually, and the 2000 edition is 1,503 pages long. The table of contents includes the following listings:

✔ Who's Who in Investment Banking

✔ Geographic Preference Index

✔ Business Intermediaries

✔ Industry Preference Index

The *Sourcebook* covers most sizes, shapes, and types, from Goldman Sachs to shops employing only one professional. There's no listing of lower-tier players or boutiques, however. You need to segregate the candidates by geography and industry type. Beyond that, you have many potential candidates to choose from. Careful investigation is called for.

Boutiques like to arrange private institutional financings for mature companies, in some cases public companies, but they don't have the capital or the inclina-tion to join in syndicates underwriting public offerings. They also do occa-sional private placements at the early stage level, depending on the market. Obviously, a robust market is more attractive than a stingy and skeptical one, particularly if a boutique is considering, say, a $3 million to $5 million private placement.

Boutiques ordinarily have low overhead. Each partner is, in effect, a one-man band, without an entourage of assistants. They tend not to locate in the highest-rent districts in the city. When the engagement is appropriate, how-ever, they can be effective.

No specific list of boutique investment banks exists. Most are listed in the *Corporate Finance Sourcebook* but not identified as such. They're mixed in with the Goldman Sachs of the world.

Here's a checklist of things to remember about boutiques:

✔ They'll work with any company within the field of expertise of one of their partners.

✔ They require no particular funding minimum, but $3 million is about as low as most of them will go.

✔ They're open for business for early stage firms.

✔ They can't manufacture investors out of whole cloth. If a deal is too early for a placement agent, it's too early for a placement agent, period.

Some so-called boutiques are groups of curious individuals who have little aptitude for fundraising but nonetheless publicize themselves as successful intermediaries. They apparently exist on retainers, with little hope of earning the remainder of the fee for a successful transaction.

The fifth tier: Boiler rooms and bucket shops

At the next level is an amorphous group of firms that consist mainly of a retail sales force engaged largely in promoting *penny stocks* — public securities of issuers listed on the NASDAQ Small Cap Market and the OTC Bulletin Board and Pink Sheets. These issuers are too small or shaky to be listed on a national market exchange such as the New York Stock Exchange (NYSE). Some of these firms are legitimate and perform necessary market functions in maintaining some liquidity in public securities that the big guys don't deign to pay attention to. Others, though, are what are known in the trade as *bucket shops* or *boiler rooms*. These brokers cold-call potential customers and attempt to push questionable securities on an unsuspecting public for no reason other than the commissions the trades will garner.

On occasion, these firms attempt to place private equity, and many of them are not particularly picky about the size of the offering. That can be good news for a legitimate entrepreneur because, as they say, all money is green. And despite questionable stock sales practices in the public markets, a bucket shop sometimes knows where the appropriate buckets are. However, astute professionals don't recommend doing business with firms in this bracket. Even if you successfully raise private equity, there's no telling what kind of story the salesperson told to the investor. A group of angry and disappointed investors can be worse than no investors at all.

Here's a checklist of things to remember about fifth-tier placement agents:

- They'll work for any company.
- They require no funding minimum.
- The only good news about them is that you can be sure they'll take you on.
- The bad news is the same as the good news.

The new tier: Incubators

Recently, a new category has been added — organizations are styling themselves as incubators. The term *incubator* includes a couple of possibilities:

- ✔ **Physical incubators** are office and conference facilities set up to house emerging growth firms in a quasi-private, quasi-communal environment. A typical physical incubator comprises an entire floor or floors of an old loft building — split into cubicles occupied by early stage firms — and provides shared conference, reception, phone-answering, and cafeteria facilities. Incubators are particularly useful for firms specializing in information technology because the space typically includes access to broadband Internet capability.

- ✔ **Virtual incubators** also serve a multitude of clients and provide an array of services, including business consultation (they will help with a business model), technical work (they will help design a Web site if that's part of the model), recruiting, financial management, and strategic advice.

"Finders" Beware!

The Securities Exchange Act of 1934 defines a *broker/dealer* as any person (which includes individuals and firms) effecting transactions in securities for the account of others. Ignoring for the moment some technical exceptions, anybody in the business of trading stocks and bonds as an agent — whether public or private — falls within that definition and therefore is required by the 1934 Act to register and be subject to a variety of rules having to do with training and qualification of personnel, regulation of sales practices, possession of adequate capital, and, through required membership in the National Association of Securities Dealers (NASD), compliance with codes of conduct. Most placement agents are currently registered with the SEC and members of the NASD.

It's important to understand that 1934 Act registration, together with membership in the NASD, a self-regulated organization, is not a guarantee of a firm's efficacy or integrity. Regulation can do only so much in weeding out unethical practices and incompetence. For example, a number

of so-called bucket shops are members in good standing of the NASD.

Moreover, a number of the intermediaries at this level are *not* registered under the 1934 Act and/or are not members of the NASD. They operate on the theory that they are distinct from broker/dealers because they are "finders." Their main line of business is something other than placing private equity, or they do it on such an occasional basis that they believe they are not required to register. Language in the standard treatise on securities regulation has encouraged legitimate parties to believe that they are exempt from registration, but straws in the wind indicate that the SEC may take steps to require registration among players in this sector.

If you want to check on a firm's standing, go to www.nasd.com where you can ask for information about individual firms, their brokers, and complaints, violations, or penalties. Allow ten days from the date of your request to receive the report from NASD.

Some of the more visible firms that style themselves as incubators are in fact sources of capital — the equivalent of venture capital funds. These firms create synergies among their portfolio companies by, for example, introducing a Web site design firm in which the incubator has invested to an investee firm that's looking for Web site design services. We mention firms operating under this label *were* very much in fashion because many so-called incubators are actually placement agents in the classic sense. By calling themselves incubators and offering ancillary services — business consultation, for example — the incubator can charge a higher fee, particularly a fee expressed in terms of equity participation in the entrepreneur's company.

Our intent is not to denigrate a phenomenon that has been highly useful to a number of emerging growth companies in terms of advice and capital, but simply to point out that a rose by any other name smells as sweet. A placement agent, whether it's called a finder, an investment bank, or an incubator, functions most usefully as a placement agent. Emerging growth companies can use business advice and share office space, technical services, financial management, and overall strategic direction; however, in the final analysis, the most prominent need is the need for investment capital. And if a firm called an incubator can meet that need, then so be it.

Understanding the Role of Placement Agents

If you think that the primary job of placement agents is finding the capital you seek, then you are right. Placement agents do much more than simply find capital, but there are a number of things that they most definitely do not do. Just to make sure that you're clear on both in the review that follows about what placement agents do and don't do.

What placement agents do

A placement agent is useful (often critical) in identifying sources of financing that a company wouldn't have stumbled upon itself. A good agent has a sense of what the market wants and can give useful advice about the business plan and how to present it. Moreover, a placement agent can help reduce the hidden costs of raising capital at this stage — the time that managers must devote to fundraising.

Early stage fundraising is seemingly constant. And emerging growth companies are not ordinarily overpopulated with managers — they run lean and mean. Almost everyone has more than a full-time job, often working around the clock to achieve the company's goals. Therefore, raising money is an expensive diversion for managers, particularly when they have to find prospective investors on their own.

By identifying likely prospects, a placement agent can save precious time in two respects:

✔ The company's managers don't have to do it and therefore can devote more time to running the company.

✔ The time between the start of the hunt and the end is shorter, often a life-or-death matter for companies operating from payroll period to payroll period.

A placement agent's role should not, however, be exaggerated. If you think that all you'll have to do is hand over a business plan to your friendly local placement agent and wait for the dollars to come in, you're suffering from a financially fatal self-delusion — one that can mean a quick end to your entrepreneurial dream.

What placement agents don't do

Let us make one thing perfectly clear: No placement agent in the early stage space — no matter how skillful — actually sells the security in the conventional sense, the way one might sell a computer or used car. In private equity, the sales are one-on-one, with the investor on one side of the table and the managers of the company on the other. The agent's function is

✔ First, to give advice on what the market is looking for

✔ Second, to locate potential investors

✔ Third, and last, to introduce the two sides and then step back and let nature take its course.

Private investors at this level are not terribly interested in hearing what the agent has to say about the company, other than the spiel given when the opportunity is being introduced. After the courtship starts, the investor wants answers directly from the company's managers. In fact, the agent often looks to the founder for a so-called *friends list* — that is, potential investors already known to the founder. Moreover, an agent acts only on a best-efforts basis. A firm commitment in the early stages of a company — indeed, a firm commitment on a private placement of any kind — is encountered only in special circumstances.

No matter what a placement agent may tell you, your company sells its own stock.

Decisions, Decisions: Do You Need a Placement Agent?

Here's at least one compelling reason to retain a placement agent: It may mean the difference between getting the job done and coming up empty-handed. And coming up empty-handed may mean closing the shutters on your business venture. Remember: The market is incredibly inefficient at this level, and successful financings often are the result of chance encounters. A good placement agent may take some of the chance element out of the equation.

Here are a number of other reasons to hire placement agents:

- They can save you time by doing much of the legwork involved in finding potential investors and making arrangements.

- They lend an air of professionalism to your company. You're more attractive to potential investors if you have a professional placement agent presenting your public face.

- They can tutor you in the rules of the game. For example, they can remind you that all capital raised goes straight into your company — no luxury vacations!

- They can help with preparing the placement memorandum and the deal terms that you offer.

When you're considering whether to hire a placement agent, you must approach the situation realistically. Most mainstream investment banks aren't going to do any more than be polite, and by being polite, they're wasting your time. The trick is looking at the opportunity with an objective eye and figuring out whether the agent working with you:

- Will listen to your story.
- Can do something with the opportunity.

This judgment is hard to make, particularly when you can wind up with a charlatan or an incompetent — someone who will take your money and, perhaps even more damaging, waste your time. When in doubt, avoid the crowd and aim at the most likely target — placement agents in the tier that will welcome your business.

Learning by example

To give you a horrible example (without naming the firm) of asking a placement agent to bite off more than it can chew, an Israel-based dot-com engaged the services of a firm that was not a bucket shop or a boiler room but nonetheless did not appear to have the appropriate credentials to get the job done. Despite advice to the contrary, the parties forged ahead and signed a deal. The agent's partners invested some of their own money and got an initial portion of financing raised — more or less as a pump primer, because it wasn't enough to get the company to its end point, where cash flow breakeven would be in sight. The parties strained to complete the financing, but it simply couldn't be done with the agent in question at the controls.

That doesn't mean that another agent would have done a better job, but rather that during the period in which the agent and the company were struggling to find money, nothing much was going on at the company, and the business languished. Finally, after months of trying, the agent gave up and recommended (as the lesser of two evils) that the company try a back-door public offering by merging into a public shell. This was in a period when public markets were delirious with joy. But, as we have predicted on any number of occasions (based on a public survey conducted under our auspices) the shell game did not work out satisfactorily. The last the company was seen, it was in liquidation.

We've explained the potential positives of using placement agents, but there are some negatives as well:

- ✔ A good placement agent can be hard to find. You may find no placement agent, at least of good quality, available for a given financing. And the hunt for an agent can be time-consuming.

- ✔ You may make the wrong choice and wind up with a weak placement agent (or worse, an outright faker).

- ✔ You can be deemed undesirable by association. An entrepreneur seeking capital is often known by the company he or she keeps. A second-rate placement agent can be off-putting to experienced investors. The occasion does not arise often, but it can be a dirty shame when a placement agent drags you down in a potential investor's eyes — not only not helping, but also hurting you.

- ✔ Placement agents cost money. Preparing the necessary placement memoranda and locating the right cadre of investors takes a lot of time. It should come as no surprise, then, that the compensation that a placement agent seeks is not a trivial percentage of the money raised.

> ✔ Placement agents occasionally bite off more than they can chew. Induced by a retainer and the *possibility* of completing a financing, they set sail on uncharted waters with the company's management in tow, waste everybody's time, and risk the company's ultimate fortune in the process. Often, the company's management will start counting on the equity to be raised simply because the placement agent is on the job. Doing so is, of course, unwise! You don't want to substitute the wish for the deed, but it frequently happens and the result often is disaster.

Placement agents generally do not take on assignments if the target raise is less than, say, $5 million. Most prefer larger amounts because they can charge larger fees. Early stage placements are not usually mini/max offerings such as, "We will raise $10 million or nothing." However, if you expressly target $10 million, it is hard to close on $2 million. After all, you said you needed $10 million. You can have a first closing, particularly when capital for a private equity fund is being raised; most second closings are tag end affairs topping off the round. If you didn't raise enough at the first closing to get the job done, you shouldn't take down any money.

Fees: Coughing Up the Cash

Make no mistake about it: Placement agents don't work for free. In fact, a placement agent's fees can entail a significant diminishment of your ultimate funding. Not only that, but the placement fee can become a troublesome issue when the placement agent brings in fewer than the necessary number of investors, and your company brings in the rest with no help at all from the agent. Fortunately, if you do your homework in advance and find a good placement agent, chances are that everyone will be happy with the result.

So, exactly who pays for the services of a placement agent? The three possible sources for payment of the placement fee are

> ✔ If the company pays the fee, *everybody* (the founder, other shareholders, and investors) ends up paying a piece of it.
>
> ✔ If the fee is deducted from an investor's capital contribution, the investor pays.
>
> ✔ If the founder reaches into his or her own pocket, then the founder pays.

When you surf the Internet in search of a placement agent, it's unlikely that you'll find anyone offering to get you $1 million in funding for a set fee of, say, $19.95. There is no standard schedule of fees for placement agents at this level — everything is negotiable, and deals vary considerably. There are, however, some typical elements in placement agent compensation:

- ✔ A cash retainer
- ✔ A success fee
- ✔ Equity, usually in the form of warrants to buy stock in the future at a set price

Who you select to act as your placement agent and the nature of the investment opportunity itself will have a large bearing on the fees you'll be expected to pay. Investment banking fees for public offerings and institutional private placements are more or less set — within a range, of course — but those fee structures are irrelevant in the early stage sector. Why? Because of the relative difficulty in placing an early stage investment opportunity.

If your opportunity looks like it will jump off the shelf and a number of placement agents are competing for it, the fees (including equity) will tend to be lower. For a "sticky" placement — one that's less desirable (most early stage placements are) — the fees will tend toward the upper end of the spectrum.

The retainer

Most placement agents want a *retainer:* a fee that you pay upfront to secure the agent's services. Why? Because, if the project turns out to be a dud and the agent can't get it done, he or she needs to defray expenses in some way. This part of the fee usually is fixed by what the issuer can afford — an amount that's often not much more than $25,000. The retainer cements the deal and presumably gets the placement agent going. At least that's the idea.

Retainers come in two varieties: They are or are not set off against the success fee. For example, if a success fee is 5 percent of a $1 million raise, the total cash consideration can be either

- ✔ $50,000 — $25,000 on closing plus the $25,000 that has already been paid
- ✔ $75,000 — 5 percent of $1 million, or $50,000, plus the $25,000

The placement agent's compensation usually includes reimbursement of monthly expenses as well. Be sure, however, to put a cap on expenses and require full documentation just as you would for your employees. Fortunately, most deals at this level are local, so you shouldn't have to cover exorbitant travel expenses.

The success fee

The *success fee* — paid to the placement agent when he or she lands a deal — comes in two parts: cash and equity.

Cash

The cash fee generally ranges from 2 percent to 10 percent (or more) of the money raised. That calculation needs to be drafted carefully because money often comes in over a period of time, and some of the investment may be contingent on benchmarks or milestones. It isn't unusual for some of the investors to contribute property, and/or the equity placement may be accompanied by a layer of debt on top of it. Is the fee charged against equity only or equity and debt? How do you value the investment of, say, intellectual property? If the investment comes in over time, is the whole fee paid upfront?

The cash success fee also requires attention in the placement agent agreement. It is ordinarily expressed as a percentage of the amount raised. If the placement agent comes up with $1 million and the success fee is 5 percent, the equation is simple — $50,000 payable when the deal closes. Difficulties may arise, however. If a placement agent raises $1 million but the capital is payable in two installments of $500,000 each, it's in the company's interest to stagger payment of the fee, $25,000 on each closing, instead of paying one lump sum to the agent at closing.

You need a lawyer's attention in calculating the benchmark against which the cash fee is measured. Be sure to have an attorney help you with fee-related issues.

Equity

The cash portion of the success fee can be lucrative to the placement agent, but the equity element — usually expressed in terms of warrants to buy stock in the company at a set price — can be much more significant in the long run. Depending on the bargaining leverage between the two parties, the equity fee can range from a small percentage (say, 2 percent to 4 percent of the company's outstanding stock) to as high as *80 percent* for some incubators. How do incubators justify such high fees? As we point out earlier in this chapter, some incubators claim (and sometimes rightly so) that they are putting the entrepreneur in business — that the incubator is, in effect, the founder and is taking the risk, with the entrepreneur defaulting into the smaller role of key manager.

In the real world, a typical figure for equity subject to the warrant hovers between 5 percent and 10 percent of the equity raised. This is potentially a big number. Assuming a $2 million placement and the postmoney valuation of the company at $5 million, a 10 percent warrant position (assuming a nominal exercise price) entails a call on close to 4 percent of the entire company, or $200,000 (+/-) in notional value (we are not doing a Black Scholes calculation here).

Add to that 10 percent of the cash raised, or $200,000, and you get $400,000 in consideration on a $2 million raise. This is pretty close to the kinds of percentages that your friendly local loan shark might find familiar. On the other hand, the cash outlay is only $200,000, leaving $1.8 million prior to lawyers' fees. And that $1.8 million may mean the difference between success and failure.

You have other important points to consider when it comes to the equity component of the success fee. Here are a few:

- ✔ The term of the warrant and the exercise price have to be set. The placement agent wants the term to be as long as possible to postpone the decision of when to put up its capital; the company wants it to be as short as possible. The exercise price of a warrant is key: A warrant to buy the underlying stock at its then fair value (the price the investors are paying) is valuable because the stock value is expected to go up and be worth more when the warrant is exercised. A warrant to buy one share at $5.00 is worth nothing when the value of the stock is only $5.00 and the warrant must be exercised right away; but if the warrant term is 10 years out, exercisable at any time, then the stock can go up to $100 (for techies, the way of calculating value is called the Black Scholes Method, and Black and Scholes got Nobel prizes for their work).

- ✔ A principal objective of the company's negotiators should be to require the warrants to be exercised, "use them or lose them," on the eve of an IPO or other exit event, such as the sale of the entire company.

- ✔ Occasionally, a placement agent asks for special antidilution protection, which means either that automatic adjustments ensue in case a stock split or stock dividend is declared (technical and therefore, noncontroversial adjustments) or that the warrant holder automatically gets more stock for the same price if the company has a problem and has to issue stock in a subsequent financing at a price lower than the warrant holder's exercise price.

  This last provision is highly controversial, particularly because the placement agent did not pay cash for the warrant. In terms of negotiations, it's considered a "jump ball" — one that can go either way depending on the relative leverage of each party.

- ✔ The company may not want the warrant to be transferable, the idea being that while the company is private, it should control what kinds of individuals or firms can wind up as stockholders. Occasionally, the placement agent asks for a provision in the warrant that enables it to take advantage of what's called *cashless exercise*. Instead of exercising the warrant for cash, the warrant holder gives up the warrant and in exchange receives stock, the value of which equals the so-called *spread,* meaning the fair market value of the stock subject to the warrant as of the date of the transaction minus the exercise price, and translated into shares of stock.

  To illustrate, if a warrant entitles the holder to buy 10 shares of stock at $1 per share and, at the point of exercise, the stock has gone up in value to $5 per share, the warrant is deemed to be "in the money," and the value of the spread is 10 times the $5 fair market value per share, minus the $1 exercise price, or $40. The $40 at a fair market value of $5 a share buys eight shares of stock, so the cashless exercise privilege entails the holder giving up the warrant and receiving in return 8 shares of stock. This is a tax-advantaged transaction to the holder and thus is highly desirable. However (and this is the minus from the company's standpoint), the holder doesn't have to put up any money to obtain the value of the spread, meaning that the company doesn't get any money.

The understandings between your organization and the selected placement agent are critical to the success of your search for capital. Always put them in writing. Although we recommend that you enlist the help of competent legal counsel to draft and/or review any written agreement with a placement agent before you sign on the dotted line, we have included a sample agreement at the end of this chapter. Remember that every agreement has its own unique terms and conditions. Also keep in mind that more than a few owners have lost control of their businesses when they signed an agreement that gave away too much of the business away for too little in return.

Due Diligence: Avoiding Rip-Offs and Failures

Finding the cash to grow a business — or simply to keep it afloat — is important for almost every business at one time or another. Getting funded can be the catalyst that makes your business take off for the stratosphere, while failure to raise capital can mean filing for bankruptcy. That makes the process of qualifying your placement agent and checking his or her references particularly important.

Qualifying a placement agent

The process of qualifying a placement agent involves what the law calls *due diligence* — checking behind and around statements that the candidate makes to see whether they are accurate. Although qualifying your placement agent may appear to be simple and straightforward, all too often important details are overlooked.

When a placement agent claims that it has placed $30 million in equity in 12 separate transactions during the past 12 months, validating that number is difficult. However, with a little research, you can better your odds against getting duped, just by doing the following:

✔ Insist on a sampling of the transactions claimed with the names and contact information of the players.

✔ Make a few phone calls and find out whether the agent's customers are satisfied with the services that they received in return for their hard-earned cash and equity. That so many companies neglect this tire-kicking process is simply perverse.

✔ Consult LexisNexis (www.lexisnexis.com) to see whether the candidate has been in the newspaper in the last four or five years and, if so, in what capacity. You'd be surprised at the kinds of gruesome stories that can turn up when you take the opportunity to mine the data available at the click of a mouse.

✔ Inquire with the SEC (www.sec.gov) and the NASD (www.nasd.com). These searches also can turn up interesting information.

Keep in mind, however, that you don't need to insist on a squeaky clean record. Even the best of firms encounter regulatory issues from time to time. But there are violations of the rules and then there are *violations*. After you obtain a write-up of an incident, figuring out what kinds of people are involved is usually pretty easy.

Being realistic about valuation

Your company's goals, in terms of premoney valuation, should be realistic, not farfetched. Too many entrepreneurs read stories in the financial press about deals that seem like the financial equivalents of another gold strike at Sutter's Mill. Remember that some journalists are trained to write about the exceptions and not the rule — man bites dog rather than vice versa. The fact that a given company raised a ton of money at a heroic valuation does not mean that you can do the same. It only means that every lottery has a winner.

The pricing of any product has to be realistic if the placement agent is to perform his or her job effectively. A good agent makes that clear before taking on an assignment.

Stay flexible

You must be flexible. Listen to the marketplace when it says that the price of the offered securities is too high. The early stage private equity universe is not a place for hardheads. When the placement agent brings back news that your security is overpriced, don't shoot the messenger. Instead, pay attention and adjust your sights accordingly.

Be candid with your placement agent

You have to be candid with your placement agent. This is probably the most important point we can make. Your job is to pitch to the investors, not the placement agent. Assuming that, a placement agent will be equipped to turn around and sell the investors a proverbial bill of goods if you can somehow talk the agent into believing a suspect story is a mistake. Give the placement agent the whole story, warts and all. Nothing is more embarrassing or destructive than investors finding out (as they inevitably will) that the placement agent has been kidding them. The investors disappear, your placement agent is angry, everyone has wasted time, and you're out of business — not exactly the outcome that you had in mind.

Finally, keep in mind that any placement agent worth his or her salt will likely seek further concessions from you when it comes time to sign a contract. This means that:

- In the agreement between the issuer and its placement agent, the agent expects indemnities against claims arising out of failures to disclose material information (an indemnity is of dubious worth when dealing with a founder with little money and a start-up company).

- The placement agent usually insists on a right of first refusal to lead subsequent rounds of financing — a provision that you should approach thoughtfully. If an investment bank known only to a few loyal adherents on Wall Street is willing to help out in a first-round financing — but at a cost of controlling subsequent rounds — you may find that price too high. On the other hand, it's unrealistic to expect an investment banker to work enthusiastically on the earliest, most difficult financing and then take his or her chances at being remembered with gratitude when subsequent, more lucrative rounds are being discussed.

A good placement agent is worth perhaps more than his or her weight in gold — especially when the agent succeeds in lining you up with the capital that your business needs. Spend lots of time interviewing agents before you settle on the one, and then work hard to create a long-term relationship that will benefit you, your business, and your agent.

Sample Agency Agreement

WARNING: *This sample copy is provided only for purposes of illustration. The provisions are highly complex and technical, and may vary depending on controlling law; you should consult your own lawyer rather than use this sample unadvised in an actual transaction.*

Acme Electronics Limited
New York, NY
Ladies and Gentlemen:

This engagement letter confirms our agreement (this "Agreement") that Acme Electronics Limited (the "Company"), a Delaware corporation, hereby retains Adviser & Co. Inc. ("Adviser") as exclusive financial advisor to the Company in connection with the proposed sale (the "Placement") by the Company of Series A convertible preferred stock (the "Stock") to a group of accredited investors (the "Investors").

Advisor will assist the Company in searching for prospective Investors and, if requested by the Company, in analyzing, structuring, negotiating, and effecting a Placement with the prospective Investors in the Stock. In this regard, we propose to undertake certain activities on your behalf, including, if requested, the following:

Advising the Company as to the structure and form of the Placement;

Counseling the Company as to strategy and tactics for negotiating with the potential Investor or Investors and, if requested by the Company, participating in such negotiations;

As compensation for its services hereunder, the Company shall pay to Adviser a nonrefundable fee of $25,000 upon the Effective Date. In addition, the Company agrees to reimburse Advisor, up to a maximum of $5,000 per month, for all reasonable out-of-pocket expenses it incurs in carrying out the terms of this Agreement, including telephone, travel, facsimile, courier, computer time charges, and reasonable attorneys' fees and disbursements.

If the Company consummates with one or more parties a Placement or series of Placements for aggregate consideration of at least $10,000,000 (the "Consideration") at any time during the period beginning on the execution hereof and terminating upon the delivery of written notice of termination by either party (the "Engagement Period"), or not later than two years after the expiration of such Engagement Period with any party (or any entity controlled by or affiliated with such party) identified to the Company by Advisor or as to which Advisor has rendered any services hereunder, Advisor shall receive, in addition to the amounts set forth above, a fee (the "Closing Fee"), contingent upon and payable in cash promptly upon receipt by the Company of aggregate consideration in excess of $10,000,000, equal to four percent (4%) of the Consideration, plus a nontransferable 10-year warrant (the "Warrant") to purchase that number of shares of the Company's common stock as shall equal four (4) percent of the Company's entire outstanding common stock, fully diluted, including in this calculation the exercise of all nonvested employee options, the exercise price to be one cent ($0.01) per share equal to the conversion price of the stock issued in the Placement.

(**Note:** It's customary to define *consideration* carefully for purposes of calculating the fee. See the following language for an example.)

Consideration paid with respect to the Stock shall be equal to the total of all cash, assets, stock, or other securities paid to the Company. Consideration shall also include future investments by the Investors obligated either absolutely or upon the attainment of milestones or financial results ("Future Payments"). The fee paid as a result of Future Payments shall be paid at closing and shall be valued at the present value of the Future Payments. For the purpose of calculating the present value, the Company and Advisor agree to discount all Future Payments by a discount factor equal to fifteen percent (15%) per annum and, where necessary, to use the projections that have been provided by the Company in the course of this placement to quantify these amounts and their timing.

If any employee of Advisor is required to give testimony or otherwise provide information in any pretrial proceeding or the trial of any action in which the services rendered by Advisor pursuant to this Agreement are the subject of examination, the Company agrees, as part of its obligations as set forth in *Appendix A* annexed hereto, to pay to Advisor the sum of $2,500 for each day or portion of a day that any of its Managing Directors; $1,500 for each day or portion of a day that any of its Vice President and/or Associates; and $500 per day or portion of a day that any of its Vice-Presidents and/or administrative employees make themselves available to give such testimony or provide such information or spend time in preparation to do any of the foregoing; provided, however, that the foregoing obligation shall not apply to any testimony or the provision of any information by Advisor or its employees in connection with the Approval by the Authorities of (i) this Agreement or (ii) the Placement.

If during the Engagement Period (including any extensions thereof), or not later than two years after the expiration of such Engagement Period (including any extensions thereof), the Company elects to undertake any underwritten public offering(s) of equity securities, Advisor shall have the right of first refusal to represent the Company as lead manager of such offering(s). Such right of first refusal shall be subject to the execution of a separate underwriting agreement between the parties providing for fees payable to Advisor that are normal and customary for placements of this type among firms qualified to perform such services. The terms and conditions of any such public offering, as well as the timing of such public offering, shall be subject to general market conditions.

If during the Engagement Period (including any extensions thereof), or not later than two years after the expiration of such Engagement Period (including any extensions thereof), the Company elects to undertake any additional private placement(s) of equity securities, Advisor shall have the right of first refusal to represent the Company as placement agent for such private placement(s).

Any advice, written or oral, provided by Advisor pursuant to this Agreement will be treated by the Company as confidential, will be solely for the information and assistance of the Company in connection with its consideration of a placement of the type referred to in the first paragraph of this Agreement, and will not be used, circulated, quoted, or otherwise referred to for any other purpose, nor will it be filed with, included in, or referred to in whole or in part in any registration statement, proxy statement, or any other document, except in each case with our prior written consent.

In order to coordinate our efforts with respect to a possible Placement satisfactory to the Company, during the period of our engagement hereunder neither the Company nor any representative there (other than Advisor) will initiate discussions regarding a Placement except through Advisor. In the event that the Company or its management receives an inquiry from Advisor, it will promptly advise Advisor of such inquiry in order that Advisor may evaluate such prospective Investor and its interest and assist the Company in any resulting negotiations.

In addition, if at any time prior to 12 months after the termination or expiration of this Agreement a Placement is consummated, or if at any time prior to 24 months after the termination or expiration of this Agreement a Placement is consummated with any party contacted regarding a Placement during the period of this engagement, Advisor will provide the Company with written notice of the parties contacted by Advisor regarding a Placement during the period of this engagement.

It is understood that if the Company completes a placement in lieu of any placement for which Advisor is entitled to compensation pursuant to this Agreement, Advisor and the Company will in good faith mutually agree upon acceptable compensation for Advisor, taking into account, among other things, the results obtained and the custom and practice of investment bankers acting in similar placements.

The Company acknowledges and agrees that Advisor has been retained solely to provide the advice or services set forth in this Agreement. Advisor shall act as an independent contractor, and any duties of Advisor arising out of its engagement hereunder shall be owed solely to the Company.

In order to enable Advisor to provide the services requested, the Company agrees to provide to Advisor, among other things, all information reasonably requested or required by Advisor including, but not limited to, information concerning historical and projected financial results with respect to the Company and its subsidiaries and possible and known litigious, environmental, and contingent liabilities. The Company also agrees to make available to Advisor such representatives of the Company, including, among others, directors, officers, employees, outside counsel, and independent certified public accountants, as Advisor may reasonably request. Advisor does not assume responsibility for the accuracy or completeness of the information to which reference is made herein.

The services herein described are to be rendered to the Company. They are not being rendered by Advisor as an agent or as a fiduciary of the shareholders of the Company, and Advisor shall not have any liability or obligation with respect to its services hereunder to such parties or to any other person, firm, or corporation.

The Company and Advisor hereby agree to the terms and conditions of the Indemnification Agreement attached hereto as *Appendix A* with the same force and effect as if such terms and conditions were set forth at length herein.

This Agreement sets forth the entire understanding of the parties relating to the subject matter hereof and supersedes and cancels any prior communications, understandings, and agreements between the parties. This Agreement cannot be terminated or changed, nor can any of its provisions be waived, except by written agreement signed by all parties hereto or except as otherwise provided herein. Commencing upon the Effective Date, this Agreement shall be binding upon and inure to the benefit of any successors and assigns of the Company.

This Agreement shall be governed by and construed to be in accordance with the laws of the State of New York applicable to contracts made and to be performed solely in such State by citizens thereof. Any dispute arising out of this Agreement shall be adjudicated in the courts of the State of New York or in the federal courts sitting in the Southern District of New York, and the parties hereto hereby agree that service of process upon it by registered or certified mail at its address set forth above shall be deemed adequate and lawful. The parties hereto shall deliver notices to the other parties by personal delivery or by registered or certified mail (return receipt requested) at the addresses set forth herein.

Please confirm that the foregoing is in accordance with your understanding by signing in the space below and returning an executed copy of this Agreement to Advisor.

Very truly yours,

ADVISOR & CO. INC.

By:

Its:

Chapter 9

The Small Business Administration

● ●

In This Chapter

▶ Exploring SBA loan programs

▶ Qualifying for an SBA loan

▶ Understanding the SBA loan application process

▶ Looking at Small Business Investment Corporations (SBICs)

▶ Finding other sources of government-sponsored financing

● ●

*F*or many business owners — especially *small* business owners — raising capital means getting a loan from or guaranteed by the Small Business Administration (SBA). The SBA was chartered in 1953 with the express purpose of providing financial, technical, and management assistance to people starting up new businesses in the United States. The SBA specializes in serving small businesses — large businesses need not apply. It's the largest single financial backer of small businesses in the United States, with a portfolio of business loans, loan guaranties, and disaster loans valued at more than $45 billion. The SBA also holds a venture capital portfolio worth more than $13 billion.

Why all the attention directed to small businesses? Because American business is very much a story of small business. Check out these facts from the SBA:

- ✔ Approximately 25 million small businesses are located in the United States today.

- ✔ 99.7 percent of all employers are small businesses.

- ✔ Small businesses provide approximately 75 percent of the country's new jobs.

- ✔ Small businesses develop 55 percent of the country's innovations.

- ✔ Small businesses comprise 96 percent of all United States exporters.
- ✔ Small businesses employ 53 percent of the United States' private workforce.

In other words, small businesses are an essential element of the U.S. economy. In fact, some would argue that as a source of new jobs and innovations, small businesses are *the* essential element of the U.S. economy. Because of the importance of small business to the country's prosperity, the Small Business Administration does everything it can — including providing a variety of loans, loan guaranties, and other financing programs — to ensure the health and well-being of American small businesses.

But why bother with an SBA loan? Wouldn't it make more sense to try one of the many other approaches for raising capital presented in this book? The answer depends on your situation, but SBA loans often provide advantages over loans from private financial institutions. For example:

- ✔ SBA loans often offer longer repayment terms than loans from other sources.
- ✔ A small business may qualify for an SBA loan even if it does not qualify for a loan from other sources.

Many different kinds of SBA loans and lending programs exist, each with its own unique purpose, application requirements, and eligibility standards. In this chapter, we explore each type of SBA loan. We also take a look at finding capital through other government agencies and sources, including Small Business Investment Corporations (SBICs) — a major source of capital for small businesses in the United States.

Choose One from Column A and One from Column B: Exploring SBA Loan Programs

When you hear someone say that he or she is going to apply for an SBA loan, you may believe that all SBA loans are created equal. Nothing could be further from the truth. Many, many different SBA loan programs exist, and if you want to be successful in getting Uncle Sam to loosen up his purse strings, you want to be sure that you're pursuing the right kind of loan, that you're filling out the right forms and submitting them to the right place at the right time, and that you meet all the requirements for approval.

The three main categories of SBA loan programs are Section 7(a), Section 504, and microloans. The following sections take a closer look at the different kinds of loans available under each program.

Section 7(a) loan programs

Section 7(a) loan programs (*Section 7(a)* refers to the part of the Small Business Act authorizing these particular loan programs) — of which there are many different kinds — are the heart and soul of SBA business financing. They comprise the majority of money provided to loan applicants. In fiscal year 2000, for example, approximately $10.5 billion out of a total of $12.3 billion in loans and loan guaranties — or 85 percent — were provided under Section 7(a) loan programs.

The SBA doesn't actually provide the cash for loans made under the Section 7(a) loan program; instead, the agency acts as a guarantor of loans made by banks and other approved private-sector lenders. If a borrower defaults on a Section 7(a) loan, the SBA reimburses the lender for the remaining loan balance. As a result of this guaranty, lenders are generally much more willing to loan funds to small businesses that otherwise might not be considered eligible.

SBA Section 7(a) loans are limited to a maximum of $2 million, with a maximum SBA guaranty of $1 million. Small loans (of $150,000 or less) are guarantied up to 85 percent; larger loans (of more than $150,000) are guarantied up to 75 percent.

Here's a bit of background on how the various Section 7(a) loan programs differ from one another:

- **7(a) loan guaranty:** The bread and butter of the SBA loan program. When people say that they're going to apply for an SBA loan, this is usually what they're talking about. The SBA doesn't actually supply the cash for these loans; private lending institutions do. The SBA's role is to act as guarantor for the loan in the event of a default. Obtaining a loan through the 7(a) program can take from several weeks to several months.

- **SBA LowDoc:** Just like a regular 7(a) loan guaranty, but lots faster and limited to a $150,000 maximum loan amount. The SBA must respond to an application within 36 hours after receipt. The term *LowDoc* refers to the fact that loans granted under the program require less paperwork (documentation) than other loan programs.

- **SBA Express:** Even faster than an SBA LowDoc loan, the lender uses its own application forms and approves the loan. SBA Express loans are limited to a $150,000 maximum loan amount, and the SBA guaranties only 50 percent of the loan amount. Lenders can approve an unsecured line of credit of up to $25,000 under this program.

- **SBA Export Express:** Similar to an SBA Express loan but geared to small businesses hoping to finance entry into a new export market or expand an existing export market. The maximum loan amount is $150,000, and the SBA guaranties 85 percent of the loan.

✔ **Community Express:** Similar to an SBA Express loan but geared to areas with a predominance of low- and moderate-income individuals and SBA New Markets (which are defined as Hispanics, Native Americans, Asians, veterans, and women), the maximum loan amount is $250,000 with a 50 percent guaranty by the SBA.

✔ **CAPlines:** Designed to help small businesses meet their working capital needs, CAPlines loans are available in amounts of up to $1 million, with the SBA guarantying up to 75 percent. Five different kinds of loans are available under the CAPlines umbrella:

  • **Seasonal line:** Advances against anticipated purchases of inventory for businesses with seasonal sales fluctuations, such as the holiday season.

  • **Contract line:** Used to finance direct labor and material costs expended under assignable contracts.

  • **Builders line:** Used to finance direct labor and material costs for building or renovating commercial or residential buildings.

  • **Standard asset-based line:** Provides a revolving line of credit for the cyclical growth of small businesses that can't meet the credit standards for long-term loans issued by regular lenders.

  • **Small asset-based line:** Similar to the standard asset-based line, but some of the more stringent servicing requirements are waived.

✔ **International trade:** Another loan program designed for small businesses that are engaged in international trade (or are adversely affected by competition from imports), loans under this program are available in amounts of up to $1.25 million for a combination of fixed-asset financing and Export Working Capital Assistance (EWCA).

✔ **Export working capital program:** A joint program of the SBA and the Export-Import Bank, these loans are designed to provide short-term working capital to small business exporters. Loan requests of $833,333 or less, are processed by the SBA, while loans for more than that amount are processed by the Export-Import Bank.

✔ **Pollution control:** Need to finance the planning, design, or installation of a pollution control facility? Need to prevent, reduce, abate, or control a particular form of pollution or get involved in recycling? If so, this is the loan for you. Eligible businesses can receive up to $1 million under this program, with an SBA guaranty of 80 percent for loans that are $100,000 or less and 75 percent for loans in larger amounts.

✔ **DELTA:** DELTA, short for Defense Loan and Technical Assistance Program — a joint program of the SBA and the Department of Defense — was developed to provide assistance to small businesses negatively impacted by reductions in the national defense budget. Loans can be made in amounts of up to $1.25 million under the 7(a) loan program (with a guaranty of up to 80 percent of the loan value) or up to $1 million under the Section 504 loan program (with a guaranty of up to 100 percent).

As you can see, plenty of different opportunities for landing a 7(a) loan exist. New programs are added to the mix from time to time, increasing your chances of getting the capital that you need if you own or operate a small business. If you have specific questions about these loans or want to get the latest and greatest information about new loan programs, visit the Small Business Administration's Web site at www.sba.gov or contact a local lending institution that offers SBA loans.

Section 504 program

The intent of the SBA Section 504 program (*Section 504* refers to the part of the Small Business Act that authorizes this loan program) is to provide growing businesses with long-term, fixed-rate financing for the purchase of major fixed assets, including buildings and land. Money is provided by the SBA to Certified Development Companies (CDCs), which are nonprofit corporations created to spur economic development in their communities. If you want a loan under this program, you need to apply directly to the appropriate CDC. CDCs are usually comprised of community groups, banks, utilities, private investors, and professional organizations. By banding together, these organizations spread out the burden of risk if an investment goes bad.

The maximum SBA participation (the most the agency can contribute to the loan) is limited to $1 million, or $1.3 million for meeting a public policy goal. Public policy goals include

- Business district revitalization
- Expansion of exports
- Expansion of minority business development
- Rural development
- Enhanced economic competition
- Restructuring because of federally mandated standards or policies
- Changes necessitated by federal budget cutbacks
- Expansion of small-business concerns owned and controlled by veterans
- Expansion of small-business concerns owned and controlled by women

The SBA generally requires a business receiving a Section 504 loan to create or retain one job for every $35,000 provided by the SBA.

Section 504 funds may not be used for working capital or inventory, consolidating or repaying debt, or refinancing debt. Section 504 funds are intended for use on bricks-and-mortar and fixed-asset projects, such as

> ✔ Purchasing long-term machinery and equipment
> ✔ Constructing new facilities
> ✔ Renovating or modernizing existing facilities
> ✔ Purchasing land and improvements

Loan terms are either 10 or 20 years, and the interest rate is set at an increment above the current market rate for five-year and ten-year U.S. Treasury issues. Project assets (including machinery, equipment, and other capital items) are usually pledged as collateral for the loan, and the principal owners are also required to sign personal guaranties.

You can find a complete, up-to-date list of Certified Development Companies at www.sba.gov/gopher/Local-Information/Certified-Development-Companies/

Microloan program

Do you have a really, really small business? Can you get by with $35,000 or less for your financing needs? If so, the SBA microloan program may be just the thing for you. Through its microloan program, the SBA provides funds for start-up or expansion through local, community-based nonprofit groups. These groups — which the SBA terms *intermediaries* — pool the money with other local funds and then lend it out to eligible small businesses. Depending on the geographic area in which your business resides, the appropriate intermediary might be a community development corporation (CDC) or a non-CDC community-based organization, such as Chicago's Women's Self-Employment Project or the Nevada Microenterprise Initiative.

Applications must be submitted directly to microloan intermediaries, which are responsible for making credit decisions and for setting terms and conditions for the loans, including interest rates and collateral requirements. Applications generally can be processed in a week or less. According to the SBA, the average size of a microloan is $10,500, and the maximum allowable loan term is six years.

The SBA intends microloan funds to be used to purchase supplies, inventory, furniture, machinery, and equipment, and as working capital. In addition to providing capital, microloan intermediaries are required by the SBA to provide borrowers with technical assistance and business-based training. In some cases, completion of such training may be a requirement for receiving a microloan.

SBA loan statistics — that's a lot of money!

In fiscal 2000, the SBA played a role in more than 48,000 individual loans totaling more than $12 billion. That's a lot of money! Here's where all that money went (dollars in thousands), according to the SBA:

Loan Type	Number of Loans	Total Amount Distributed
7(a) Loans	43,748	$10,523,437
Development Companies	4,565	$1,819,630
International Trade	978	$351,788
1013-EWCL	311	$116,364
1018-IT	169	$78,850
Under $100K	20,242	$1,105,738
LowDoc	9,622	$755,575
PLP Loans	15,063	$6,031,572
Fastrak	9,294	$508,747
CLP Loans	2,269	$838,521
DELTA	25	$15,213
All Loans	48,313	$12,343,066

The SBA maintains an up-to-date list of microloan intermediaries at www.sba.gov/financing/microparticipants.html

Maybe Yes, Maybe No: Understanding SBA Requirements

Not every business is eligible for an SBA loan. Qualifying businesses must meet the criteria that the SBA has established for small businesses. To begin with, qualifying small businesses must meet specific size standards. Table 9-1 shows these standards, which apply to all SBA loans, regardless of whether they are Section 7(a), Section 504, or microloans. Ranges in the categories reflect differing standards for specific business types within overall industries.

Table 9-1	Size Requirements for SBA Loans
Industry	*Size*
Retail and Service	$3.5 million to $13.5 million (annual revenues)
Construction	$7.0 million to $17.0 million (annual revenues)
Agriculture	$0.5 million to $3.5 million (annual revenues)
Wholesale	No more than 100 employees
Manufacturing	500 to 1,500 employees

To qualify, a small business must also

- Operate for profit
- Do business in the United States
- Have "reasonable" owner equity available for investment
- Use alternate financial resources first, including personal assets

Funds secured through SBA loan programs must be used for the purposes specified by the loan type. Any other use may cause the SBA to cancel the loan and require immediate repayment. Depending on the loan program, these uses include

- Real estate
- Construction
- Fixed assets
- Working capital
- Furniture
- Fixtures
- Renovation
- Leasehold improvements

Getting an SBA loan has its downsides. SBA loans can have restrictive terms and covenants that many entrepreneurs don't understand or don't see until the last minute of the deal. And we *are* talking about working with the government, so expect to fill out a lot of forms and provide a lot of paper to your loan officer during the course of the loan application process. We can guarantee that, at a minimum, your patience will be tested.

Still interested in applying for an SBA loan? Yes? Great! In the next section, we discuss exactly how to go about doing just that.

Be Prepared: Applying for an SBA Loan

Generally, two different approaches can be used to apply for an SBA loan: You can either apply directly to the SBA or apply through an approved lender that handles SBA loans. In addition to filling out and submitting the SBA loan application, be prepared to provide the following information and documents:

- An overview/history of the business
- A business plan
- Financial statements for the past two or three years
- A current financial statement (within the past 90 days)
- Résumés of the business's management team
- Business projections

Despite the relaxed qualifying requirements, not every business will be granted an SBA loan. Every business that applies for an SBA loan must meet the lending institution's (and the SBA's) requirements in the following areas:

- **Collateral:** The borrower must provide valuable consideration that he or she is willing to give up in the event of a loan default. Collateral is most often the equipment or fixed assets to be purchased with the loan proceeds but can be almost anything of value.
- **Management ability:** The borrower must demonstrate that he or she has the ability to run a successful business or to hire a team that can run a successful business.
- **Repayment ability:** The borrower must be able to show evidence of good creditworthiness demonstrated by having successfully made regular payments on previous loans and avoiding defaults or bankruptcy. The borrower also must prove that he or she has sufficient current resources to make loan payments.
- **Equity:** Expect to invest a minimum of 10 percent of the loan's value from your own funds to create a favorable loan-to-value ratio.

The loan process generally works like this:

1. You complete and submit an application.
2. You participate in an initial interview with the lending institution.

3. You respond to a request for further information, including W-2 forms and pay stubs.

4. The loan receives preliminary approval from the lender.

5. The lender verifies the information that you provided.

6. The lender creates a loan package containing the forms and information required by the SBA.

7. The lender submits the loan package to the SBA for approval.

8. The loan is funded — mission accomplished!

Depending on which type of SBA loan program you apply for, loan approval can occur relatively quickly — sometimes within just a few days. You can obtain SBA loan applications from local banks, community development corporations, or community-based organizations that handle SBA loans, or you can get a form through the SBA Web site (www.sba.gov/library/forms.html).

And Don't Forget Small Business Investment Corporations (SBICs)

Although the most significant and perhaps the most visible program of federal government assistance to small business is the loan and loan guaranty program that the SBA has run since 1953, one other program provides almost as much capital to small businesses: Small Business Investment Companies (SBICs), which utilize funds obtained from the federal government at favorable interest rates.

Figuring out how SBICs can help you

SBICs are privately organized corporations (or partnerships) regulated by the SBA, and they're a booming business. According to SBA statistics, the SBIC sponsored 4,639 financings in fiscal 2000 — up 50 percent from fiscal 1999 — for a total of $5.46 billion (up 33 percent from fiscal 1999). In fiscal 2000, $1.35 billion of those financings went to small businesses located in low- and moderate-income areas.

So how can Small Business Investment Companies help you obtain the capital that you need for your business? That's exactly what you're about to find out.

SBIC investments: Cutting through the red tape

SBICs are privately capitalized and managed by private citizens and institutions. They are, nonetheless, funded, on top of the private capital, and regulated by the Small Business Administration. The government funding carries with it various obligations designed to ensure that the public's money is well spent. The SBICs, as the name implies, invest equity and offer loans in *small-business concerns,* which are defined generally as firms with a net worth of not more than $18 million and an average annual net income of not more than $6 million. The regulations governing SBICs are complex and subject to a number of exceptions. If you're interested in obtaining SBIC financing, a visit to a local SBA office, or to a lawyer or advisor specializing in SBIC financings, is a must.

The three general types of SBICs are

- ✔ Traditional firms that have provided loans and supplied equity and subordinated debt financing to a wide variety of industries and small businesses

- ✔ Specialized SBICs that focus their investments in firms with socially or economically disadvantaged ownership)

- ✔ A relatively new type of SBIC, carefully licensed by the SBA, that provides equity (typically preferred stock) to businesses that fall under the loose umbrella of *venture capital-eligible firms*

Thus, for example, if you're planning to open a fast-food restaurant, you're likely to be looking for equity and subordinated debt financing from traditional SBICs. If your company is minority controlled, you can obtain some favorable breaks on investment terms from a specialized SBIC. If you're starting a company that is developing a new drug to combat Alzheimer's disease, then an SBIC licensed under the so-called *participating securities* program could be your cup of tea.

Because an SBIC involves private capital, the decision-making process is aimed at maximizing investor returns. That is, the SBIC has stockholders (or limited partners) who've contributed capital in anticipation of making competitive returns on their investments.

One disadvantage of dealing with an SBIC is that government (actually the SBA), to protect the taxpayer's money, has imposed certain restrictions on what an SBIC can do. Thus, conflict-of-interest restrictions, plus limitations on, for example, the firms in which an SBIC may invest or to which it may loan money — only *small* businesses — are involved. The interest rate an SBIC charges to a small business concern is limited by law. This can be good news. Note, however, that regulations govern the types of eligible equity investments the SBIC may make.

Approaching an SBIC

To help you decide which SBIC to approach and how best to pitch your investment opportunity, the SBA offers the following advice (you can find this and much more at www.sba.gov/INV/howtoseek.html):

Research the SBICs

When you own or operate a small business and want to obtain SBIC financing, you first need to identify and investigate existing SBICs that may be interested in financing your company. Use this directory as a first step in learning as much as possible about SBICs in your state, or in other areas important to your company's needs. In choosing an SBIC, consider the types of investments it makes, how much money is available for investment and how much may be available in the future. You also need to consider whether the SBIC can offer you management services appropriate to your needs.

Plan in advance

You should determine your company's needs and research SBICs well in advance — long before you actually need the money. Your research takes time, and so will the SBIC's research of your business.

Prepare a prospectus/business plan

When you've identified the SBICs that you think are best suited to provide financing for your company, you'll need to prepare a presentation. Your initial presentation plays a major role in your success in obtaining financing. It is up to you to demonstrate that an investment in your firm is worthwhile. The best way to show worth is by presenting a detailed and comprehensive business plan or prospectus that includes, at a minimum, the information listed on the following page.

Identification:

✔ The name of the business as it appears on the official records of the state or community in which it operates.

✔ The city, county, and state of the principal location and any branch offices or facilities.

✔ The form of business organization, and if a corporation, the date and state of incorporation.

Product or service:

✔ A description of the business performed, including the principal products sold or services rendered.

✔ A history of the general development of the products and/or services during the past five years (or since inception).

✔ Information about the relative importance of each principal product or service to the volume of the business and to its profits.

Product facilities and property:

✔ Description of real and physical property and adaptability to other business ventures.

✔ Description of the technical attributes of production facilities.

Marketing:

✔ Detailed information about your business's customer base, including potential customers. Indicate the percentage of gross revenue generated by your five largest customers.

✔ A marketing survey and/or economic feasibility study.

✔ A description of the distribution system by which you provide products or services.

Competition:

✔ A descriptive summary of the competitive conditions in the industry in which your business is engaged, including your concern's position relative to its largest and smallest competitors.

✔ A full explanation and summary of your business's pricing policies.

Management:

✔ Brief résumés of the business's management personnel and principal owners including their ages, education, and business experience.

✔ Banking, business, and personal references for each member of management and for the principal owners.

Financial statements:

✔ Balance sheets and profit and loss statements for the last three fiscal years or from your business's inception.

✔ Detailed projections of revenues, expenses, and net earnings for the coming year.

✔ A statement of the amount of funding you are requesting and the time requirement for the funds.

✔ The reasons for your request for funds and a description of the proposed uses.

✔ A description of the benefits that you expect your business to gain from the financing: improvement in financial position, expense reduction, increase in efficiency, and so on.

The main advantage that an SBIC enjoys is in its ability to leverage other capital, meaning the availability of capital from the government at favorable cost *leverages* returns for the private owners. A regular SBIC leverages its private funds up to 3 to 1 with borrowings funded by the proceeds of debentures sold in the public markets and guaranteed by the United States government. The SBIC's capital carries an interest rate that compares favorably to commercial rates (generally 75 to 100 basis points more than the Treasury yield for comparable maturities), with the repayment principal of the debt postponed until maturity. For the venture capital-type (those in the *participating securities* program), an SBIC leverage of 2 to 1 is available and is in the form of a so-called *participating security,* such as a preferred stock. What does the SBIC's favorable cost of capital get you? The savings are passed through *to* the applicant — you.

All this is a little complicated, of course, but the underlying message is clear. Money from SBICs is available for all types of businesses as long as the business qualifies as a *small business concern.* The capital can take the form of debt on favorable terms, a package of equity and debt or common and/or preferred stock. The managers are private individuals with experience in making investments, like bank credit officers and venture capitalists. In fact, the SBIC managers usually are graduates of venture capital funds and commercial or investment banks. Because SBIC financing involves government money, restrictions with detailed provisions are placed on the form and sub-stance of the investments made by an SBIC. Some technically carry criminal penalties, to ensure that the government isn't being ripped off. The conflict of interest regulation is one example.

Again, stating the obvious, the way to find out whether SBIC capital is avail-able is to visit the SBA offices, get a list of the SBICs in your area and knock on some doors just the way you'd knock on the doors of your local bank or a VC.

Chapter 10

Private Equity Offerings

· ·

· ·

*I*f you're seriously considering an Initial Public Offering (IPO) to raise the cash you need to take your business to the next level (or simply to get it out of debt or cash out all your sweat equity), you'll soon find out that it isn't exactly the easiest way in the world to raise capital. In fact, it can be a real pain in the neck. An IPO involves a great deal of work: documents to create, lawyers and accountants to pay, and forms to fill out and sign. You also will constantly worry about what happens if the IPO market falls apart before *your* offering is sold.

Tough luck.

Wouldn't an easier way to drum up large sums of money for your business be nice? Actually, the private placement fits that description. In a *private placement* you sell ownership stakes in your business, such as common or preferred stock, directly to a small number of individuals or organizations but not to the general public. When executed properly, these transactions are exempt from the federal and state laws that govern public offerings of securities.

Although the private placement gets far less publicity than its much flashier cousin, the IPO, many businesses use this approach to raise all the capital that they need. In fact, when (for whatever reason) the IPO route doesn't make sense, a private placement — in the form of common stock (founders, friends, family, and angel rounds) or convertible preferred stock (Series A, B, and so on, also known as the Professional or VC rounds) — may be just the ticket. A couple of years ago, a Redmond, Washington-based telecommunications company, Metawave Communications Corporation, had big plans to go public, but ended up postponing its IPO when the market went south. Was all hope lost? Hardly. Within a few months, the company was able to raise $91 million in a private placement.

Must-have investor representations

To avoid having your private equity offering invalidated because you didn't sell your securities to the right kind of investor (accredited investors who can't complain they didn't understand the materials), here are several representations that you would be well served to require:

✔ **Rich:** The investor has the ability to bear the risk of the investment. This is the so-called *rich test,* spelled out under Regulation D in specific income and net worth tests, but running through the entire concept of the private-offering exemption. Some people believe it is incumbent on the issuer, in close cases, to obtain backup information, that is, investors' personal financial statements. If you're smart, you may too.

✔ **Smart:** The investor has the requisite knowledge and experience to evaluate the merits and risks of an investment. This is the *smart*

or *sophistication test.* Insisting on backups is open to cautious issuers. They may seek recitations of an investor's experience with venture investments and/or general business experience. The smart test must be passed by nonaccredited investors in Rule 56 offerings under Regulation D. Qualifying investors as smart and rich protects broker/dealers, who are subject to rules laid down by their respective governing bodies, the National Association of Securities Dealers (NASD), and various state authorities.

✔ **Diligent:** The investor has read (and claims to understand) all the offering materials, including, in particular, the risk factors. This representation is designed to bind the investor to the exculpatory statements in the PPM that indicate that the investment involves a high degree of risk.

In this chapter, we explain exactly what a private equity offering is and the rules that govern its uses. We tell you exactly whom to target in your own private placements — and how best to reach them — and we discuss the all-important *placement memorandum* along with a detailed examination of typical terms and conditions.

Exploring the Regulation D Exemption

The Securities Act of 1933 dictates that sales of all securities in the United States have to be registered with the Securities and Exchange Commission (SEC), except for those specifically exempted from the regulation requirements. The so-called Section 4(2) — or *private-placement exemption* — provides the basis by which most emerging business enterprises make private offerings of securities in the United States, and thus, most don't have to register with the SEC.

A couple of decades ago, however, Regulation D was enacted to provide a safe harbor for private-equity offerings — in other words, if you comply with Regulation D fully, your offering will be viewed by the SEC as a *good* private placement. Before Regulation D, offerings were limited to some (not well-defined) number of offerees who were defined as *smart* and *rich* in the jargon of the trade. Regulation D has helped many companies raise a great deal of money. It also has helped company lawyers and chief financial officers sleep better at night by providing an easy-to-follow exemption.

One note to keep in mind at the outset of this discussion: Issuances of stock to employees, directors, and consultants pursuant to a *written compensation plan* and not for the purpose of raising capital have been exempt for the past 10 years or so under a different law — Rule 701 of the Securities Act of 1933.

Keep in mind, too, that Regulation D exempts private offerings only at the federal level and that you must adhere, unless exempt, to state laws that govern securities transactions (the so-called *blue-sky laws*, preempted for most Regulation D offerings), regardless of your federal status.

With that little note behind us, we can discover a bit more about Regulation D.

Rules, rules, and more rules

Regulation D applies solely to *primary or issuer transactions*, and is made up of a number of different rules that all spell out different parts of the regulation. Here are the summaries of the rules that comprise Regulation D:

✔ **Rule 501** sets forth a number of definitions used in Regulation D. One of the more important definitions is the one for *accredited investor,* which is defined as any person within one of the following categories:

- Certain institutional investors, such as many banks, insurance companies, investment companies, broker/dealers, thrift institutions, business development companies, Small Business Investment Companies (SBICs), certain employee benefit plans, and certain 501(c)(3) charitable corporations

- Certain insiders, including directors, executive officers, and general partners of the issuer

- Natural persons whose net worth (or joint net worth with his or her spouse) at the time of purchase exceeds $1 million or whose individual income was more than $200,000 ($300,000 joint income with spouse) for each of the two more recent years, coupled with a reasonable expectation of maintaining that income level during the current year

- Any corporation, business trust, or partnership with total assets in excess of $5 million that was not organized for the purpose of making the investment, plus any trust with assets in excess of $5 million that was not organized for the purpose of making the investment and is directed by a *sophisticated person* (someone with the experience and knowledge required to adequately judge the merits and risks of an investment and to safeguard his or her interests).

- Aggregates of the previous four definitions, including any entity whose equity owners all are accredited investors under any category.

- Another key definition in Rule 501 relates to the calculation of the number of purchasers allowed to participate in a Regulation D offering. Accredited investors are excluded from that count.

✔ **Rule 502** sets forth the general terms and conditions for a Regulation D offering. It specifically addresses *integration of contemporaneous offerings* (in other words, when you have — or have had — another securities offering that is integrated with your current offering, the investment and amount raised count against the limits of your Regulation D offering), the information to provide to investors, and the limitations on the "manner" of the offering and/or resale.

✔ **Rule 503** provides the requirements about how and when your Form D (the form that announces the securities sale and the issuer) needs to be filed.

✔ **Rule 504** specifies parameters for an exemption for issues of $1 million or less.

✔ **Rule 505** specifies the parameters for an exemption for issues of $5 million or less.

✔ **Rule 506** specifies parameters for offerings of more than $5 million (and can apply to offerings of up to $5 million when you don't want to comply with the requirements of Rule 504 or 505).

✔ **Rule 507** disqualifies you from relying on Regulation D in the future when you fail to comply with Rule 503 (filing of notice).

✔ **Rule 508** provides forgiveness for issuers who commit violations of Regulation D that are "insignificant" and occur despite a "good faith attempt" to comply.

Antifraud provisions still apply to all transactions, and therefore Regulation D doesn't do away with the necessity for disclosure. See our discussion about "Creating a Winning Private-placement Memorandum" later in this chapter.

Regulation D (with exceptions having to do with the way prospects are identified) is not *technically* offended when the placement is made available to an unlimited number of offerees, as long as they all are accredited investors. This is a dramatic departure from the SEC's former view, which focused heavily on a number that was hard to track — the number of offerees.

Complying with the ban on "general solicitation"

Everything sounds pretty good so far, right? It is, but now is the time for a word of caution.

Regardless of the number of purchasers (maybe even none) or offerees that you approach to buy your private equity offering, if the placement is made on the basis of either a *general solicitation* or *general advertising,* the exemption is lost, and you've officially screwed up in a big way!

Unfortunately, making this simple mistake is all too easy. The problem is that getting a deal in front of even a limited number of potential purchasers without participating in some kind of activity that is reasonably viewed as solicitation is difficult. The problem facing a business founder approaching Regulation D is how to keep from running afoul of the ban on general solicitation, and yet getting an offering memorandum out to a wide enough audience to have a chance of raising the money.

So, how can you be sure that you don't end up on the next television episode of *Wanted by the SEC!?* The following sections present a few areas where you need to be sure to pay extra close attention.

Recordkeeping

The first rule of recordkeeping almost goes without saying, but it bears constant repetition: Keep careful records. Here, we'll say it again: Keep careful records.

Why? An analysis of cases in which issuers went too far in soliciting or advertising their securities shows one consistent theme: The issuer and its agents didn't keep careful records and therefore couldn't state with certainty, when challenged in court, exactly how many and what type of people were offered the opportunity. And, if you can't prove with a high degree of certainty exactly who has seen your opportunity, how can you prove that your offer hasn't been widely distributed?

The simple answer is: You can't.

No advertising

Don't be lulled into a false sense of security, thinking that because the ban on advertising is stated in terms of a ban on *general advertising,* anything short of advertising in a newspaper or on radio or television is okay. It isn't. In fact, the ban on general advertising actually means no advertising whatsoever.

Because conjuring up a practical scenario involving "nongeneral" advertising is difficult, any sort of advertising for a private equity offering is strictly off limits. Thus announcements of the offered opportunity in the newspapers, on the radio, on television, and so forth, are not in order.

You may think this constraint is clear enough — either you loudly announce the investment opportunity in the media or you don't — but nothing in life is simple when securities laws are involved.

What happens, for example, if technology being exploited by a firm doing a private offering is interesting enough for the press to want to interview the founder (who is naturally proud to have come up with a scientific break-through)? Does this interview constitute advertising? In theory, if the founder limits his conversation with reporters only to the technology, and makes no mention of the fact that he's out hustling to find funding, the media haven't been used in connection with the sale of a security.

The problem, however, is that the founder doesn't have control over what the reporter actually publishes. The article can end up coupling the inter-view with a mention that the business has a pending offering (an offering in progress). Just this single mention in the press of the pending offering can inadvertently blow Regulation D's ban on general solicitation. Long story, short: Steer clear of the media when you're in the process of seeking capital under Regulation D.

Mailings

Even when you keep careful records, you still may be accused of a forbidden solicitation because the word "general" isn't a precisely measurable term. For example, a founder may want to mail her business plan to a list of, say, all venture capital funds named in *Pratt's Guide to Venture Capital Sources,* the most common reference book in the field. So, if a mailing does go out to 1,000 names, is that a general solicitation?

The SEC helped illuminate this issue through a series of *no-action letters* (so named because the SEC indicates in the letter, it is hoped, that it won't take enforcement action against the issuer for engaging in a specified course of conduct). Taken together, these letters indicate a staff view that *general solicitation* does not occur when the solicitor and his targets have a *substantial preexisting relationship.*

So, the answer to our question about a mailing to 1,000 names taken from *Pratt's Guide* is: Yes, the mailing can be considered a forbidden general solicitation, if no substantial preexisting relationship existed between the issuer and the targets of the mailing (which is probably the case).

Some placement agents have devised a way around this restriction, however. To establish meaningful pre-existing business relationships between the agents and prospects, agents send out cold mailings well in advance of deals — questionnaires asking individuals to fill in certain financial information thereby establishing a record of their sophistication in such transactions.

It is SEC staff's view is that an offering that is not in existence at the time the cold mailings can be sent out widely without running afoul of the general solicitation constraint, assuming that it's only sent to prequalified individuals, such as those who answered the questionnaire and were appropriately qualified as accredited and interested. (Note: The National Association of Securities Dealers, Inc., or NASD, to which agents must belong, has specific rules governing the prequalification practices to be followed by its members).

These strategies are only minimally helpful in the venture context. A founder doing his first, and perhaps only, deal of his lifetime usually has no access to a list of prior prospects. Absent such a list, the founder is left to soliciting friends, business acquaintances and parties with whom he can conjure up a prior relationship of some kind. That list, it is presumed, can be expanded by the founder, — perhaps at some risk to running afoul of the law — by asking his lawyer, accountant, and/or banker to make the material available to potential purchasers with whom they're acquainted. How much further the founder can go, however, still is unclear.

But don't forget, keeping careful records is absolutely critical in helping to identify all offerees, even though the names don't appear on a master mailing list. And if an intermediary party — a lawyer, an accountant, a broker, an agent, whoever — is asked to help, keeping detailed records of that intermediary's activities also is important.

Inadvertent violations

Rule 508 under Regulation D says that a transaction won't be disqualified when the failure is insignificant with respect to the offering as a whole and a "good faith and reasonable attempt" is made to qualify.

That's nice, but according to the text of Rule 508, violations of the general solicitation requirement — the fuzzy area where most violations occur — will not be deemed *insignificant*. So, although inadvertent violations of Regulation D may not cause a major problem for the issuer in a private placement, if the violation has to do with any ban on general advertising and solicitation, then he or she is likely to be out of luck.

Avoiding nonaccredited investors

Believe us when we say that a placement under Regulation D will be much smoother when purchasers are limited only to accredited investors. Whenever a single nonaccredited investor is allowed to purchase your securities (other than employees receiving compensatory equity), two bad things happen:

- For offerings exceeding $1 million, specified disclosure is mandated; the issuer must prepare information as if the issuer were offering the securities publicly.

- In a holdover from Rule 146 (the SEC's old and now superseded rule on private placements) nonaccredited investors in a financing deal where Rule 506 is relied on must (alone or together with his or her purchaser representative) have "sufficient knowledge and experience in financial and business matters" to evaluate the investment's merits and risks — be *sophisticated*.

Moreover, the mandatory disclosure requirement — specifying the particular items to be included when nonaccredited investors participate — opens up a Pandora's box of issues that must be considered and adds up to one thing: Nonaccredited investors may be more trouble than they're worth. If you still don't believe us, consider this fact: Rare is the professionally managed placement that includes nonaccredited investors.

There's a reason for that.

Wait, There's More! Important Regulation D Considerations

Aside from the previously mentioned points regarding Regulation D, when planning a private placement, you may want to consider a few more of the following factors, which, depending on your situation, may or may not have an impact. Regulation D is complex, and exceptions to the following general statements mean you need to consult an attorney.

- Small financings, those less than $1 million, are the least heavily burdened with legal red tape. Purchasers need not be accredited, and, under certain conditions, no limit is placed on the number of buyers. No specific disclosure is mandated, but antifraud rules apply.

- Larger financings ($1 million or more) limit the number of unaccredited investors to 35 and, when any unaccredited investors participate, require specific disclosure. Indeed, whenever any unaccredited investors participate in financings where Rule 506 is relied on, they (or their representatives) must be sophisticated enough to evaluate the investment's merits and risks.

✔ Securities acquired in Regulation D financings under Rules 504 (in most offerings), 505, and 506 are *restricted,* meaning that they are subject to limitations on resale and can't be freely resold like, for example, stock acquired in an IPO. In other words, when the purchaser wants to resell, he or she must either register the sale or find an exception from the 1933 Act regulation requirements.

What this limitation also means is that purchasers (or their representatives) must sign an *investment letter* acknowledging that the purchaser isn't "taking (the securities) for resale" and understands that the securities are restricted.

✔ A notice of sale on Form D must be filed by the issuer in connection with each Regulation D placement.

Also keep in mind that disclosure obligations in Regulation D are potentially extensive. Although Regulation D provides some relief when information can't be obtained "without *unreasonable* effort or expense," the problems entailed with crafting an offering document that has the same kind of information normally included in a public prospectus suggest substantial expense. The preferred solutions, wherever possible, are

✔ Limiting the offering to less than $1 million.

✔ Selling only to accredited investors.

Presenting tips for Regulation D transactions

Although Regulation D is a boon for companies that decide private placements are the better way to raise the capital they need, running afoul of the rules is all too easy if you're not careful. Here are tips to help you, as the issuer, stay on the *right* side of the rules and minimize the risks of making an inadvertent error. Remember: The more closely you're able to follow these tips, the more headaches you can avoid on the road to completing your private placement.

✔ Keep accurate records. We've said it before in this chapter, and we're saying it again, because it's important. Appointing an individual — one and only one — to serve as your official recordkeeper is a good idea. All solicitation must be preapproved by that individual, who:

- Maintains careful records of the destination of every item of sales literature and of all meetings and telephone contacts — who was present and what was said.

- Decides — on advice of counsel — whether a purchaser is eligible as an accredited investor, whether the investor's certification to that effect has been properly filled out, and whether to go beyond and behind that certification in close cases, which means asking for tax returns or other evidence of different assets or income.

- Sends out (and collects) purchaser questionnaires, ensuring that Form D is filed on time.

- Qualifies, as necessary, that a purchaser is smart, because he or she is unaccredited.

- Patrols the blue-sky issues, finding out whether making an offer in a given state is legal under the local statute.

✔ Insist that each purchaser fill out a questionnaire attesting to, among other things, his or her accredited status, and then keep it in a permanent file. Note: You, the issuer, must reasonably believe the investor is an accredited investor.

✔ Specifically inform each investor that the securities being offered are restricted, and therefore obtain:

- An undertaking from the investor to sell *only* in a public offering or pursuant to an exemption from registration.

- A series of representations (including, in particular, that the buyer has read the private-placement memorandum; see "Creating a Private-placement Memorandum" later in this chapter) designed to preserve the exempt status of the offering and prevent later lawsuits.

✔ Give no press interviews during the selling period.

✔ Restrict the list of prospects to only those people with whom someone on the sell side of the transaction — you, the issuer, and your officers and directors, placement agent(s), lawyers, and accountants — has a pre-existing business relationship.

✔ Raise enough money so that no financings are necessary for at least six months after the date of closing, thus avoiding the problem of integration discussed in the section about "Rules, rules, and more rules" earlier in this chapter.

✔ Make available to investors all pertinent information concerning the issuer, and keep track of all information furnished or accessed. Regardless of whether some or all of the information is included in a private-placement memorandum, be sure that each investor gets a list of the risk factors — in the subscription agreement if necessary.

You need *not* depend on the private-placement memorandum as the only source of investor information — record each specific invitation to investors to meet with the founder and his key employees to ask and receive answers to questions. This is *not* recommended, however, because using a placement memo as the sole source of information avoids the issue of one investor getting material information not provided to other investors.

The Big Blue Sky: State Regulation

State securities laws routinely are referred to as *blue-sky statutes*. The first was a 1911 Kansas statute, the stated purpose of which was to protect local citizens against fraudulent offerings. The term *blue sky* actually was apparently taken from a commentary by the United States Supreme Court that indicated state securities laws were enacted to protect investors from securities transactions that had no more substance than so many feet of blue sky.

Although in the not-too-distant past, blue-sky statutes were a major pain in the neck (a virtual minefield of nonuniform rules that were hard to comply with and hard to keep up-to-date with) when it came to working with private equity offerings, we have some good news for you: Most blue-sky statutes now are relaxed when an offering is exempt under Rule 506.

In a major display of lawmaking prowess, the United States Congress pre-empted most blue-sky statutes by way of the National Securities Markets Improvement Act of 1996, meaning that layers of bureaucracy and expense may be avoided.

And that *is,* indeed, good news.

Creating a Winning Private-placement Memorandum

Although public equity offerings require significantly less paperwork than IPOs or other public offerings, a tree (or two) still must sacrifice its life to facilitate your transaction. One key step in conducting a private equity offering — in fact, perhaps the most important step — is producing a private-placement memorandum (PPM).

Why prepare a private-placement memorandum?

Two main reasons for preparing a private-placement memorandum are:

- ✔ To avoid liability for misstatements or, more important, omissions under the antifraud provisions of state or federal law. The PPM, including disclaimers, is a written record of what was and wasn't disclosed to potential investors.

- ✔ Regulation D may require its use.

Regulation D generally requires that, if a placement memorandum is necessary, it must contain the same type of information that a public registration statement, such as Form SB-2 or Form S-1, provides.

If an issuer is not required to provide a private-placement memorandum (PPM), it may choose not to do so for a variety of reasons, including that:

- ✔ Except for antifraud provisions, the SEC doesn't require any specific amount of information for the exemption to apply when the offering is only to accredited investors and otherwise fits within the four corners of Regulation D.

- ✔ The preparation of a document containing all the information required by Form SB-2 (and by reference in such form, Regulation S-K) is expensive. If the issuer wants to go to that expense anyway, why not register the offering publicly?

- ✔ Antifraud cases, taken as a whole (and not many exist outside the area of actual fraud) rarely hang on the issue of inadequate disclosure if smart investors are exclusively involved.

- ✔ When counsel purports to follow Regulation S-K and Form SB-2 and makes a mistake, it can be argued the issuer is worse off — trapped by an undisputed omission in a document counsel concedes should have been prepared — than if counsel had simply put all the information about your company in a file cabinet and shoved it in the general direction of investors.

The question of whether to prepare a PPM, except where one is required, has no right answer. Thus, when a placement in excess of $1 million is made to one or more nonaccredited investors, a PPM obviously is in order. Although Regulation D doesn't specify that information must be assembled in one document, neither is any reason apparent why not to do it that way. Indeed, every reason exists for following Regulation S-K and Form SB-2 as closely as possible.

You, the issuer, are bound to inform investors of the risks, but less expensive — and perhaps more effective — methods of informing investors than slavishly following the SEC form can be found. An all-day seminar at a company's headquarters — with participants from company management, accountants, counsel, and financial consultants, for example — may serve this purpose quite well, as long as *all* prospective investors attend and *stay* for the entire presentation.

In deciding what information to disclose, ask yourself these questions: What kinds of information would I want if I were investing my own money? And what is the most efficient way to provide it to them? As these questions suggest, the answers depend on the type of offering and type of investors involved.

The most compelling legal case in favor of preparing a PPM occurs when an issuer isn't dealing face-to-face with every investor, which often is true of prefabricated partnerships offering interests in managed assets such as real estate and oil and gas. Caution dictates that measures must be taken to ensure that investors farthest out in left field get all available information. Remember, the fact that a lead investor knows all is not a solid defense against a suit by another investor not formally represented by that knowledge-able party. On the other hand, when you're dealing with only a few offerees and they're sophisticated and able to interrogate the issuer efficiently, the balance of risks obviously changes.

Starting an offering with rudimentary documents — perhaps even none at all — is common. The full-dress private-placement memorandum then is delivered (with the intention of bulletproofing the offering from a liability standpoint) prior to the closing to all investors who actually are going to purchase stock. The theory is that if each purchaser obtains the requisite information, the threat of liability is diminished.

Preparing the contents of the PPM

The following assumes you are preparing a PPM not because it is required under Rule 502 (which requires basically the same disclosure as a prospectus for a public offering) but because the private-placement memorandum is the norm in most deals. The person preparing the PPM needs to keep in mind — as you would with any legal document — the variety of potential audiences that are being addressed:

✔ The audience composed of potential plaintiffs (and, theoretically at least, the SEC enforcement staff) who will interpret the document by comparing it against requirements contained in cases imposing liability.

✔ The audience composed of investors who will read the document for its substantive content: "What are the terms of the deal?"

✔ The professional investors who are interested enough to become potential buyers. Thus, the PPM is a handy collection of only some of the information they're interested in, plus a lot of surplus verbiage — the empty language about suitability standards, for example.

✔ The issuers who see the PPM as a sales document, putting the best face possible on the company and its prospects.

✔ The managers who view the memorandum as a summary of the business plan. Indeed, it may incorporate the business plan as an exhibit or serve as a wrapper for the plan itself — a memorialization of how the business is to be conducted.

The cover page

The first page of the PPM — the cover page — contains some of the information that you see on the front of a prospectus used in a public offering of securities. Such things as:

✔ The name of the issuer

✔ A summary description of the securities to be sold

✔ The price per share

✔ The gross and net proceeds (minus selling commissions and expenses)

✔ A risk factor or two (for example, the offering is highly speculative or the securities will not be liquid)

Some argue that including the date is important because, legally, the document is a statement as of a certain time. However, if a PPM becomes substantively stale between the offer and its closing, it is critical that the issuer circulate an updated version — omission of material information as of the closing is inexcusable based on the theory that the memo displays an earlier date. Moreover, a memorandum appears to be dated after months elapse and the issue remains unsold.

A related issue is whether to specify that a minimum amount of proceeds must be subscribed if the offering is to be allowed to move forward. Whenever financing is subject to such a minimum, a reference to it belongs on the cover page.

It makes common sense that a critical mass exists in most placements. However, a *stated* requirement that all subscriptions will be returned unless X number of dollars is raised inhibits an early closing strategy. (The idea is that you see what amount of investment you can obtain, and, if that amount is close enough, you close). Closing early, if only in escrow, with the most eager of the issuer's potential investors may not be substantively meaningful; the deal may be that the closing will be revisited if more money isn't raised. However, a first closing can have a healthy shock effect on overall financing, shaking loose (sometimes interminable) negotiations on the terms of the deal and creating a bandwagon effect that drives the deal.

A handwritten number must be inscribed on each cover page to help record the destinations of each PPM. It also is customary to include self-serving language (of varying effectiveness in protecting the issuer) to deflect any blame aimed at the issuer by a disgruntled investor (or as sometimes required by applicable securities laws). This includes language such as:

- ✔ The offer is only an offer in jurisdictions where it can be legally made and then only to persons meeting suitability standards imposed by state and federal law. (The offer is, in fact, an offer whenever and to whomsoever a court designates.)

- ✔ The memorandum is not to be reproduced

- ✔ No person is authorized to give out any information other than that contained in the memo.

- ✔ The PPM contains summaries of important documents (a statement of the obvious), and the summaries are qualified by reference to the full documentation.

- ✔ Each investor is urged to consult with his own attorney and accountant.

- ✔ The offering has not been registered under the 1933 Act, and the SEC has not approved it.

Most of these statements are reasonable and necessary, but certain legends are mandatory as a matter of good legal sense, for example:

- ✔ A summary of the risk factors

- ✔ A statement that investors may ask questions, review answers, and obtain additional information (an imperative of Regulation D)

- ✔ Any language required by various state securities administrators

A tip that investors will be required in the subscription documents to provide statements purporting their wealth and experience also is desirable.

However, in our opinion, a cover page loaded with superfluous statements may signal to readers that the deal is borderline. So be judicious when choosing what language to include on your cover page.

Offering summary

A well-written PPM follows the cover page with a summary of the offering. This section corresponds to a *Term Sheet* (a nonbinding summary of the terms under which an investor is willing to invest his or her money in a venture), except that the language usually is spelled out, not abbreviated. These important, briefly covered points are

- A description of the terms of the offering
- A description of the company's business
- Summary financial information
- A restatement of the investor suitability standards (the definition of an accredited investor)
- A reference to the risk-factors section
- Additional terms (for example, antidilution protection, registration rights, and control features)
- Expenses of the transaction

Making the offering easy to read and understand is the purpose of the offering summary. As you can imagine, suppliers of capital are absolutely inundated with business plans and private-placement memoranda; so, the sales-conscious issuer must get all the salient facts in as conspicuous a position as possible if he or she wants them to be noticed.

Issuers need to approach offerings that have stated maximums and minimums with caution. The SEC makes its position clear. When an issuer elects to increase or decrease the size of the offering above or below the stated maximum/minimum, each of the investors who has signed a subscription agreement must consent to the change in writing. Sending out a notice to the effect that, "We are raising or lowering the minimum and, if we do not hear from you, we assume you consent," is not an option for the issuer. Instead, the issuer must obtain affirmation from each investor, which can be a bit difficult, especially when an investor, at that point, decides to embark on a yearlong trek somewhere in Katmandu.

Risk factors

If the issuer's lawyers are careful, one sentence that the memorandum *will not* contain is the name of the issuer's counsel; if named, the law firm involved may be assuming responsibilities in the eyes of the purchasers of the securities.

For maximum caveat-emptor (let the buyer beware) value, the risk factors section needs to be referenced on the first page (not the cover page, which generally has only the name and address of the issuer) and reproduced in-full in a position in the PPM prior to sections in which the attractiveness of the opportunity is trumpeted. Several recitations are standard and, indeed, their absence would be conspicuous, namely:

- ✔ The company is in its development stage — that is, most highly vulnerable; its products haven't been proven or marketed.

- ✔ The company's success is highly dependent on a few key individuals, none of whom have run a company of any size before.

- ✔ Fearsome competitors are on the horizon.

- ✔ The company needs more than one round of financing to survive.

- ✔ The securities are illiquid.

- ✔ Substantial dilution is involved.

- ✔ A few major customers form the backbone of the order bank.

- ✔ The technology is not entirely (or at all) protected by patents or copyrights.

These factors need to be fleshed out with risks specific to the issue: environmental problems, the possibility of technical obsolescence, difficulties in procuring drug licenses from the FDA, and so forth. The specific risks should be cross-referenced and perhaps even repeated next to the statements they modify . . . in other words, whenever you boast that your technology is unique, a statement about potential substitutes needs to accompany your boast.

Substantive terms

Following the risk factors section, the PPM needs to set out terms (previously summarized) of the deal — for example, the special features of the securities being offered (preferences, voting rights, conversion privilege, dividends, and so forth), pricing terms (payable all at one time or in installments), and what the placement agent is being paid.

Many private-placement memoranda don't include — in either the summary or the early discussion — an upfront disclosure of the expenses of the transaction, particularly the legal fees. That information usually can be determined from the pro forma financials, but straightforward disclosure also is necessary — even though embarrassingly high placement and legal fees may mean to the experienced reader that the offer is sticky and has been out on the street for a while.

Understanding the use of proceeds and dilution

Regulation S-K, which applies to public offerings, requires that a prospectus (used in a public offering) be drafted discussing how proceeds from the offering are to be used. However, unless the issuer plans to pay down debt or use any proceeds for the benefit of an insider (in which case the discussion should be quite specific), the initial draft of this language usually is cryptic and stylized — "working capital" or "general corporate purposes" — to provide for maximum flexibility.

"Bespeaks caution" doctrine

Significant recent cases have upheld (albeit not yet at the Supreme Court level) the *bulletproofing effect* of language that "bespeaks caution" in a disclosure document. *Bulletproofing*, in this case, means a document on which may be founded a successful motion for disposing of a complaint on the pleadings and prior to trial. The judicially treated doctrine has been largely formalized by Congressional action in the Private Securities Litigation Reform Act of 1995, which gives protective effect to "meaningful cautionary statements which qualify 'forward looking' information." The 1995 law was extended to state courts in 1998. Based on judge-made law and legislative action, most courts have, of late, been stingy in allowing claims to proceed based on "forward-looking" statements that turn out to be inaccurate — claims of "fraud by hindsight," as Judge Henry Friendly puts it — provided there is prominent disclosure of the risks. The decisions have involved public and private offerings. The defense, however, is not absolute, particularly in light of the Supreme Court's dictum in Virginia Bankshares that "not every mixture with the true will neutralize the deceptions."

As one commentator put it: Drafting good risk factors takes time, effort, and creativity, because they cannot generally be taken from a standard form or borrowed from disclosures made by another registrant. The effort of crafting well-tailored risk factors is rewarded, however, not only by better risk-factor disclosure but also by improved insight into the business of the registrant. Such insight can favorably impact the quality of the disclosure in the prospectus, PPM, or report as a whole.

Some practitioners take the view that covering risks once in the risk factors section fully satisfies the registrant's disclosure obligation. A better view, however, is that risk factors are primarily excerpts from the disclosure document and that each risk, or at least each of the more significant ones, also needs to be discussed elsewhere in the document, accompanying the positive statements with the risk factors that qualify them.

On occasion, the founder argues with counsel that a given risk factor is stated too negatively. In our view, that argument generally is a waste of time. Few sophisticated investors are influenced by the risk factors section. They form their independent judgments on the issues; its utility is more prophylactic than educational.

To be sure, once negotiations begin, the use of proceeds often becomes a heavily negotiated item for a private placement for a start-up. Investors often want a concrete menu — in part to meet the problem when the start-up has too much money. However, the policing of how proceeds are to be used won't necessarily result in a sharpened description in the private-placement memorandum. That sort of provision usually is written in the form of a promise in the Stock Purchase Agreement that is either tied to a specific schedule of expenditures, or indicates that expenditures of more than, say, $25,000 will be subject to an advance-approval process.

Regulation S-K also requires disclosures relating to dilution, in other words, when a substantial disparity exists between the public offering price and the prices paid by officers, directors, promoters, and other insiders in the recent past. The SEC is serious about this disclosure, so it isn't to be taken lightly. Although a savvy investor can dope out the dilution without a table or narrative in the PPM leading him through the calculations, the SEC states that disclosure of dilution shouldn't be a "jigsaw puzzle" that investors must piece together.

With that position on the record, simple prudence dictates that the dilution calculations also needs to be set out in a prominent, early place in the PPM. Dilution in later rounds (or any round if the deal is hot) can be a formidable number: for example, stock priced at $10 per share that the founders sold to themselves and other insiders for 10 cents a share. Sophisticated investors typically aren't intimidated by dilution, because it often is the function of a desirable offering.

Financial disclosure

The most significant section of the PPM is the financial section: historical and projected financial results. A threshold issue — whether financial statements in the PPM need to be audited — often arises on the eve of the financing. Is paying the accountants for a certified financial statement (with a financial opinion) necessary when the statements haven't customarily been certified? If historical results have not been significant, common sense suggests that the certification isn't worth the expense. On the other hand, all financial reporting needs to be done in a form that looks just like an audited version will look — audited financials will be needed sooner or later, so no reason exists for not starting out on the right foot.

Hiring accounting firms can be enormously expensive, especially if, for them to render a clean certification at some later date, it becomes necessary to recreate the entire financial-reporting system from day one forward. In addition, the certification is expensive because it exposes the accounting firm to liability. That expense may be too great a burden to bear unless operations are so significant that the issuer and other participants in the offering think the certification is required to protect them from liability. The question, of course, is moot in offerings in which investors insist on a certification. Moreover, if nonaccredited investors are admitted to a placement that depends on Regulation D for its exemption, the disclosure requirements of Rule 502 may require audited balance sheets.

Projections are not required in public financings, and although the SEC encourages their use in that venue, they seldom appear. As discussed in Chapter 15, regarding IPOs, the SEC's safe harbor for forward looking statements hasn't attracted many takers.

Nevertheless, although not a required component of your PPM, forecasted goals and projections are essential in a placement. Investors usually won't bite unless these projections are included prominently in the presentation.

Well-run businesses routinely prepare forecasts and statements of objectives, so investors have come to expect such material on a continuing basis and, therefore, have no reason to be shy in insisting on seeing that kind of information before they put up their money.

Because estimates and projections of future — not present — performance cannot be audited, management and the issuer are therefore responsible for their content — the accountants cannot be the scapegoat.

Preparing the forecasts on three tracks, best case, worst case and most probable, is one sensible way of warding off trouble. That way, the actual results are closer to at least one curve on the graph — the worst case scenario — than if only one forecast is presented. This method of presentation, incidentally, jibes with the way some venture investors go about analyzing opportunities. They weight each alternative and then take the average of the three. Moreover, as we mentioned earlier, all projections need to be drenched in cautionary language. The Private Securities Litigation Reform Act is focused on "forward looking" statements, of which projections are the classic examples.

Description of the business

The heart of the PPM is the description of the business. Some practitioners like to draft this section afresh, as if preparing a prospectus. The contrary view is that the issuer's business plan needs to be incorporated more or less verbatim into the PPM by attaching it as an exhibit and/or inserting it as the inner core of the PPM, wrapping the boilerplate around it. The business plan is the meat inside the standard disclosures.

The argument that favors rewriting the business plan in legalese stems from the fact the language in the plan may be overly optimistic and, therefore, needs to be sanitized before its thrust is incorporated into a disclosure document. The counterargument is that, if a case over the offering ever goes to trial, witnesses for the issuer may spend days on the stand, lamely attempting under hostile cross-examination to explain differences between the document produced for investor scrutiny and the one that management used for its own purposes.

Management

One of the more widely read segments of the PPM is the discussion of management — the résumés of the directors and senior officers, together with an exposition of how they're compensated. In the start-up world, nothing is tranquil. Thus, in describing the management team, even the disclosure of names may on occasion be dicey — some people agree to join the officer corps of a start-up, if and only if the financing is successful.

Prudent issuers need to fully set forth compensation for all senior employees:

- ✔ The terms of the employment agreement
- ✔ Any understandings concerning bonuses
- ✔ The parachutes (that is, the severance benefits paid if the employee is dismissed, or bonuses paid if the stockholders controlling the company change)
- ✔ Any stock arrangements

Because investors are likely to zero in on the agreements between the firm and its key managers, the memo needs to disclose how the managers have had their wagons hitched to the company with noncompete clauses and *golden handcuffs*.

The potential for embarrassment in this section is relatively high for those charged with due diligence. For some perverse reason, résumés often contain easily checkable lies (X claims a doctorate in chemical engineering from Purdue when he didn't complete the course). Moreover, federal and state laws contain so-called *bad boy* provisions, meaning that disclosures are required and exemptions from registration aren't available if anyone connected with the issue (or the issuer) has, in the recent past, been convicted of crimes or subjected to administrative proceedings that are relevant to the sale of securities. These provisions are included, for example, if you're relying on Rule 505 for your Regulation D exemption. An overlooked felony conviction for mail fraud (particularly if a computer search on the Nexis system would've disclosed it) thus can be more embarrassing than a phony degree.

Certain transactions

In this section of the PPM, the compensation issue overlaps with a section on conflicts of interest. This section, which is mandated by rule in public offerings and by prudence in private placements, requires the disclosure of any transactions between the issuer and its insiders, such as the company leasing its offices from the founder. Tax implications lurk below the surface. If goods or services are exchanged with an employee at bargain prices, for example, the bargain element may be considered taxable compensation.

Corporate law also imposes a gloss. Insider transactions may be voided later as a result of a lawsuit by a disgruntled stockholder, unless the transaction is approved by disinterested directors and/or stockholders or is *objectively fair* to the corporation. The preliminary planning for an offering, public or private, often is an occasion for reviewing and canceling some of those *sweetheart* deals. The disclosure requirement can be therapeutic and educational, enlightening the founder about what it means to have partners.

Due diligence and tradeoffs

The level of diligence required in presenting the facts in a private placement is not as well defined by case law and controlling authorities as is a public offering. In the final analysis, the PPM is a compromise document, entailing a tradeoff between the durability of a bulletproof statutory prospectus versus the expenses that preparing such a presentation for investors entails.

Founders and their advisors must face the problem squarely. If the financing involves no more than, say, $750,000, a line is drawn that counsel cannot cross in spending time drafting the PPM. A business plan coupled with prudent caveats — for example, the risk factors — may be the best anyone can do in the circumstances. Anything more formal (such as a full-blown prospectus) may simply not be cost effective.

The tradeoff issue shouldn't suggest that the problem of antifraud liability is insignificant. Many comforts and safeguards for the issuer that are built-in to a public offering — the SEC staff's letter of comment, the use of Regulation S-K as a guide, the existence of audited financial statements, and other expertise portions of the registration statement — aren't available in a private placement that utilizes a stripped down PPM. Furthermore, many law firms won't issue a formal opinion from the firm (called the "negative 10b-5 opinion") that attests that the firm is not aware that the PPM does not (notice the double negative) contain complete and accurate information.

Subscription documents

Prudence suggests that, in a private placement, each purchaser needs to be required to fill out and submit subscription documents to the issuer that help the issuer claim exemptions from federal and state laws that otherwise would require the securities to be registered. Furthermore, statements made by a purchaser in these subscription documents also prevent him or her from later claiming that he or she didn't read the PPM or was too unsophisticated to understand it.

The inclination of issuers — and it appears to be sound — is to load up the subscription documents with a combination of *exculpatory language* (concessions by the investor as to his or her status as a smart and rich investor) and representations that he or she has, in fact, done the sorts of things — read the memo and consulted her own advisors — that the PPM urges him or her to do.

The core minimums to include in subscription documents are:

✔ That the securities are being bought for investment, not resale. This helps protect the issuer's exemptions from the registration requirements under the Securities Act of 1933 and with a number of states. Even though the initial sale is exempt, the issuer may be responsible for the investor reoffering shares to the public, all part of one distribution. The issuer must demand this representation, which in turn can and needs to be translated, as a policing mechanism, into a legend on the stock certificates themselves.

✔ That the investor realizes his or her investment is nonliquid.

✔ That Regulation D suggests that purchasers be given the opportunity to ask questions and receive answers concerning the terms and conditions of the offering and to obtain additional information. Thus, a representation that an investor concedes that the issuer has complied with the access rule routinely is demanded.

Chapter 11

Venture Capital

● ●

In This Chapter

▶ Venture capital: The basics

▶ Understanding the lingo

▶ Landing a venture capital deal

● ●

1 t isn't certain who coined the term *venture capital,* and no standard definition exists. But in common usage, *venture capital* simply means money made available to growing firms by people ("venture capitalists") who take a major stake in the company's ownership (and often management) in exchange for their cash. In more specific terms, venture capital refers to pools of money contributed by unrelated investors to a structured activity that conforms to definite (albeit changing) patterns and rules and that is organized into separate legal entities that are managed by experts according to stated objectives set forth in a contract between managers and investors.

If you're thinking about expanding your business and you need some funding to get the job done, venture capital may be an option.

Back to the Basics: Venture Capital

Venture capitalists usually are experienced professionals with formal academic training in business and finance as well as on-the-job training as apprentices with venture funds or financial institutions. Their universe still is relatively small, but they and their advisors (lawyers, accountants, and so forth) tend to work on a first-name basis, veterans of a deal or two together. Their work is hard, particularly because on-site visits impose an enormous travel burden.

Because venture capital funds are private, no precise numbers are available to describe the amount of capital venture capitalists spend in any given period. Recent estimates published in *Angel Investing* magazine suggest that the amount of capital raised in 2000 by venture funds in the United States was $70 billion. Not million — *billion.*

Queen Isabella, the first VC?

Stanley Pratt, whose annual *Guide to Venture Capital Sources* made him the recording secretary of the venture capital business, refers to Queen Isabella as the first venture capitalist, inasmuch as she staked Columbus to an adventure into unknown territory, a voyage entailing high risk and promising big rewards. Pratt makes the point that the venture capital process is as old as commercial society itself. In this century, for example, Vanderbilt interests financed Juan Trippe in the organization of Pan American Airways, Alexander Malcolmson financed Henry Ford, and Captain Eddie Rickenbacker organized Eastern Airlines in the 1930s with backing from the Rockefellers. It was General Georges Doriot's group, however [American Research and Development (AR&D), the first true venture capital firm] that heralded the age of professionally managed venture capital.

Because of the numerous stories in the press about venture capital firms that have turned countless young entrepreneurs into millionaires — even billionaires — inexperienced observers may erroneously conclude that a well-managed venture capital portfolio concentrates on one investment that will return 200 or 300 times the initial layout of cash, usually to justify a drab performance by the rest of the portfolio. This often fosters the notion that an ultrahigh-risk strategy is characteristic of venture capital investing, the managers plunging exclusively into new and untried schemes, hoping to win big every now and then. But in fact, most venture capital strategies are diversified and, more important, disciplined in their investment selection process, carefully evaluating each potential deal one by one.

Not all (not even most) venture funds focus on early stage companies. Venture funds come in all shapes and sizes, and each has its own area of specialty:

- Some venture capital pools focus on late-round investments — infusions of cash made to companies on the verge of going public.

- Buyouts of mature firms are another popular venture capital strategy, as are so-called *turnarounds,* or investments in troubled companies.

- Some venture funds are hybrids, pursuing more than one strategy and even investing a portion of their assets in public securities.

The point is that a venture capital manager balances risk against reward: A preseed investment needs to forecast sensational returns to balance the risk, while a late-round purchase of convertible debt promises a more modest payoff but is safer.

Dealing with venture capital is an intense business. The relationship between venture capitalists and the companies they invest in is such that each VC professional can carry a portfolio of no more than a handful of companies.

If you hope to raise the capital you need by taking the venture capital route, you need to have a firm understanding of what makes venture capitalists tick and what gets their attention in a crowded financial marketplace. In this chapter, we give you the information you need to succeed in the venture capital arena.

Understanding VC Lingo

Every profession has its own unique language — the terminology that enables its practitioners to communicate difficult concepts to one another in a concise way. The venture capital business is no different, relying on more than enough VC jargon to create an entire dictionary. To help you survive in the wonderful world of venture capital, we'll first turn our attention to some of the more important concepts and lingo.

Looking at the term venture capital

Originally, the term *venture capital* described a process — the making, managing, and ultimate selling of certain types of investments. The term grew into an adjective describing players in that game, as in *venture-backed companies*. Likewise, its use has expanded as a noun describing the people behind the capital provided by individuals, families, and firms. They and the partnership managers who provide them with direction are called *venture capitalists* (sometimes abbreviated as *VCs*).

Summarizing, the term *venture capital* can be used in a number of ways, but it's more often used to describe

- ✔ **Investments:** Venture capital involves the investment of funds.
- ✔ **Legal entities:** Venture capital firms specialize in providing capital to emerging ventures.
- ✔ **People:** The men and women who work in the venture capital arena are known as venture capitalists.
- ✔ **Activities:** Venture capital involves the investment of funds, generally in illiquid (private) securities that often are high-risk.

A venture capitalist ordinarily expects that his or her participation (or the participation of one of the investors in the group he or she has joined, usually designated as the *lead investor*) in an investment will add value — the ability to provide advice designed to improve the chances of the investment's ultimate success. And, indeed, that is often the case.

Venture capital investments are made with extended time horizons required by the fact that securities involved in such transactions are illiquid (cannot immediately be converted into cash). Similarly, most independent venture funds are partnerships (of venture capitalists) scheduled to liquidate 10 to 12 years from inception, suggesting that a venture capital investment is expected to become liquid around four to six years after the initial investment.

Your venture capital decoder ring

When talking venture capital, it's easy to get lost in a bunch of unfamiliar jargon — the kinds of words and terms that are second nature to venture capitalists. Assuming that you're not a venture capitalist in your spare time (and that you don't play one on TV), here's a guide to some of the most common terms:

Funds

The entities into which capital is pulled together for the purpose of making investments usually are referred to as *funds, venture funds,* or *venture partnerships.* They resemble mutual funds but aren't registered under the Investment Company Act of 1940, because they're not publicly held and don't offer to redeem their shares.

Venture funds include federally assisted Small Business Investment Companies (which can be either corporations or partnerships) and, on occasion, business development companies. We use the term *fund* (and occasionally *partnership*) in this chapter to refer to any managed pool of capital.

Venture capital: Not just for techies anymore

Because the more celebrated rewards in the past generally have gone to investments involving advances in science and technology, traditional venture capital often is thought of as synonymous with high-tech start-ups. However, that representation is not always accurate, even in the start-up phase. For example, one of the great venture capital winners, Federal Express, relies on technology that has essentially been available since the 1920s.

Whether high-tech or low-tech, the traditional venture capitalist thrives when the companies in which he or she invests have an advantage over the potential competition in a well-defined segment of the market, often referred to as a *niche.* The product or service is as differentiated as possible, not a uniform commodity available almost anyplace. Exploiting scientific and technological breakthroughs historically has been a principal way for emerging companies to differentiate themselves from their more-mature and better-financed competitors.

The first round

The first round of venture capital financing generally is used to bring a product idea to the prototype stage. After a VC fund invests in this early stage business proposal, the resulting company that usually is organized to exploit the new product idea is called a *start-up.* Founded by an individual sometimes referred to as the *entrepreneur* or *founder,* any newly organized company routinely is labeled *Newco.*

Stock issued by a Newco founder to himself (and his key associates) usually is sold for nominal consideration. Those shares are labeled *founders stock.* The founder, as he or she pushes his or her concept, attracts professional management, usually known as the *key employees.* If this concept holds particular promise, he or she may seek from others (versus providing himself or herself) the capital required to prove that the concept works — in other words, capital invested prior to the production of a working model or prototype. This is called *seed investment,* and this stage in the process is called the *seed round,* or the *friends-and-family round.*

The second round

The second round of venture financing helps to create the organizational infrastructure needed to roll out a new product into the marketplace. Once the prototype is proven in the lab, the next task ordinarily is placing it in the hands of a customer for testing — the *beta test* (the test coming after the lab test, or *alpha test*).

The machine or process is installed at one or more beta-test sites, where customers are given free access to use and debug it during a period of several weeks or months. While the product is being beta-tested, you raise capital to develop and implement a sales and marketing strategy. The financing required at this stage is, as indicated earlier, the *first venture* or *professional round* (also known as the *Series A round*).

The third round

The third (and occasionally the last) round is a financing calculated to bring the company to *cash breakeven,* where revenues from product sales offset expenses. Whenever a robust market exists for initial public offerings, this round often is financed by investors willing to pay a relatively high price for the security, based on the theory that their investment soon will be followed by a sale of the entire company in an IPO. This round often is called the *mezzanine round.*

The term *mezzanine* has more than one meaning in the world of venture capital. As used in venture finance, mezzanine financing directly precedes the occasion on which the founder and investors become liquid — an initial public offering (IPO) or sale of the entire company. Measures taken to become liquid are referred to as *exit strategies.*

Burn rate

One critical element in venture investing is the rate at which a firm incurs expenses, because most financings occur at a time when the business has insufficient income to cover expenses. The monthly expense burden indicates how long the company can exist until the next financing. That figure is color-fully known as the *burn rate.* If a company burns its venture financing too quickly, it soon may find itself either begging for more financing or out of business.

Taking a Closer Look at How VCs Work

If you're planning to seek venture capital, understanding what venture capital firms look like and how they work is a good idea. A VC fund ordinarily is a limited partnership. It can be a limited liability company, but in any event (at least in the United States), it is an entity exempt from taxation at the fund level, meaning that as a partnership it isn't taxed at all. The tax obligation, if there is one, is passed on to individual VC partners.

The reason for this is relatively straightforward. A high percentage of the investment capital committed to the funds comes from pension and endowment plans in the United States, which themselves are tax exempt. Structuring the fund so that it pays taxes on income and gains when the partners are exempt is a severe disincentive to fund investing. Moreover, even if the fund's owners are all taxable, double taxation drags down the returns for capital providers.

The structure of a typical fund involves three entities:

- A limited partnership, also known as the *investor partnership,* to which the capital is committed

- Another partnership (or a limited liability company looking much like, and formed as, a partnership) that acts as the general partner of the limited partnership

- An incorporated management company that receives the management fee and handles all the administrative details — paying employees, collecting withholding tax, securing medical and retirement benefits, and signing leases and other supplier contracts

The partnerships usually have a limited term — ten years, for example — with provisions for a couple of extensions of one year each to enable the general partner to clean out inventory and liquidate any sticky investments still hanging around in the portfolio.

What exactly is a venture capitalist?

No professional examination or state license is required for an investor or anyone to qualify as a venture capitalist. You can become one just by saying that you are and hanging out a shingle — on the Internet, if you like. That probably won't cut it, however. By and large, VCs are stewards of other people's money; they're asset managers who've raised capital from a group of investors subscribing to buy interests in (ordinarily) a limited partnership that they (the VCs) manage.

The sizes of the partnerships vary, but in today's climate, they run from roughly $50 million in committed capital to as much as $1 billion. Some venture funds are smaller, $5 million to $25 million, but because management fees customarily charged against committed capital are in the 2 percent range, understanding how a venture capital fund could long pay its rent and hire skilled personnel for 2 percent of $10 million, or $200,000 for example, is hard to fathom.

Even if the VCs work for free, they must travel to perform due diligence, pay lawyers, and do the kinds of things that maximize the opportunities for getting the best deals. As a consequence,

the term VC usually is synonymous with a substantial ($50 million and up) VC fund . . . one of the 600 or so funds that are listed in the standard guide to venture funds, *Pratt's Guide to Venture Capital Sources*.

Other institutions and individuals, of course, are entitled to the label venture capitalist. One of the earliest and best venture capitalists is an individual, Arthur Rock. Playing with his own money, Rock was instrumental in founding some of the major high-tech players in Silicon Valley in the 1950s, 1960s, and thereafter. Today, Paul Allen, whether investing individually or through a private label fund, is a quintessential venture capitalist. Allen is a cofounder of Microsoft.

Many financial professionals, including partners in entities that manage venture capital funds, invest for their own accounts, often in opportunities that are too early or too small for the fund for which they have professional responsibility. In today's parlance, however, individual investors (unless they're of the VC stature of a Paul Allen) usually are referred to as *angels* (see Chapter 4 for more on angels).

How individual VCs make their money

Since the venture capital business became professionalized in the late 1950s and early 1960s, compensation for individual VCs (that is to say, the professional owners of the tax-transparent entity called the *general partner*) has remained roughly unchanged. In the old days, the owners organized themselves as a general partnership, but now most venture capital organizations are structured as a *limited liability company (LLC)*, which, in effect, is a general partnership for tax purposes but a corporation for limitation of liability purposes. An LLC serves as the general partner of the investor partnership, which receives the capital that has been committed and disburses it to make the investments.

VCs invest principally for capital gains; they put the investor partnership's capital into privately held companies, known as portfolio companies, that they hope to incubate and help mature until what's called the *exit* or *liquidity event,* meaning an initial public offering of the portfolio company shares (which, in turn, eventually melts everybody's shares in that company into liquid assets), or a sale of the portfolio company for cash or stock.

In either event, the holding period usually is in excess of a year. That qualifies any profit (if there is one) from the ultimate exit transaction as taxable at capital gains rates. However, if the holding period is five years or more, the capital gains rate may be reduced by as much as 50 percent. Incidental income from dividends and interest can be ignored for present purposes. The play for the VCs and their capital-providing partners is in the potential for a big capital gain.

If gains are to be made, the action for the individual members of the VC fund is in the so-called *carried* or *promoted interest,* meaning that general partners typically enjoy profits from interests that they do not pay for and therefore *carried* in the investor partnership, which is pegged at 20 percent of net gains over the life of the partnership.

For example, if $100 million is invested and that $100 million turns into, say, $400 million, when all the hits, runs, and errors have been totaled up, the general partner recoups 20 percent for itself, or $60 million ($400 million minus the initial $100 million cost basis, times 20 percent) for its management of the portfolio. The $60 million is then split up among the owners of the overseeing general partnership, or LLC. If, for example, six such owners split the carried interest equally among themselves, each takes home $10 million, taxable at an effective rate of, say, 25 percent to 30 percent (state and federal). That means they put $7 million or so in their pockets. Nominally, that $7 million is pocketed *after* the ten-year term of the partnership expires, but in fact, distributions are made in the interim.

With the pace of the business being what it is today, the general partner often is deemed *fully invested* by year four, and the remaining balance of the partnership term is devoted to making follow-up investments. After four or so years, assuming that the first investment has been successful, the general partner has likely put together another investment partnership to oversee; therefore, that $7 million may wind up in an individual VC's wallet much sooner than the tenth anniversary of the fund.

In addition, a management fee of between 2 percent and 2½ percent is assessed annually against committed capital. So if $100 million is committed, 2 percent, or $2 million, per year goes to paying expenses for rent, travel, secretarial help, telephone, and so on, and the salaries of the members of the general partner. Although it seems like a big number, $2 million doesn't go a long way in that regard. No VC is getting rich at compensation of, say, $200,000 a year. But it does enable those managers to keep the wolf away from the door while the promoted interests in profits are building up . . . and, in fact, from time to time being distributed.

A note on change by Joseph W. Bartlett

In 1988, when I wrote my first treatise on venture capital, I mentioned a phenomenon that had become apparent to me (and to other experienced players in this space) over the years — a problem that can be called "the too much money problem." It reads:

> One imperative remains constant in venture finance: survival. The death toll of venture capital start-ups is ominous; above all the founder must keep the business on the road until something good happens or until it becomes clear the cause is hopeless. And the open road to survival is uncomplicated, at least in theory: cost control. It is a truism that costs should be controlled, true in any business. The problem is that, like Mark Twain's weather forecast, so many people talk about cost control and so few really do anything about it. Some founders, reared in a big company atmosphere, simply do not understand what cost control implies. The idea of doing without the paid services of a chief financial officer means to them that they aren't in business at all. More insidious is the siren call of the often-repeated venture capital strategy known as *the early and preemptive strike*. A founder in command of a new technological wrinkle correctly perceives that he is a lone adventurer among titans, giants who will seize the first opportunity to steal his idea and exploit it with their unlimited resources to the point where he's unable any longer to compete. The *first strike strategy*, and it is often the right and correct strategy, can beguile the founder into thinking *that he should maximize the impact of his entry by spending money*, the *big bang theory*. (Emphasis added.)

Yet again, the pigeons have come home to roost, as they say. The so-called dot-com/NASDAQ meltdown, and the failure of a number of high-flying venture-backed public and private companies in the 10 months following the market breakdown in March of 2000, has been attributed by various pundits to a variety of factors. Among those often cited (with which I strongly disagree) is that *all* the failures were the product of flawed business models. Many of these companies, in my view, represented solid and sound business opportunities. Where the model got off track, I suggest, is a function of the delirium in the public and private markets in late 1999 and early 2000.

What happened was that a bunch of companies got too much money and they got it too soon. They staffed up, awash in money from the VCs and from the public stock markets, and started spending it at exorbitant *burn rates* (monthly cash outflow) on the theory that the market conditions of the day would continue indefinitely. They tried, thusly, to seize the so-called *first-mover advantage,* get to be the *category killer* or the *killer application* (sometimes the *killer ap*) at Internet speed.

The first mover, according to the thinking of the day, would own the niche market at which the business model was aimed. Conventional wisdom indicated that only one player would survive in each of these Internet-related niches and, therefore, the race went to the swift, which implied significant spending on people, marketing, and infrastructure . . . even though cash flow (let alone profits) was not projected to start becoming respectable until some date way out in the future. The entrepreneurs took the money for one reason, and in many cases only one: It was available. And, they spent it on the theory that it always would be available.

(continued)

(continued)

When the market broke down, of course, the money dried up. The companies in trouble were incapable, despite the soundness of their original model, of scaling back economically. One cannot, as they say, put the toothpaste back in the tube. Firms weren't sufficiently mature, and thus were unable to forecast to investors a solid and reliable date when cash flow breakeven would be reached.

The fact, in short, is that firms took the money before they were ready for it. They did so deliberately, because they were beguiled by the first-mover advantage and, to repeat, on the theory that one can extrapolate the past into the future — then-current market conditions would continue indefinitely. It's as if VCs were the parents and had spoiled their children by giving them, in their adolescence, a lavish lifestyle, which, upon attaining maturity, the kids couldn't maintain. The dirty shame is that the failure of many of these companies (some would've failed regardless of circumstances) is purely financial, a failure showing a (perhaps even understandable) lack of discipline and an imprudent and overly lavish deployment of resources.

Rule No. 1 (and 2 and 3)

Don't take the money until you're ready to spend it productively. In the interim, keep your burn rate as low as possible. Scrimp, save, start working your plan as if every dollar was your last one, and get the company to a stage where a venture round of financing makes sense. Timing is everything, in other words. If the company has enough periods under its belt, enough pain, strain, energy, and (in particular) testing of the business model in the beta stages, then going out to look for big bucks makes sense.

And, in my opinion, those big dollars are available. An enormous amount of liquidity is in the system; however, according to early indications, it's being invested in the *back to basics model* — in companies that have gone through the sometimes agonizing, sometimes exhilarating process of testing the business model, attracting customers, approaching and penetrating the market to the point where it appears the start-up has a real future — with cash flow breakeven within sight. Managers have taken a careful look at what's going on around them; they've been in constant communication with customers and potential customers; they've been paying attention (on the so-called *launch, listen and learn theory)* to customer reactions. They've also been consulting their advisors, thinking long and hard about the advice they're getting. They've tweaked the business model and are ready for the *second mover advantage.* If you want to hear the jargon and clichés in this business, they've avoided the so-called *LST effect,* a reference to the cold fact that the first soldiers out of the LSTs (Tank Landing Ships) on D-Day were caught in the brunt of enemy fire; the survivors generally were those who hit the beach in the second wave.

Many of the back-to-basics companies are coming into their prime, ripe for venture funding. Pricing is back to what it was three or four years ago and, indeed, what it was 15 to 20 years ago. VCs are hard bargainers. They always have been (or at least almost always), and are exacting their pound of flesh in terms of valuations and deal terms. However, they *are* coming out of their traumas (at least some of them) and *are* ready to write checks for the appropriate opportunities.

How often VCs really turn $100 million into $300 million

If you look at the placement memoranda of venture capital funds, you get the impression that tripling or even quintupling your investment in five years is normal. A 300 percent return in five years works out roughly to a 25 percent compounded *internal rate of return (IRR)*, a sophisticated method of computing the yield on a particular investment, taking into account interim dividends and interest and how those interim distributions, if any, are reinvested.

The returns during the last 30 or 40 years probably haven't averaged 25 percent. In fact, 25 percent compounded annually on a large amount of capital can, in a relatively short period, wind up being more money than there is in the world. However, returns have been handsome, in the mid- to high teens, on the portfolios of the serious players in this business.

Finally, the average return is significantly higher than the median, spiked upward year in and year out by significant positive returns among the so-called trophy funds — the oldest, best, and largest at the top of the pyramid. In other words, venture managers do well, thank you very much, or at least, they have in the past, particularly those in the top firms.

On the hunt: How VCs find venture opportunities

The key to successful venture investing is finding good deals. The methodology varies, of course, from VC to VC. However, with rare exceptions, one way that VCs certainly do *not* find the deals they favor is from so-called over-the-transom submissions. Venture capitalists rarely fund unsolicited business plans.

Some of the more active funds receive something like 1,000 business plans a month, and they either elect not to review most of the plans or to summarily eliminate the great bulk of them. Once in a great while, a venture capital firm will investigate an over-the-transom deal, but it doesn't happen often, leading us to recommend against money seekers cold-calling the venture capital community.

Landing a VC

In spite of the speed with which venture capitalists threw all kinds of money at Internet start-ups a few years ago — when it seemed no idea was too far out to attract a crowd of hungry venture capitalists — obtaining venture capital is not an easy proposition. It takes a great deal of work, schmoozing, and no small amount of luck. But make no mistake about it: If you have the right idea at the right time, venture capital may be just the source of financing you're looking for.

Now that you're ready to go prospecting for your piece of the venture capital pie, we want you to know just one more little thing: The better prepared you are when you meet with VCs, the greater your chances of landing the kind of deal that makes sense for you and your company.

Understanding how VCs get their deals

Venture capitalists get to the deals in many different ways. Here are some of the more common ones:

- ✔ VCs often rely on advisory boards, the members of which have impressive scientific credentials. For example, a VC fund focused on biotech discoveries may learn from its advisors about what's going on in genomics and reached for a particularly promising piece of science.

- ✔ Some funds have relationships (formal or informal) with research-generating institutions, such as Stanford and MIT. They get early looks at products from institutional laboratories.

- ✔ VCs typically keep an eye on individual managers they think are particularly gifted. The mantra in this business is, "Bet the jockey and not the horse." If someone has put together a successful company and made money for the shareholders by bringing the company from embryo to IPO, VCs are liable to bet that he or she can do it again, thus they put their money where their mouth is.

- ✔ A venture firm, in a sense, invents deals itself, by spotting an underserved market, looking around for some technology, and then finding a manager — packaging the company piece by piece, in other words, and then investing.

Another well-known fact, to insiders at least, is that a high percentage of VC funds aren't early stage investors and don't look seriously at seed-stage opportunities. They tend to wait until someone else has spent time, effort, and money getting the company to its adolescent stage. Then they come in with mezzanine or later-stage investments. In that sense, it's easy to figure out how many VCs find investments; they get them from other VCs. "You show me yours and I'll show you mine" turns out to be a productive use of time and energy.

Gaining access to VCs

If you want to get venture financing, you first must get into the hearts and minds of venture capitalists. Getting on their radar screens isn't enough; you must have a plan for making your opportunity more attractive than hundreds or even thousands of other opportunities vying for the VCs' attention.

Here's a step-by-step approach to gaining access to venture capitalists:

✔ **Get an introduction.** If you're serious about landing a venture capital deal, you do the same thing you'd do if you were fishing in an unfamiliar stream. Consider hiring a guide. VCs review plans submitted by professionals in whom they have confidence, sometimes a placement agent (see Chapter 8 for the lowdown on placement agents) and sometimes a well-known law firm, accounting firm, or technical consultant.

To be sure, you can't count on a law firm raising money for you; that isn't its business. Those that are candid about the process don't pretend to be good at it, and they generally don't charge for the introductions they make. However, odds are that, with the right law firm, the plan will get read. If your lawyers can't do it, how about someone on your advisory board? Your board of directors?

You need an introduction. No blind dates.

✔ **Attend events.** Submitting to the local event-sponsoring organization in your area is a good use of your time. A bunch of events are being scheduled all the time. Go online and look for what's going on in your area; take a look at *Alley Cat* (www.alleycatnews.com), *Red Herring* (www.redherring.com), and so on for lists of upcoming events, and contact the sponsoring organization for its rules for submission. You're likely to see some VCs in the audience.

✔ **Tell your story.** If you can get your story told in the trade press (anything from *Bloomberg* to *The Silicon Alley Reporter*), do it yourself. E-mail your story to the bylined reporter or have a PR firm do it. Give the reporter a hook — what's newsworthy about your company. Your goal is getting people to talk about your company and about your products. This step is so important that if you're not experienced in getting media attention, you need to seriously consider hiring a public relations or investor relations expert to help you out. Good help isn't cheap, but a talented professional or firm will get your message to the right people in the right format at the right time, preventing you from having to learn your lessons the hard way.

Certain legal constraints apply to raising capital through "general advertising" and "general solicitation." Please read Chapter 10 carefully before talking to the press.

Figuring out what VCs want from you

Venture capitalists are like everyone else in business: They want to make a reasonable return on their investments. For every VC hit, many investments don't meet expectations, and some outright fail. In addition to making money, venture capital firms want a few other things from you in exchange for their hard-earned cash.

VCs customarily invest in a convertible preferred stock, giving them a liquidation preference in the amount of their investment plus participation in the upside (by converting into common) when the company goes public or is sold at a price that makes conversion worth it to the preferred shareholders. The VCs usually take a board seat or two, enjoy a put back to the company of their security at cost plus accrued but unpaid dividends after five years (if no exit event has intervened), and are the beneficiaries of certain registration rights and other protections of their investment (for example, veto rights over certain major events).

VCs, in short, protect themselves as best they can with deal terms that are beneficial to them. Those deal terms don't turn a bad investment into a good one, but they can improve the VCs' returns at the margin.

Remembering some tried-and-true rules

When it comes down to it, nothing really is new under the venture capital sun. Although the speed of doing deals has increased with the introduction of high-speed computers, cell phones, and videoconferencing, the heart of how business is done really hasn't changed much in recent years. The good news is that the old rules are relatively simple to explain, and they've been in place since business began.

Based on our many years of experience in the field, the basic rules of the venture capital arena are

- You must find an idea that has a potential commercial application. It need not be novel; Federal Express and Fred Smith capitalized on an idea that's as old as the Pony Express. But a market must be out there somewhere, and it must be a market that can be penetrated by an early stage company, a firm that doesn't have resources in the billions. In other words, before you dream of venture capital money, you must sit down and think long and hard about how your idea will find a market that produces profits.

- You must write a business plan, if only for your own consumption. A number of fundamental elements are required in a business plan, and we suggest that you find a good book on the topic. *Business Plans For Dummies* by Paul Tiffany and Steven Peterson is a good one. An occasional company reaches the goal line without a business plan, but it doesn't happen often enough to be worth talking about.

✔ You must find some early stage, or seed round, financing. This, as we explain in Chapter 3, is the friends-and-family round — a Rolodex round, if you like. It is *not* a venture capital round. There's no point in going out for venture capital until it's time. Even if VCs give you the money, as they did in late 1999 and early 2000, you're likely to have made a mistake.

✔ You must use the friends-and-family money to validate the concept — that is, to beta test, which means to put the idea into at least a prototype format. You do so to see whether the technology (if the idea is technologically based) or product works, and, more important, to pursue a business strategy that someone has coined "launch, listen, and learn." That isn't a synonym for "ready, fire, aim." It is a much more nuanced way of going about your business. What it means is that you listen to your customers, potential customers, and your advisors, formally and informally.

✔ The most successful firms, the ones, again, that attract venture capital money in the long run, are the ones that have tweaked their business models as they move forward. That doesn't mean to hastily jump from pillar to post; but rather, it means paying careful attention to how your concept is being received as you initially roll it out in its prototype stage.

What are the customers saying? "It needs to be green rather than blue." "The price needs to be $100 rather than $175." "It needs to be simpler — or more complicated." You must absorb and analyze this information as you push an emerging growth company forward. This kind of interchange has no substitute; it has to happen before you solicit money from venture capitalists.

✔ Once the idea has been tested, the ultimate reality check has to do with signing up customers. All the conceptual work in the world isn't going to substitute for a test on the ground. Somebody is going to buy the product at the price point in the model. That's when the time is right for an angel round, which is somewhere between $500,000 and, say, $3 million to $5 million.

We discuss angel financing in Chapter 4. Accomplishing this round is important so that proceeds are put to work further developing the product, marketing and distributing it, analyzing competition, and, more important, hiring critical management talent.

✔ Managers in early stage companies obviously are looking to be compensated with equity, but they also have to eat. Therefore, the company must raise enough money to pay at least a living wage. Again, looking toward the venture capital round (VCs follow the mantra of "bet the jockey and not the horse"), a first-rate management team is a necessary element.

During this period, a law firm and an accounting firm are putting together organizational papers, helping set up the books and creating something that is, from a legal and financial standpoint, a viable entity.

When all these pieces are in place and momentum is starting to build, then, and only then, is it worthwhile to look around for venture capital. We discussed earlier in this chapter how (and how not) to put your firm in front of professionally managed venture capital. These remarks are designed to reemphasize those points. Don't go out prematurely. "No financing before its time."

Venture capital dos and don'ts

Landing a venture capital deal is not an easy thing to do even under the best conditions. Be prepared to do a lot of work and wait a long time before you get the capital you need. There are some things that you should keep in mind when you try to land a VC deal. Remember these basic rules:

- Over-the-transom won't work.

- Use your professionals (law and accounting firms), advisors, and directors for introductions.

- Get invited by event sponsors in your area to present at local one-day fairs, where wide audiences may feature VCs, many of whom like to shop wholesale.

- Use creative public relations. Get written up in the trade press, and VCs may come to you.

- Understand that this is a looonnng process. If at first you don't succeed, try, try again.

Chapter 12

Valuation

The art of raising capital rests in many cases on successfully negotiating appropriate values for your business. The amount of money that you'll be able to raise is dependent in large part on the value assigned to your business. Investors are willing to free up far more capital for an opportunity that is assigned a high value than they are for an opportunity that is assigned a low value. Every founder takes on the chore of establishing a value for his company for the purpose of attracting outside capital.

The principal point to keep in mind is obvious but often overlooked. What the *founder* thinks the company is worth is largely irrelevant at this stage — now that he or she's invested in the task of raising capital. When outside financing is being sought, the critical number is what the founder thinks the universe of *investors* will assign as value to the company. The founder's personal valuation comes into play only if the investment community assigns a value that is so much lower than his or her expectation that he or she is forced to rethink the question of whether the game is worth playing in the first place.

In a business context, most ideas about value deal with *fair value* or *fair market value* — a phrase usually taken to mean the price at which an interest would change hands between a willing buyer and willing seller, who are adequately informed of the relevant facts and not under any compulsion to buy or sell.

As you develop an approach for placing a value on your own company, keep in mind that:

- Valuation methodologies change depending on the company's stage of development and the purpose of the valuation.

- Values at any given time are somewhat industry dependent.

- An industry's values change over time.

- Valuations based on general industry metrics are adjusted for special factors unique to the company and the investor.

- Valuation of private companies is heavily influenced by valuations in the public securities markets.

This chapter highlights the valuation process in the private-equity context, with emphasis on the interesting challenges that are involved in valuing early stage opportunities, often before it is possible to pick up cues from comparable sales, historic earnings or hard assets. You'll also find all the information that you'll need to ensure that the valuation of your own company is not only accurate but also calculated in a way that makes your opportunity as attractive as it can possibly be to potential investors.

Talkin' the Valuation Talk (and Walkin' the Valuation Walk)

When you determine that it is worth your while to attempt to raise money for your soon-to-conquer-the-world-of-business-by-storm concept, the basic issue becomes one of valuation — figuring out what your concept is worth. If, for example, the business needs $500,000 to get started, how much of the equity (ownership) in that company does $500,000 in fresh cash command? Will $500,000 buy 10 percent or 50 percent of the company? To successfully navigate the valuation process, you'll need to be familiar with some common valuation terminology.

The word *capitalization* (or its abbreviation *cap*) often is used in pricing start-ups, and you'll see it used in many different ways and in many different contexts when raising capital. In basic terms, capitalization is the total amount of capital possessed by a company. Depending on the discussion, however, capitalization can mean a couple of different things.

- **Market capitalization.** The value of a company on the stock market.

- **Capitalization rate.** A mathematical process for estimating the value of a property using a proper rate of return on the investment and the annual net operating income expected to be produced by the property.

Market capitalization

Market capitalization, or *market cap*, of a company refers to the result obtained by multiplying the number of equity shares outstanding by some assigned per-share value. If it has been determined, for example, that a share of stock in a company is worth $10 and the company has 100,000 shares outstanding, then its market cap is $1 million, or $10 multiplied by 100,000 shares.

For a variety of purposes in valuation — for example, earnings per share, determining exactly the number of shares of a given issuer that need to be considered as *outstanding* is significant. Shares actually in the hands of holders are the easy case, but questions often arise when dealing with unexercised options, warrants, and other rights to purchase shares.

Capitalization rate

The second use of the term capitalization has to do with the rate at which future flows of income (cash into the business) are valued, or a rate sometimes called the *discount* or *cap rate,* meaning that the flow of income is assigned a one-time value by being *capitalized.* The technical difference between a discounting process and a capitalization process is that the former refers generally to a finite series of payments — for example, ten $1,000 payments over 10 years — and the latter to a hypothetically perpetual stream of payments.

One of the more reliable indicators of value to be assigned to a fledgling (or, indeed, any) enterprise is a number that capitalizes projected future income streams. The question becomes what would an informed investor pay (that is, what sum of capital would be put up) in exchange for a promise to return to the investor, in the future, either through periodic payments and/or a lump-sum payment, a certain sum of money? You have to assume that the investor wants the initial capital returned along with a competitive rate of interest. The more that assumed interest rate is deemed competitive with other investment opportunities (adjusting for risk), the higher must be the annual payments, given that a fixed amount of capital is invested on day one.

Of course, higher rates of interest also reflect a higher-risk investment. So, if your opportunity is riskier than other alternatives, you'll need to offer potential investors a better return to convince them to part with their hard-earned cash.

Alternatively, a fixed amount and number of annual payments, or discounted rate, can be the given element in the formula; thus, the assumed amount of capital to be invested (in other words, the discounted value of the future payments) is then derived, again, as a function of the selected cap rate. As the assumed amount of interest that you'll pay — cap rate — goes up, the discounted value of the payment stream goes down, and fewer dollars are required on day one to earn the forecast income flows expected by the investor at the higher rate. Put another way, the higher the cap rate, the lower the initial valuation.

Example: In simple terms, an entrepreneur claims her company will be worth $100 million at the end of its fifth year. This valuation is called the company's terminal value. But how much is that $100 million worth today? Well, if the payoff is as certain as a United States Treasury Bond (that is, with a *cap* or interest rate of, say, 5 percent) the present (pretax) value is about $78,350,000. If, however, the venture capitalist considers the risk high, then the cap rate may increase to 25 percent. That means when the $100 million is paid on the fifth anniversary, most of it ($67,230,000 to be exact) is represented by assumed interest. The smallish remainder ($32,770,000) is the *assumed present value* of the principal. See the discussion under "The Venture Capital Method" later in this chapter for a fuller discussion.

Expressing values before and after getting the money

Another couple of expressions commonly tossed around during discussions of valuation are *before the money* and *after the money*. These expressions relate to what are simple concepts, but unless you really understand the differences between them, they can trip you up — it happens even to sophisticated analysts. The definitions that follow will help:

- ✔ **Before the money.** The value of a company *before* it receives a venture capitalist's cash investment.

- ✔ **After the money.** The value of a company *after* it receives a venture capitalist's cash investment.

Read through the following scenario to see how a little confusion about *before the money* and *after the money* can cause a great deal of trouble.

> If a founder values his company at $1 million on day one, then 25 percent of the company is worth $250,000. However, an ambiguity may exist. Suppose the founder and the investors agree on two terms: (1) a $1 million valuation, and (2) a $250,000 equity investment The founder organizes the corporation, pays a nominal consideration for 1,000

shares and, shortly thereafter, issues the investor 250 shares for $250,000. A disagreement can immediately occur.

The investor may have thought that equity in the company was worth $1,000 per percentage point. In other words, $250,000 gets 250 out of 1,000 shares, not 250 out of 1,250, shares. The *founder* believed that he was contributing to the enterprise property *already* worth $1 million. For $250,000, the investor's share of the resultant enterprise should be 22.5 percent — a bit of a disappointment to an investor who thought she was buying 25 percent of the $1 million company's shares. The issue boils down to whether the $1 million value agreed upon by the founder and investor was to be assigned to the company *prior to* or *after* the investor's contribution of cash.

The difference between premoney valuation and postmoney valuation — and its affect on ownership — can be made clear through the following example. In the first case, the company has a value of $10,000,000 *before* the money; in the second case, the company has a value of $10,000,000 *after* the money.

✔ If a company has a premoney valuation of $10,000,000 and investor cash is added to the tune of $5,000,000, then the postmoney valuation is $15,000,000 (that is, $10,000,000 + $5,000,000). The investor's resultant share of the company is therefore $5,000,000 ÷ $15,000,000, or 33.3 percent.

✔ If a company has a postmoney valuation of $10,000,000 (after the investor kicks in $5,000,000), this means that the investor's share of the company is therefore $5,000,000 ÷ $10,000,000, or 50 percent.

As you can see, this is quite a swing in the investor's ownership position, and if the method of valuation — premoney or postmoney — isn't spelled out clearly in advance of closing the deal, it's easy to see how misunderstandings can quickly arise.

Putting Different Valuation Methods to Work

Almost as many methods of calculating the value of a company exist as there are religions in the world, because the questions are metaphysical, in part, and depend on the appetites of the observers. Some methods are esoteric, requiring quite elaborate mathematics. Others are pedestrian, like the comparables system we showed you in the example in the previous section.

Comparables: The (ostensibly) simpler method

At first glance the comparable method can easily be described as the simple method of assigning a value to something. If you're trying to value, for example, a bushel of wheat in your barn, you take a look at the paper and find out what a bushel of wheat is selling for at the nearest dealer's place of business. Because one bushel of wheat is assumed to be exactly comparable to another, bushels of wheat are considered *fungible* commodities, in the language of the trade, and the comparable method is pretty much a cinch.

Of course, it's going to cost you something to get the wheat to the nearest market where it can be sold, and you have to factor in that cost when figuring out its value in your barn. But, if you're in the wheat selling business, you probably have a pretty good handle on those costs and you just about know what they'll be. If it takes you a while to get that grain to market, you also need to figure in some risk that the price will change by the time you get there; however, because the price can go up or down, you have a 50 percent chance it'll go up. You assign a value based on what bushels currently are selling for at the nearest dealer's location, subtract your costs of transportation and handling, and there you have it.

Life is not that simple, however, in the universe we're discussing. When you want to compare your company to another like it, you obviously aren't going to have the privilege of matching two bushels of wheat. Like snowflakes, no two companies are exactly alike, no matter how similar they may appear on the surface.

Recognizing the complexities

Selling wheat's pretty straightforward. But measuring the value of a company is more like determining the value of real estate. That kind of complexity can be introduced by taking a familiar set of examples in residential real estate, where comparables are the preferred way of dealing with the valuation issue and some of the imponderables can be shared.

Say you're in the market to buy or sell a home and you want to get an idea of what you ought to pay or charge. Your first and best instinct is to go to an experienced broker in the area and ask him what's happening all around you. If you own a three-bedroom home on half an acre of land in a desirable neighborhood, you look around for another three-bedroom home on a similar amount of ground that recently sold. Then, you inquire into the price at which that item changed hands.

Looking at some problems

The problems of determining an accurate value for real estate are pretty obvious:

- ✔ Maybe you cannot find a recent sale of a house in an area that looks exactly like yours.

- ✔ Maybe the closest example to yours has only two bathrooms and yours has four.

- ✔ The age of the house may make a difference and so may the exact location.

- ✔ What school district is the house in? Everyone these days is concerned with the quality of the schools for their children.

- ✔ The market moves fast. The value yesterday may not be the same as it is today or will be tomorrow.

- ✔ The seller may have been desperate or indifferent, or the same can be said about the buyer.

In fact, you have to take into account a number of variables when you're trying to compare value, and quantifying them is often difficult.

Variables continue to multiply, particularly when you're dealing with early stage private companies. Often these companies display none of the usual indicators of value — net after-tax earnings or, indeed, even gross revenues. Moreover, if the comparable calculation amounts to your private company versus another, how do you know exactly what the valuation of the other company is? If it's a private company like yours, using comparables creates an obvious problem.

Even if your comparable is a publicly held firm with a market cap you can trust, what kind of a discount do you apply to your company because shares of your company aren't liquid and cannot immediately be converted into cash? Your company may be worth $10 million, but, unless you can sell the entire operation for $10 million in cash, a certain touch of the hypothetical is involved. The shares, which represent your interest in the company, and which we'll call 100 percent for purposes of simplifying the example, cannot be traded on any auction market. Likewise, you probably have a long way to go before your shares become liquid. Accordingly, an apples-to-apples comparison between your private and a similar public company entails a discount — which may be as much as 85 percent — to account for the illiquidity, your inability to convert shares immediately into cash. In other words, your privately held company is worth less than a comparable public company with stock that can be bought and sold quickly and easily.

The comparables method, in short, must be construed only as a quick and dirty way to obtain a ballpark valuation for a given firm.

The venture capital method: A bit more esoteric

The venture capital method is one of a family of valuation processes that depend on working backward from an *assumed terminal value,* that is, the sale of the investment at some future time. With the venture capital method, you take a company's terminal value and add it to the sum of interim distributions (if any) to find what it's worth to the investor, expressed in today's dollars. To understand the technique better, you first need to review the process.

Using a crystal ball to see the future

If an investor plans to invest X dollars (say, $50,000) in your enterprise today for some yet-to-be-determined percentage of the company's equity, the first chore is to see if the company can be valued on the basis of existing numbers and other evidence, such as comparing it with similar companies. Maybe it looks just like another firm for which investors, or the public market, have established a value. That is the easy way: a valid comparable.

Okay, now assume the company lacks enough shape and texture to complete a comparable analysis based on today's facts. In that case, you must look into the company's future through your crystal ball.

Assume that management's projections predict that the company will enjoy X dollars of net after-tax earnings as of the day the exit strategy is accomplished — the day the company is sold or goes public — and that happy day is five years out. To determine what amount of money a company's stock might sell for in a merger or IPO five years down the road, a financial analyst then picks an exact multiple of earnings per share.

Unfortunately, because you have no way of knowing for sure what that particular multiple is going to be five years from now, the next-best strategy is using existing multiples in the given industry. So you'll want to find out what the price-earnings ratios (or PE) of companies in comparable fields are today.

Assuming that the average of those multiples is 10 (a nice round number to work with), that means, when applied to your company, its projected total market capitalization — the total market value of all the company's stock immediately prior to the IPO — will be 10 times the net earnings for the year in which the projections were made.

The investor then chooses that return on her investment, which corresponds to the risks that she deems the business is encountering, taking into account the return on competing investments, again a subjective judgment. She may believe that she is entitled to a 38 percent *compounded rate of return* (the percentage interest earned on an investment, which is then compounded — or added to the original amount — for subsequent calculations). This means that the company's forecast needs to be holding out the expectation of a five times earnings return; that is, the investor gets back $5 for every $1 invested, before taxes.

The valuation formula, therefore, is relatively simple: If the investment is $250,000, then five times $250,000 is $1.25 million. If the company is forecast to be worth $10 million in year five (in other words, 10 times projected net earnings in year five of $1 million), then the investor's $250,000 commands 12.5 percent of the company in year one.

If five years is the time horizon, then:

- ✔ To triple one's investment in five years, you need a 25 percent compounded pretax rate of return.

- ✔ To quintuple one's investment in five years, you need a 38 percent compounded pretax rate of return.

- ✔ For a return of seven times one's investment in five years, you need 48 percent.

- ✔ For 10 times one's investment you need a 58 percent compounded pretax of return.

Venture capitalists use any number of rules when determining whether the potential payback from an investment will be worthwhile to them — in part because the universe of possible opportunities is so large that some handy, ready-to-wear criteria are necessary to separate the wheat from the chaff. When talking with a venture capitalist about the value of *your* company, be sure that you know which method he or she is using, and that you understand how the result is calculated.

Adjusting the forecast: The First Chicago method

Some investors work with not one but three forecast scenarios: best, middle, and worst case. They weight each of the three according to probability of occurrence and come up with a weighted average result. This sometimes is referred to as the First Chicago method, because Stanley Golder prominently employed it when he was managing the portfolio of the venture arm of that bank holding company. To be sure, attaching probabilities to the occurrence of a given projection is conceptually impure, because probability theory requires that no statement whatsoever can be made about the probability of a single event. In other words, no probability is attached to one fair flip of a coin. Nonetheless, the practice is useful when it is taken for what it is . . . a way of helping an investor in reaching a decision, rather than purporting to make that decision for him with scientific exactitude. When businessmen measure value using methods such as First Chicago, they're described as using "personal or subjective probabilities."

Considering dilution

Using the venture capital method accurately, you must figure in the likelihood of subsequent rounds of financing, which (unless the investor participates) dilutes his or her ultimate interest. The investor must participate in subsequent rounds of financing to preserve his or her initial percentage.

Discounted Cash Flow — The Basics

So what is $10,000 after taxes a year from now actually worth to you today? How much less would you take today instead of waiting a year to get your $10K? In other words, what is its *present value (PV)* to you today? The answer depends on estimates of inflation during the next year, how certain you are that you'll actually receive $10,000 in a year (in other words, the risk you're taking), and your opportunity costs (in other words, what else you could do with the money if you had it now). Money has a value that changes with time — not surprisingly that's called the *time value of money.*

Broadly speaking, this is a fairly common business problem. In fact, these sorts of questions arise anytime that you're making a decision or comparing alternative options that involve costs and/or benefits that stretch over a period of time. A technique called *discounted cash flow (DCF)* analysis is used to make the rational and quantifiable part of your decision. It takes a number of forms. We'll show you two of the more common ones here — *net present value (NPV)* and *internal rate of return (IRR).* Whether you're trying to value an investment opportunity, deciding to purchase or lease a new piece of equipment, or evaluating the launch of a new product or marketing campaign, a form of DCF analysis quantifies your options. You're then left only with the qualitative aspects to assess in your decision.

Figure out, for example, the best that you can do if today you had put the money into a certificate of deposit that earns a guaranteed 5 percent during the next year. What amount of money invested today at 5 percent becomes $10,000 in a year? That ought to be the PV for the $10K, or $10,000 ÷ (1+ 0.05), which is $9,523.81. Check your work: $9,523.81 + ($9,523.81 × 0.05, or $476.19) = $10,000. Thus the present value (PV) of $10,000 received a year from now *discounted* at 5 percent is $9,523.81. *Discounting* is the inverse of *compounding.*

So having today invested $9,523.81 in a 5 percent CD is equivalent to getting $10,000 in cash in a year — right? Yes, but not really! Don't forget that Uncle Sam will tax away some of your interest. Because we care only about the net cash we'll receive, we must take taxes into account. So, if your federal plus state marginal income tax rate is 40 percent, that means you'll have to send

40 percent of your interest to Uncle and his Nephew. You'll really earn only 3 percent (60 percent of the 5 percent interest you earned). Thus the *after-tax PV* for the $10,000 will be $9,714.57, or $10,000 ÷ (1 + 0.03)! So investing $9,714.57 in a 5 percent CD today is equivalent to getting $10K a year from now.

Nevertheless, perhaps you have a better alternative investment that is risk free and earns 10 percent. Because you'll keep only 60 percent of your earnings after taxes (taxes eat up the other 40 percent), your after-tax *discount rate* is 6 percent. With these assumptions, the PV for the $10,000 equals $10,000 ÷ (1+ 0.06) or $9,433.96. So you'd prefer receiving any amount that is greater than $9,433.96 today to receiving $10,000 in one year if you known you can earn 10 percent (pretax) on your money now. The effect of using a higher discount factor is to decrease the PV of the expected *future value (FV)* — you need less now because you can earn more.

All this assumes that receiving the $10,000 in one year carries no risk. In reality, however, at least some risk almost always accompanies such an investment. To account for this, investors and decision makers often increase their discount factors to much higher percentages — even as high as 30 percent or 40 percent in venture capital scenarios. The $10,000 return discounted at 30 percent and a marginal tax rate of 40 percent has a PV to the investor of $10,000 ÷ [1+ 0.3 × (1 - 0.4)] = $8,474.58. After considering taxes, the investor in this case is expecting an 18 percent (60 percent of 30 percent) *risk-adjusted rate of return*.

Modifying the example to say that you'll receive the $10K in 2 years rather than one and expect to earn an *after-tax risk-adjusted rate of return* of 12 percent on alternative investments, how much would you pay for the $10K offer now? Here's where *compounding* comes in. You earn income on the money you receive after the first year during the second year and so forth. So now the calculation is $10,000 ÷ [(1 + 0.12) × (1 + 0.12)] = $7,971.94. Check it on your calculator by multiplying $7,971.94 by 1.12 twice. Given the choice then, you'd prefer to have $7,971.95 today (one penny more than the PV) than to get $10,000 in two years. Actually the DCF analysis in this case would be too close to call a winner. You'd have to consider other qualitative factors and carefully review your assumptions — even a slight change in assumptions in a DCF analysis can significantly affect the result, and by much more than mere pennies.

In most situations you'll be considering an investment followed by varying returns over a number of years. The same techniques are applied. The cash flow elements listed in Table 12-1 and its general format need to be used to define the assumptions in almost all DCF problems. The numbers here can apply to many business problems ranging from a company valuation to budgeting for capital equipment. Estimating your cash flows can be the most challenging part of a DCF analysis. Here's some background (corresponding to lettered items) on the example in Table 12-1:

A. Of the initial $12K investment, $10K goes into equipment that will be depreciated over five years at $2K per year; inventory and receivables less payables and payroll (in other words, working capital) will require another $5K of cash after the first year as sales ramp up.

B. The operating cash flow is the *net change* in your overall *cash* flow after making the investment; don't consider noncash items such as depreciation here.

C. Ending value (often called *terminal value*) is the residual value of the investment at the end of your planning horizon; here we assumed that we'd sell the equipment after five years.

D. Considering taxes is best done in a table like this; here we've assumed a 40 percent marginal tax rate and $2,000/year tax deduction from cash flow for depreciation. (For example, in Year 2 taxes are 40 percent of $6,000 operating cash flow less $2,000 in depreciation, which equals $4,000 × 40 percent.)

Table 12-1				DCF Analysis					
Cash Flow Elements	**Note**	**Years: 0**	**1**	**2**	**3**	**4**	**5**	**TOTAL**
Investments	(A)	(12,000)	(5,000)					(17,000)
Operating Cash	(B)	5,000	6,000	8,000	7,000	Flow	6,000	32,000
Terminal Value (salvage)	(C)					2,000	2,000	
Taxes	(D)		(1,200)	(1,600)	(2,400)	(2,000)	(2,400)	(9,600)
Net Cash Flow		(12,000)	(1,200)	4,400	5,600	5,000	5,600	7,400

So, is this a good investment or not? If your decision criterion is that you want to make at least 10 percent after taxes, it is. You can determine this by calculating the *net present value (NPV)*, which is the sum of the present values of the *net cash flows* using, in the example depicted in Table 12-2, your target 10 percent discount rate. You simply discount each of the net cash flow amounts back to the present time using your target discount rate. Use this general formula: PV = FV ÷ (1+ target discount rate) Number of years. For example, the PV for the $5,600 FV (future value) in year three is $5,600 ÷ (1 + 0.10)3 = $5,600 ÷ (1.1) 3 = $5,600 ÷ 1.331 = $4207.36.

The NPV of $1,645.05 is the sum of the PVs (discounted FVs) in Table 12-2. In this example you'd beat your 10 percent investment criterion by that much. Positive NPVs are good. They mean you'll earn more than the amount you set for your goal rate of return. If the NPV is negative, you're looking at an investment that earns less than your target. Each PV amount in the table can be calculated by hand — a little tedious — or you can use the NPV function in a spreadsheet program such as Microsoft Excel. Just enter the Net Cash Flow amounts from Table 12-1 into your spreadsheet and let it calculate the NPVs for future cash flows (FVs) for years one through five. Once those are discounted to PV's, net their total that against year 0 PV amount.

Table 12-2			**Net Present Value**					
		Year:						
Element	**Rate**	**0**	**1**	**2**	**3**	**4**	**5**	**NPV**
Discounted Cash Flow	10%	(12,000)	(1,090.91)	3,636.36	4,207.36	3,415.07	3,477.16	1,645.04

But sometimes folks (investors, for example) want to know the rate of return on an investment. That's called the *internal rate of return (IRR)*. Generally IRR, the compounded rate of return, has to be calculated by *iteration* — trial and error. For our example, you'd create something like Table 12-3.

IRR is the discount factor that yields zero NPV. As is true of the NPVs shown in Table 12-3, you can see that the IRR must be slightly below 14 percent because the NPV at 14 percent is slightly less than zero. The precise IRR (13.95 percent in our example) can be calculated as with the NPV in a spreadsheet program by entering the amounts from Table 12-1. NPV and IRR decision rules are interrelated. If your target discount rate (often called the *hurdle rate*) had been 14 percent rather than 10 percent in Table 12-2, the NPV (–$18) and IRR (13.95 percent) would miss your goal.

Table 12-3			**Internal Rate of Return**					
		Year:						
Element	**Rate**	**0**	**1**	**2**	**3**	**4**	**5**	**NPV**
Discounted Cash Flow	12%	(12,000)	(1,071.43)	3,507.65	3,985.97	3,177.59	3,177.59	777.37
Discounted Cash Flow	14%	(12,000)	(1,052.63)	3,385.66	3,779.84	2,960.40	2,908.46	(18.27)

(continued)

Table 12-3 *(continued)*

Element	Rate	Year: 0	1	2	3	4	5	NPV
Discounted Cash Flow	16%	(12,000)	(1,034.48)	3,269.92	3,587.68	2,761.46	2,666.23	(749.19)
Discounted Cash Flow	18%	(12,000)	(1,016.95)	3,160.01	3,408.33	2,578.94	2,447.81	(1,421.85)

Forecasting Five Years Out: Experienced Hockey Players Are Wary of High Sticks

Forecasted earnings are, in effect, a proxy for current earnings — a proxy made necessary by the fact that no current earnings exist or that earnings, such as they are, are not deemed representative of what the company can and will do in the future. However, the problem with forecasts in the early stage phase is that they're based on incomplete knowledge.

All forecasts are based on estimates and assumptions, of course, but, when a company is in its seed stage, that information is scarcer even than hens' teeth. Typically, an entrepreneur's projection extends over a five-year span (going out any further doesn't make any sense to anyone) and, in just about every instance that you'll encounter in that amount of time, the projection is of the *hockey stick* variety. We'll explain.

Imagine, if you will, a graph of forecasted earnings extended over five years on the horizontal line and ending on the fifth anniversary. The curve starts at zero in the first year and usually — because who in their right minds will believe an early spike, given the problems that early stage firms typically face — moves only marginally upward through years two through four. Then, *mirabile dictu*, the earnings curve spikes upward in the fifth year, often reaching the stratosphere.

The curve, therefore, looks like a hockey stick with its blade lying flat on the ice and its handle extended upward. The blade represents the first four years and the handle represents the fifth. The reason that the spike upward in the fifth year is thought to be (or hoped by the preparer to be) acceptable is that nobody knows what is going to happen five years out: therefore, a dramatic uptick in the forecast is as plausible as any other silhouette.

So much for the hockey stick scenario. The venture capitalists are wary of hockey sticks, but they consistently use them as a factor in computing terminal values, controlling fifth-year exuberance, if you will, by employing a high hurdle — that is, a 50 percent return.

Nonnumerical factors of forecasting for non-math majors

Before you get too excited about using your high-powered calculator to determine whether investors are going to find your business opportunity worthy of their attention, the *net present value* calculation is not relied on in isolation, despite its seeming mathematical certainty. Despite the seeming exactitude of a discounted earnings formula, professional venture managers understand that elaborate valuation techniques aren't ends in themselves in venture investing. That's because of the enormous uncertainties involved. Instead, they're considered tools, inputs that contribute to (but do not determine) a composite judgment based, in the final analysis, on judgment and experience.

Accordingly, a number of nonnumerical factors routinely are taken into account when estimating values. As an obvious example, the investor must consider the outlook for the industry as a whole, including:

- The likely competitive position of the issuer
- Trends in customer tastes
- The company's copyrights, trademarks, patents, and trade secrets
- Dependence of the business on a few major customers or suppliers
- Possible product obsolescence
- Likely capital needs
- The ability to leverage
- The existence of any tax loss carryforwards
- The potential impact of changes in the regulatory climate.

Much attention is focused on likely market share because of its significant influence on a company's ability to become a *cash cow* — a company that generates lots of cash with minimal effort on the part of its owners and management. Valuation based on the discounted value of projected earnings is then adjusted up, down, or sideways depending on the analyst's judgment as to the effect of the nonnumerical factors. The outcome is a product only partly of mathematics and principally of judgment and experience.

Using cash flows as the basis of valuation

When it comes to assigning a value to a business, most everyone uses cash flow as the basis for valuation. And, when it comes to using cash flow to value a business, EBIDTA is king, especially when conducting first-order calculations or when comparing a business to others in an industry group.

EBIDTA stands for means *earnings before interest, depreciation, taxes and amortization,* and it specifically excludes capital purchases (plant and equipment) and working capital requirements.

The best way to explain that (EBIDTA) number is that it consists of operating cash flow before deductions for:

- Depreciation (a noncash item)

- Amortization (for example, of good will, which can be quite large)

- Taxes, a highly variable item among otherwise similar businesses (and, sometimes, if the company is highly leveraged, not an item at all)

- Interest and amortization (otherwise known as debt service).

The idea, of course, is finding value indicators that enable the valuator to make apples-to-apples comparisons between the company under scrutiny and one or more companies in the same business. To buyout funds, looking at operating cash often is the best way to compare apples to apples. By using a multiple of operating cash that is customary within a particular industry, you can figure out the so-called *enterprise value* of each firm.

If Company A has a market capitalization of $100 million and cash flow of $20 million, then it's selling for five times cash flow. Taking an average for the industry, for example, if Company A is selling for five times cash flow, Company B for three times, and Company C for four times, you can use simple arithmetic to determine that the average cash flow multiple is four times. Then, and at long last, you come to the publishing company — a private company — that you're wanting to buy. But, how do you value it?

It's pretty simple. Look at the target's cash flow of, say, $10 million, and apply the average multiple in the industry (four times), and you come up with a $40 million number. The effect of taxes is factored out, because, for example, you may decide to borrow the entire purchase price in a leveraged buyout and interest expense would eat up any taxes. The depreciation is factored out for a number of reasons: First, it's a noncash item and, of equal importance, it may vary widely depending on the company's depreciation policies. Again, indicators that are in the control of the management of the company are awkward when you're working toward apples-to-apples comparisons. Then debt service is factored out, because, again, one company may be highly leveraged and another not leveraged at all. In short, EBIDTA often is the more relevant value indicator in the buyout universe.

Without question, a company's debt ultimately enters into any pricing formula: If companies A and B each have operating cash flow of $10 million, and the multiple is four, their enterprise values are identical at $40 million. Company B, however, has $10 million of debt on its books. Thus, when the sale event occurs, shareholders of Company A receive net proceeds of $40 million for their company. The purchase price of Company B, on the other hand, is split between shareholders who get $30 million and holders of the debt who get

$10 million. These calculations, of course, can become a great deal more complicated, but the central point to remember is that when dealing with mature firms, operating cash flow or EBIDTA is a number that contains fewer discretionary elections and, therefore, may lend itself to better and more accurate comparisons.

Indeed, more than a few reasons can be cited for shunning *net profits* as *the* bellwether indicator. Public and private companies have considerable latitude in presenting earnings and earnings per share, quarter by quarter — or, as cynics call it, "cooking the books" — all within the parameters of Generally Accepted Accounting Principles (GAAP). That latitude provides all the more reason to rely upon cash flow, a number that is a good deal more difficult to fake or tweak.

Other indicators of value

In some businesses and under some circumstances, professionals believe that other numbers are more reliable to indicate future values, or at least need to be factored into a composite analysis. If the company is in the oil and gas exploration business, proven and probable reserves sometimes are used as the most reliable indicator . . . or at least a major contributing element. The company will sell as a function of its assets that are in the ground, so to speak.

For a while anyway, dot-coms were selling as a function of the number of the eyeballs connected to their Web sites. *Unique visitors* stopped and took a look as they surfed the Internet on a daily (or monthly, or quarterly) basis. A *unique visit* is a visit by the same visitor regardless of the number of pages he or she turns. Sometimes the number of visitors is weighted by the average amount of time a visitor spends on the site, creating a degree of *stickiness* for each visit. The idea, therefore, is that a long-term visitor is more likely to buy products that are advertised on the site, assuming that advertising revenue is at the heart of the revenue model.

By way of example, professional service businesses usually are valued on a *multiple of revenues* — for example 1 times revenues or 0.5 times revenues, and so on — depending upon their particular market niche and a bit on their relative size within their industry. Usually multiples such as these are expressed like this: 50 percent of revenues *below* a certain threshold revenue level (say $500M) and 1 times revenues *above* that threshold.

Industry factors are so important that most senior (nonfinancial) managers constantly are using them to compare assessments of their companies against the competition. They're easy for nonfinancial types to use and the data is more readily available — no one publishes EBITDAs, you have to analyze statements to get them. Engineers and marketers (and CEO's) often consume the better part of their evenings (and more) at trade shows and association events discussing industry and competitor valuations in these terms.

The comme il faut method

Comme il faut is a fancy valuation method that seldom appears in textbooks on the subject and rarely is taught in schools of business or finance. Accordingly, we've labeled it with an exotic French phrase. What it means is that valuation, in the final analysis, is driven in many cases by fashion — and by what some economists refer to as the *herd instinct.*

The economic theory behind the herd instinct goes back to the greatest economist of the 20th century, John Maynard Keynes, who explained how public stock markets behave and then advised investors how they needed to adjust their perspectives. Keynes made a personal fortune himself by speculating in the market. He pointed out that the way to make money in the stock market was not (at least in the final analysis) to attempt to figure out the intrinsic value of a publicly traded stock. He viewed an investor in the stock market in the same category as someone trying to handicap the outcome of a beauty contest, where the winner was determined by the vote of, say, five judges, including the investor. Because all the contestants were attractive, it made no sense for an individual to attempt to estimate which one was more attractive in his mind. What really counted, Keynes pointed out, was how the judges would vote as a group. Rather than trying to identify the individual *you* thought was more beautiful, you needed to spend your time trying to figure out the individual that the judges favored.

Keynes used the same concept with the stock market. Rather than figuring out the absolute value of a security and picking that one as the winner, you're better off trying to dope out what the other players will find more attractive. Once you have that data in mind (if you can forecast it), you have a lead on which stocks are going up and which are going down. Because each individual investor has only a handful of votes compared to the number of votes of the herd, the trick is to figure out which way the herd is moving. Your own opinion is not as important as your opinion of what the herd's collective opinion will be; that is the decisive variable.

In short, we submit that many, if not most, valuations, at any given time, have a certain intrinsic regularity to them, despite the day-to-day underlying factors. This is not an iron rule, of course, but it needs to enter into the expectations of anybody who's looking for capital in the private equity markets. Consulting the voices of experience is useful when trying to figure out where the bell-shaped curve sits, vis-à-vis the angel round, the Series A Round, and so forth. If the distribution of valuations for current rounds of angel financing sits inside a bell shaped curve that starts at $1 million and ends at $3 million, then the trick is either to follow the herd and price your company somewhere inside that range (arguing, of course, for $3 million, the right-hand edge of the curve, based on your special talents and so on), or else be prepared, if you're outside the curve (particularly on the high side), to encounter significant resistance and have compelling arguments ready to overcome that resistance.

It needs to be noted that an industry valuation metric rises and falls through the years depending on the attractiveness of that industry to investors. Thus, during the Reagan defense buildup, which started in the early '80s, the defense industry's valuation metric, a multiple of sales, more than doubled to more than 1X by the mid-80s. Timing can be everything. The early '80s were good for many of these companies, because they could sell out to larger competition at the 1X-plus multiple. However, by the early '90s you were lucky if you could sell one for 30 percent of sales. Thus the value for the same company dropped by more than 70 percent in a period of less than 10 years, without much else changing at that company.

To repeat, the issue of value is in the eye of the beholder. Market share may be a trivial asset to one inquirer but a highly significant one to another. Similarly, cash flow can be all-important in the valuation process, or only a supplementary factor.

Chapter 13

Lease Financing

*L*ease financing, a long-term form of renting equipment, has taken the business world by storm. The leasing business is booming, and for good reason: Leases offer a variety of advantages to companies that use them. Although most leases don't generate capital (sale-leaseback is an exception), they do make it possible for businesses to acquire the equipment they need without a large cash outlay upfront — enabling companies to leverage their cash into a variety of capital needs.

So who leases equipment instead of purchasing it? You may be surprised by the answer. According to industry statistics, 85 percent of U.S. businesses currently lease at least some of their equipment — anything from locomotives to computers to desks and chairs. They spend $233 billion a year in the process, double the number of a decade ago. Chances are your company already leases at least some of its equipment, perhaps a copier or telephone system.

In this chapter, we take a close look at how leases work, explain the pluses and minuses of lease financing, and tell you how to find the best lease for your business needs.

Introducing the Basics of Lease Financing

A *lease* is a contractual arrangement whereby an individual or company that owns specific business equipment or property (the *lessor*) allows another business (the *lessee*) to possess and use the equipment or property in exchange for cash payments or other agreed-upon compensation. Leases have a fixed term *(duration),* and lessees usually make payments on a monthly basis.

What's the difference between leasing equipment and renting it? Actually, there is no legal difference between the words *lease* and *rent.* A lease is usually considered to be a relatively long-term arrangement (one year or more), however, whereas a rental agreement is a relatively short-term arrangement — anywhere from an hour or two to a day, a week, or a month.

You've got to speak the language: Common terms and conditions

Leasing contracts tend to be fairly complicated agreements. But, while every leasing agreement is almost guaranteed to have page after page of legal requirements, a few key items are part of the majority of lease agreements. These key items — all of which are subject to negotiation — are the following:

- **Lease term:** Lease agreements are in effect for a specific period, generally from a minimum of one year up to ten years or more for expensive, long-life equipment. The longer the term of the lease, the lower the monthly payment, with all other things being equal.

- **Residual value:** Most leases specify the value of the equipment at the end of the lease term — its residual value — an amount that is estimated at the inception of the lease agreement.

- **Rental rate:** The rental rate is the amount of money you'll pay the lessor each month for the privilege of leasing your equipment. You determine the rental rate by multiplying the cost of the equipment by a rental rate factor representing the cost of money (similar to the interest rate in a loan).

- **Purchase option:** This contractual condition spells out whether you have the right to purchase the equipment at the end of the lease term and, if you do, how much it will cost to do so.

- **Early termination:** Terminating a lease before the termination date set forth in the leasing contract. Obviously, the lessor would prefer you to maintain your lease for the full duration of the leasing agreement and will push for substantial penalties for early termination.

- **Closed-end lease:** In a closed-end lease, you owe nothing at the end of the lease term — you can simply walk away, assuming that you have returned the equipment and that it has suffered no damage beyond normal wear and tear.

✔ **Open-end lease:** In an open-end lease, you pay the difference between the fair market value of the equipment and the residual value established in your lease agreement (only if the fair market value is less than the residual value) if you decide to return the equipment to the lessor at the end of the lease term.

The two most common types of leases

Two major types of leases exist. Each has advantages and disadvantages depending on your particular situation:

✔ **Operating lease:** The term of an operating lease is shorter than the expected life of the leased equipment. For example, a two-year lease on a computer with an expected life of five years would be considered an operating lease. Operating leases are classified as expenses, not debts, on a company's balance sheet — an advantage for many companies that use lease financing because they can be completely written off for tax purposes in the year they occur.

Not only that, but the lessee does not have to depreciate the equipment obtained under operating leases — again, allowing the equipment to be fully expensed. Operating leases are considered to be "true" or "straight" leases; that is, the lessee has no ownership interest in the property — the lessor retains ownership.

✔ **Finance lease:** The term of a finance lease extends over most or all of the expected life of the leased equipment. For example, a five-year lease on a postage machine with an expected life of six years would be considered a finance lease.

Unlike operating leases, finance leases are considered debts and not expenses on your company's balance sheet, and you must depreciate equipment obtained under these leases in the same way you depreciate equipment that your company owns outright. You do so because with a finance lease, the lessee, not the lessor, retains ownership of the property.

Certified Public Accountants (CPAs) have long and involved standards they use to define these two types of leases, and how they will be shown on your financial statements. Their key reference is FAS 13 (and related Standards). If this is a large transaction, the classification may seriously impact your credit. To avoid being surprised by this later, either read the references on this or get your CPA to evaluate the lease *before* you sign. A present value analysis will have to be made.

Within the category of finance leases, there is a type of lease that can actually generate cash for a firm that already has substantial investments in capital equipment. In this kind of lease, known as a sale-leaseback, a company purchases and then uses capital equipment — say, furniture, computers, production machinery — for a period of time, and then sells it to a leasing company.

The leasing company then turns around and leases the capital equipment back to the company that originally owned it. Sale-leaseback agreements (most commonly used for real estate and buildings) often contain a provision that gives the lessee the option of buying back the equipment at the end of the lease term for an agreed-upon amount of money.

Other, less common forms of leases are available as well, and new twists on familiar themes are being developed all the time. You can keep up on these changes by reading the business press or by visiting leasing association industry Web sites, such as the Equipment Leasing Association site at http://www.elaonline.com.

Does your equipment qualify?

Businesses in every industry can acquire all sorts of equipment under lease financing. Table 13-1 presents some of the most common kinds of equipment leased in a number of different industries.

Table 13-1	Types of Leased Equipment by Industry
Industry	*Type of Equipment*
Agriculture and forestry	Harvesting and planting equipment, tractors, dairy machinery, and livestock equipment
Banking	ATMs, check scanners, sorters, and encoders
Computer	File servers, networks, personal computers, peripherals, printers, software, and workstations
Construction	Bulldozers, cement trucks, excavators, surveying equipment, and tractors
Industrial and manufacturing	Forklifts, grinders, injection molding machinery, lathes, production equipment, and welding equipment
Medical	CT scanners, heart monitors, lab testing equipment, physical therapy equipment, X-ray machines, office equipment, furniture, and postage machines
Professional	Copiers, fax machines, file cabinets, furniture, postage machines, telephones
Restaurant	Bar equipment, food warmers, fryers, furniture, grills, and ovens
Transportation	Aircraft, automobiles, buses, passenger vans, tow trucks, and trailers

What kinds of big-ticket equipment does your business require to function efficiently? Before you lay out a large sum of money to make your next major acquisition, consider leasing it rather than buying it. Chances are a lease is available for the equipment that you need at terms that will make the transaction attractive, while enabling you to direct your funds elsewhere.

Some Good Things about Lease Financing

Although most leases, with the notable exception of sale-leaseback arrangements, which we discuss later in this chapter, do not actually generate capital for the companies that enter into them, they nevertheless do offer a variety of financial benefits that enable companies to conserve their precious capital and apply it to other purposes.

The benefits of lease financing are that it:

✔ **Protects against obsolescence.** Short-term operating leases enable lessees to upgrade to better or more current equipment on a regular basis.

The advantage of this kind of arrangement becomes particularly obvious when you consider purchasing technology such as computers. If you buy 100 computers for your business, you probably aren't going to be eager to replace them when, in two years' time, they are virtually obsolete. If you lease your computers, however, you can simply turn them in to the lessor at the end of the two-year lease term to be replaced with the latest technology acquired under a new lease.

✔ **Increases flexibility.** When you purchase equipment, it's yours, period. Leases enable you to customize the terms of the transaction to meet your needs in such ways as

- The duration of the lease

- The amount of cash you put down

- Provisions for buying out the lease

Not only that, but you have a chance to try out a specific piece of equipment for a limited time instead of committing to buying it and then hoping that it works out for you.

✔ **Improves cash flow.** Purchasing expensive equipment can put a major dent in your cash flow as the amount of cash that flows out of your business temporarily exceeds the amount of cash that flows in, which often happens when you buy something big. Depending on how quickly the cash is replenished from revenues, the impact can be negative for some time. Many leases require no money down, with payments due monthly. The less cash you put out to acquire the equipment you need to run your business, the better your cash flow. And don't forget: Happiness is a positive cash flow.

✔ **Preserves capital.** Because leases often require little or no money down and you make payments on a monthly, pay-as-you-go basis, you can leverage an equal amount of cash to acquire much more capital equipment than you can in an outright purchase. While you might pay $100,000 in cash to purchase four new vehicles for your business, for example, leasing may enable you to acquire not only the four new vehicles, but also a new telephone system, new furniture for the home office, and new computers for all employees.

✔ **Treats payments as expenses rather than debts.** Accountants consider payments made under certain kinds of leases to be expenses rather than debts, enabling the companies to keep the equipment off of their balance sheets. This approach minimizes the company's debt and leads to more favorable debt ratios (and a more favorable climate in which to approach banks and other financial institutions for loans and other financing).

✔ **Comes with tax advantages.** Payments made under short-term operating leases are fully tax deductible, as are many of the costs (if any) of initiating these leases. You write off payments immediately, and fully realized tax savings don't have to await a five- or seven-year depreciation schedule.

✔ **Enables your company to acquire more/better equipment.** Because leasing cash often goes much further than purchasing cash, using a lease to acquire equipment may significantly reduce your initial cash outlay. Although you can retain the money you save in the process, you may choose to use the extra cash to acquire even better (and more expensive) equipment.

✔ **Makes getting credit easier.** All things being equal, a company generally has a much easier time qualifying to lease a million-dollar piece of equipment than obtaining a commercial loan to buy it. For relatively young companies, or companies without an established track record, leases can offer a tremendous financial advantage. Not only that, but many bank loans also have quirky loan covenants. Sometimes leasing is somewhat overlooked in the debt to equity ratios and debt coverage ratio. On the other hand, you will almost certainly have a ceiling on the amount you can borrow.

All in all, lease financing offers many advantages for the firms that choose to pursue it. Of course, there are disadvantages as well. To make sure you get *both* sides of the story, we address those in the next section.

Some Not-So-Good Things about Lease Financing

Despite all the glowing advantages about lease financing that we detailed in the preceding section, leasing also has its disadvantages. Depending on your situation, these disadvantages may be deal killers, or they may simply become nuisances as your lease term wears on. At a minimum, you should consider them carefully as you explore the possibility of pursuing a lease.

The potential negatives of lease financing include the following:

✔ **The property being leased isn't yours.** When you acquire equipment under an operating lease, the equipment belongs to the lessor, not to you. Not only do you have to return the property in good operating condition when your lease ends, subject to normal wear and tear, but your lease may place a variety of restrictions on how and where you use your equipment (vehicles, for example, may have mileage restrictions, buildings may have restrictions on leasehold improvements).

✔ **You must pay penalties for early lease termination.** If the equipment you acquire under a lease doesn't work out for you or your company, terminating your contract and returning the equipment may not be easy. Depending on the terms of your lease agreement, you may have to pay a substantial penalty for terminating the lease early.

✔ **It's expensive.** Leases are almost always more expensive in the long run than buying items with cash, and leases are sometimes more expensive than obtaining commercial loans to buy the same items. How much more expensive depends on a number of factors, such as

- The cost of funds (interest rate) used to calculate lease payments. The higher the interest rate, the more the item will ultimately cost you.

- The length of the lease term. The longer the lease term, the smaller the incremental payments.

- The residual value of the equipment. The estimate of what the equipment will be worth at the end of the lease.

- Lease initiation fees. Fees that must be paid at the start of the lease, including necessary deposits and processing fees.

- The capitalized cost of the item. The negotiated price of the equipment.

Although the disadvantages of leasing may not be overwhelming for most organizations, be sure that they aren't going to be a problem for *your* organization before you even get close to signing a leasing contract. Every organization is different, and an advantage for one may be a disadvantage for another.

Making the Lease-Buy Decision

In general, leasing offers numerous advantages over the outright purchase of equipment. Every company is different, however, and you should conduct a thorough financial analysis of the alternatives before you decide to go one way or the other. The Small Business Administration offers the following approach to conducting the financial analysis necessary to make an informed lease-buy decision:

> You can analyze the costs of the lease versus purchase problem through discounted cash flow analysis. This analysis compares the cost of each alternative by considering: the timing of the payments, tax benefits, the interest rate on a loan, the lease rate, and other financial arrangements. To make the analysis you must first make certain assumptions about the economic life of the equipment, salvage value, and depreciation.

> To evaluate a lease you must first find the net cash outlay (not cash flow) in each year of the lease term. You find these amounts by subtracting the tax savings from the lease payment. This calculation gives you the net cash outlay for each year of the lease.

> Each year's net cash outlay must next be discounted to take into account the time value of money. This discounting gives you the present value of each of the amounts. The present value of an amount of money is the sum you would have to invest today at a stated rate of interest to have that amount of money at a specified future date. Say someone offered to give you $100 five years from now. How much could you take today and be as well off?

> Common sense tells you that you could take less than $100, because you'd have the use of the money for the five-year period. Naturally, how much less you could take depends on the interest rate you thought you could get if you invested the lesser amount. For example to have $100 five years from now at 6 percent compounded annually, you'd have to invest $74.70 today. At 10 percent, you could take $62.10 now and have the $100 at the end of five years.

Fortunately, there are tables that provide the discount factors for present value calculations. There are also relatively inexpensive special purpose pocket calculators programmed to make these calculations. And better yet, most spreadsheets such as Excel, Lotus123, or QuattroPro have present value calculations built in and even have templates to use for analyzing a lease versus a purchase.

Why bother with making these present value calculations? Well, you have to make them to compare the actual cash flows over the time periods. You simply can't realistically compare methods of financing without taking into account the time value of money. It may seem confusing and complex at first, but you'll begin to see that the technique isn't difficult — just sophisticated.

The sum of the discounted cash flows is called the net present value of the cost of leasing. It is this figure that will be compared with the final sum of the discounted cash flows for the loan and purchase alternative.

Evaluation of the borrow/buy option is a little more complicated because of the tax benefits that go with ownership through the investment tax credit, loan interest deductions, and depreciation. The interest portion of each loan payment is found by multiplying the loan interest rate by the outstanding loan balance for the preceding period.

As noted earlier, the salvage value is one of the advantages of ownership. It must be considered in making the comparison; however, it is discounted at a higher rate (the firm's assumed average cost of capital, 9 percent). This rate is used because the salvage value is not known with the same certainty that the loan payment, depreciation, and interest payments are.

 The major difference in cost, of course, comes from the salvage value. If you ignore that value (a highly conservative approach), the alternatives are very close in their net present value of costs. Naturally, it's possible that salvage costs for each asset can be very high or next to nothing. Salvage value assumptions need to be made carefully.

Ten questions to ask before signing a lease

According to the Equipment Leasing Association (www.elaonline.com), businesses should ask the following ten questions before signing a lease. You ask these questions at three different stages of the leasing process: before, during, and after.

Before:

1. How am I planning to use this equipment?

2. Does the leasing representative understand my business and how this transaction helps me do business?

During:

3. What is the total lease payment, and do I could incur any other costs before the lease ends?

4. What happens if I want to change this lease or end the lease early?

5. How am I responsible if the equipment is damaged or destroyed?

6. What are my obligations for the equipment (such as insurance, taxes, and maintenance) during the lease?

7. Can I upgrade the equipment or add equipment under this lease?

After:

8. What are my options at the end of the lease?

9. What procedures must I follow if I choose to return the equipment?

10. Are there any extra costs at the end of the lease?

Always sleep on the lease offer! Being pressured by the lessor's salesman ("You have to sign it today to get this one-time great deal") and not reviewing the contract in detail lead to most leasing errors. Sit quietly in your office or at home and go over everything carefully after sending the salesman away.

Lease Financing — Where to Look

All kinds of organizations, from banks and traditional financial companies to equipment manufacturers and dealers, offer lease financing. Of course, each source has its advantages and disadvantages, so it's in your best interest to understand your own financial needs and then match your needs with lease financial sources that most closely meet your needs.

Looking at the big picture, three major sources of lease financing exist: captive leasing companies, independent leasing companies, and banking institutions. In this section, we take a look at each source.

Captive leasing companies

Say you're in the market to buy a General Electric jet engine to keep as a spare at your Chicago aircraft maintenance facility. Where do you turn to lease the engine? Well, General Electric has an entire group — General Electric Engine Leasing (GEEL) — devoted to nothing more than making it as easy as possible for the company's customers to lease its products.

Many manufacturers — especially manufacturers of big-ticket items — include captive leasing operations (called "captive" because they most often exclusively finance products produced by their corporate parents) within their organizations as a way to increase product sales and make a little extra money while they're at it. Ford Motor Credit, Cat Financial (Caterpillar), and IBM Global Financing are just a few examples.

Captive leasing companies often offer special deals, particularly on closeout equipment or last year's models. If you have a specific brand of equipment in mind, check out what kinds of deals the manufacturer's captive leasing company offers before you agree to go with another source of financing.

Banking institutions

Just as banks, savings and loans, credit unions, and other banking institutions offer loans, most now offer leases on capital equipment as well. Although many have provided the financing behind the leases offered by independent leasing companies and retail businesses such as auto and heavy equipment dealers for years, more and more banking institutions are beginning to offer leases directly to the public.

If you're interested in leasing equipment for your business, see whether your bank offers lease financing and, if so, get a quote. When you have a long-standing relationship with a bank, you may have access to programs that are unavailable to the general public, and you may be eligible for special rates or other incentives.

Independent leasing companies

In addition to the captive leasing companies and banking institutions that offer lease financing, there are many independent leasing companies — from one-person home-based businesses to large financial corporations with thousands of employees — that would be happy to process your lease for you. Because they have access to a wide variety of funding sources, independent leasing companies often offer better deals than the competition. They can also be more flexible when negotiating the terms of the lease.

Even if leasing is a beneficial option for you, there are good lease deals out there and there are bad ones. Your number one goal when shopping for a lease is not to get caught in a bad lease. Once you sign the lease contract, you've committed your company to several years of payments on the equipment that you've chosen to finance. You'll be required to make the payments regardless of whether you actually use the equipment, whether you lose or damage the equipment, and whether it suits the purposes for which you acquired it.

Getting out of a bad lease can be much more difficult than getting into one, so take your time and review the lease terms closely. If you don't understand the agreement, by all means have an attorney or financial consultant review it for you.

To find local sources of lease financing, let your fingers do the walking through the Yellow Pages. For nationwide listings of leasing companies and for more information about leasing in general, check with the following associations of leasing companies:

- ✔ Equipment Leasing Association, 4301 N. Fairfax Drive, Suite 550, Arlington, VA 22203; 703-527-8655; www.elaonline.com

- ✔ United Association of Equipment Lessors, 520 3rd Street, Oakland, CA 94607; 510-444-9235; www.uael.org

Part III

Third-Stage Financing: Acquisition

The 5th Wave — By Rich Tennant

"The SBA called. Based on the quality of our Strategic Development Plan, we might qualify for a low-interest Disaster Loan."

In this part . . .

At some point in their lives, company founders and owners want to be rewarded for all their hard work. They do this by selling their businesses — either to the public through stock or to another company through a merger. We discuss these topics in detail along with the role of investment bankers in this process.

Chapter 14

Investment Banks

• •

In This Chapter

▶ Understanding the role that investment banks play in raising capital

▶ Finding out how investment bankers do what they do

▶ Getting acquainted with investment bankers

• •

Investment bankers serve as catalysts for almost all the major financial transactions around the world. Although every now and then corporations attempt to tap the capital markets for equity and debt without an investment banker's intervention, issuers attempt to go public through self-underwriting (no law requires an issuer to use an investment banker when registering with the SEC), and mergers take place without investment banker advisors, those instances are extremely rare.

An *investment bank* is a securities firm, financial company, or brokerage house that helps companies take new issues to market. Investment banks also generally handle the sales of large blocks of previously issued securities and private placements. Because of a number of regulations dating back to the Depression, investment banks by and large are limited to these specific roles. They really don't participate in the lending business in any major way. If you're considering raising capital through an initial public offering (IPO) or the sale of stock, you'll want to get to know your friendly local investment banker sometime in the near future.

Note: This chapter needs to be read alongside Chapter 8, which is about placement agents. Investment bankers act as placement agents, and most good placement agents are investment bankers. For starters, the more important objective is getting a sanity check. Is your deal ready for investment banking advice? If not, get back to work until it is. Don't force a relationship. If you do, you may wind up with a bucket shop type of operation, and you'll regret it. Best case, you'll have wasted a great deal of time.

Regulating investment banks

Regulation of investment banks has a good deal to do with adequacy-of-capital requirements, imposed to buttress an underwriter's ability to make good on its commitment to purchase its allocable share of the underwritten amount when participating in a stock floatation. A number of other regulatory regimes impact investment banks, including those imposed by the Securities Act of 1933, the Securities & Exchange Act of 1934, and the rules of the two principal self-regulatory organizations of which most investment bankers are members, the New York Stock Exchange (NYSE) and the National Association of Securities Dealers (NASD). These rules cover plenty of ground, governing such matters as

✔ Allowable spreads on public underwritings.

✔ Conflicts of interest (as when underwriters park stock in a *hot,* that is, oversubscribed, issue in the account of a friend or relative, or sources of commission income).

✔ Unfair sales practices (the practice, for example, of pushing shares on unsuspecting widows and orphans through so-called *boiler-room tactics, or* promoting excessively questionable issues — *pump and dump).*

✔ Experience requirements for key personnel. Brokers are required to pass an examination to achieve their Series 7 license; and supervisory personnel, Series 24 and Series 27.

✔ Trading on inside information (as when an analyst uncovers key nonpublic information on a company and passes it along to the trading desk).

✔ Pending rules that govern conflicts when analysts hype stocks the bank is promoting.

The regulations are sufficiently complex that investment banks employ extensive compliance officers and monitor investment and trading practices as carefully as they can. Nonetheless, in view of the size and the complexity of the business, a casual scan of *The Wall Street Journal* will reveal frequent lapses, resulting in not insignificant fines imposed on even the most prestigious institutions.

What Investment Bankers Do to Earn Those Big Bucks

Depending on the bank and its philosophy for doing business, different investment banks do different things. However, most investment banks share a common set of basic functions related to handling securities. These basic functions include

✔ Underwriting securities

✔ Serving as placement agents

✔ Trading for their own accounts

✔ Acting as financial advisors and asset managers

✔ Operating retail brokerages

✔ Managing buyout and venture capital funds

Investment banks are one-stop shops for companies that want to raise capital by issuing securities. Not only that, but they also often manage their own investment funds and provide investment services to institutional investors and, in some cases, high-net-worth individuals. In the sections that follow, we take a close look at what an investment bank can do for you.

Underwriting, yes; overwriting, no

Underwriting is a vital function of and for investment banks, and it's at the heart of what every investment bank does. Although the term *underwriting* is used in other financial arenas besides investment banking, in general, it means to assume financial responsibility for or to guarantee an enterprise against failure, or to set one's name to an insurance policy for the purpose of becoming answerable for a designated loss or damage in consideration of receiving a premium.

Thus an insurance company is a classic underwriter. You pay the company a premium, and it accepts a risk — that you aren't going to die right away, that your residence won't disappear in a fire or a flood. In some cases, investment banks are underwriters in the classic sense. They accept the risk, against their own capital resources, that the value of a given security or block of securities won't fluctuate in a way that defeats the expectations of the parties to the transaction, specifically the company seeking capital and the investors providing it.

Using an example in plain language to explain that high-flown phrase, an underwriter is like a bookie. It accepts bets on future market conditions. In the simplest example, a company decides to sell stock to the public or privately, and the investment bank and the company agree on a price. The bank then buys the stock from the company at that price and guarantees payment to the company — out of its resources if necessary. In market parlance, the underwriter "goes long" on the stock; it owns the shares. The investment bank is betting that it can resell the shares to the public or to a private syndicate at a higher price, in much the same way that a bookie lays off his bets in Las Vegas.

Of course, this isn't gambling in the classic sense. If the sale is a public offering, for example, pursuant to an SEC registration, the underwriter informally lines up buyers for the security in advance. In fact, prior to the effective date of an IPO, when the price of the security is firmly established, the underwriter has spent weeks soliciting nonbinding indications of interest. That way it has a sense of the market's appetite for the stock long before it *"goes firm"* — formally agrees to buy the security from the company.

On the day the registration statement is declared effective and trading commences, the investment bank accepts binding orders for the security at the established price. It is hoped that the stock has traded up on the first day. Indeed, the pricing usually has been designed to ensure (to the extent possible) an upward spike on the first day as a way of further managing risk. The underwriters deliberately, and with the company's consent, agree to buy the stock from the company and offer it on the market at a price a little bit under what they think the market will bear.

If the stock price floats up, then those investors who've agreed to buy it are unlikely to default on their contracts. A default in the securities trade is known as a *fail.* Indeed, the managing underwriter usually puts in a bid on the first day of trading just under the offered price to *stabilize the market* — ensuring that the price doesn't float down because of *flippers,* those customers who buy at the IPO price and immediately resell.

The risks to the underwriters are

- ✔ That their oral indications of intent won't turn into sufficient concrete orders (this is a risk of only a few hours).

- ✔ That the firm buyers (or some of them) will fail to close on the settlement date . . . usually three days later (*T + 3* as it is referred to in shorthand.)

One way to manage risk is to oversell the offering the way airlines overbook their flights to guard against no-shows. The *syndicate* (a group of bankers that pool their financial interests to purchase the securities) negotiates a commitment in advance (called the *green shoe* after the company in which it first appeared) to sell an added *tranche* (installment) of stock (usually 15 percent of the total) on call of the syndicate. Thus, if all the potential buyers who have indicated interest and submitted oral, nonbinding orders in fact elect to buy, there will be enough stock to go around.

As a further protection, underwriters will insert various clauses in their agreements, sometimes known as *market outs,* which give them an opportunity under extraordinary circumstances to renege on their contract. Assume war breaks out, for example, and the New York Stock Exchange is closed by order of the government or its board of governors. These causes are sometimes known as *force majeure,* or act-of-God clauses, meaning that parties need not honor contracts. Finally, underwriters distribute risk by organizing themselves into syndicates of other underwriters and spreading the obligation to buy across the syndicates.

The top ten IPO underwriters

While the rankings of the top-ten IPO under-writers change from year to year, here's the list for 2000, according to i po . com. The names on this list are considered to be among the elite investment banks in the world.

Number of IPOs by lead manager — 2000

1. Credit Suisse First Boston (89)

2. Goldman, Sachs & Company (61)

3. Morgan Stanley Dean Witter (54)

4. Merrill Lynch & Company (40)

5. Robertson Stephens (36)

6. Salomon Smith Barney (33)

7. Lehman Brothers (33)

8. Deutsche Banc Alex. Brown (33)

9. Chase H&Q (30)

10. UBS Warburg (15)

Serving as placement agents

Investment banks often serve as placement agents, a subject discussed at length in Chapter 8. Private placements can resemble public offerings if a mature company, for example, a Fortune 500 issuer, wants to float an issue of high-yield debt or medium-term notes into the capital markets. Here are some characteristics of deals where investment banks serve as placement agents:

- The transaction usually is agented by an investment banker or a syndicate of bankers.

- Buyers almost exclusively are institutional (versus an equity IPO, where the deal takes on a retail aspect — usually somewhere in a ratio of 80 percent institutional to 20 percent retail).

- The placement is essentially a quasi auction and, if limited to the appropriately sophisticated institutions, is conducted under an exemption from registration, Rule 144A.

- A prospectus — called a placement memorandum — is in place, but, because the offering is exempt from the Securities Act of 1933, it is unnecessary to go through the formal registration process.

- Buyers can be dealt with at any time during the process because of the absence of the restrictions spelled out in the Securities Act of 1933.

- The terms of the deal can be negotiated over time and the closing, therefore, may be little more than a formality, with the bankers under-taking no quantifiable risk — a pure intermediary play. Because the risk has been diminished (the principal risk being the time and energy the banker has put into the process) and the list of potential buyers limited and well known to the bankers (and presumably to the issuer as well), the spreads are much narrower.

Of course a banker may decide to buy an entire Rule 144A placement for its own account (a real *firm underwriting*), and become a principal, either reselling the security later on or holding it in its portfolio for investment. Again, however, given the institutional character of debt securities and the fact that the bond market doesn't move as dramatically as the equity markets can on occasion, the banker's risk in *going long* with the security usually is more contained.

Trading on their own accounts

Investment banks also trade for their own accounts. Most of the major banks run a trading desk, which buys and sells liquid securities in the marketplace, committing the bank's capital and (in the appropriate instance) achieving significant profits for the bank.

The trading may, of course, be in an agency capacity. For example, a client of the investment bank may want to *hedge* (protect an investment from risk) against particular currency fluctuations. A manufacturer that sells in France and expects to be paid in euros may need to protect revenues stated in dollars against depreciation of the value of the euro. To implement this protective strategy, the customer engages the investment bank in a hedging transaction. The bank agrees, in effect, to compensate its customer — for a fee, of course — if the value of the euro falls against the dollar. The bank, in turn, may retransfer that risk to someone else, trading itself in the forward market for euros.

When an investment bank trades for its own account, it takes chances, which, from the outside, may appear to be pure speculation. A large investment bank, however (like a large commercial bank), has an advantage because the people on its trading desk are highly experienced; moreover, they have a special feel for how the markets are moving as a result of the bank's regular participation in them, as principal and agent.

Playing an advisory role

Elite investment banks function as advisors in the course of various transactions, particularly corporate reorganizations. If Company A wants to merge with Company B, for example, both companies (if they are large enough) are accustomed to hiring investment banks to advise them on the terms of the merger. The acquiring company wants advice on whether it's paying too much for the target and, similarly, the target directors want assurances that their shareholders are getting a fair price.

These are lucrative assignments for the investment banks. The fees run well into seven figures and higher for the larger transactions. Some risk, of course, is involved. Aggrieved shareholders of one of the participant companies have a habit of suing everyone involved if the results don't turn out as expected. However, that risk is deemed as manageable, and the work is interesting.

The investment bank may perform advisory functions in connection with a transaction involving only one company — a classic restructuring, or, for example, a management buyout. Again, the end result of the bank's analysis (the advice you're paying for) often is a so-called *fairness opinion*, giving the directors comfort that, whatever is planned (a merger, a leveraged buyout, a swap with the company's creditors of stock for debt), the terms are fair to the company's shareholders.

Courts are particularly inquisitive into transactions where management may have been feathering its own nest at the expense of the shareholders, or acting recklessly, in violation of the so-called *Duties of Loyalty and Care,* and the investment banker's advice is a necessary preventive (*and* protective) step in most such transactions.

Functioning as a retail brokerage

For many, although not all, investment banks, a large part of their business is retail — working with individual investors, and in nearly all cases, institutional brokerage accounts. As members of the various Exchanges, including the New York and American Stock exchanges (Amex), and as a participating member in the National Association of Securities Dealers (and therefore, a trader for its own account on the NASD Automated Quotation System or NASDAQ), the investment bankers execute trades. On the New York exchange and Amex they're agents; on NASDAQ they're technically principals, although the results are essentially the same, the bank matching buy and sell orders and taking a commission — or, in the case of NASDAQ, the spread between the bid and the ask prices.

Some of top-tier investment banks, Goldman Sachs, for example, don't have a retail component, whereas others — including Merrill Lynch and Morgan Stanley — do. Typically, regional investment banks (Piper Jaffray, for example, based in Minneapolis and 23 Western states) have robust retail capacity. In the institutional end of the business, leading investment banks enjoy commission income (including spreads on NASDAQ) which is not necessarily competitive with charges for executing securities trades imposed by some of the low-cost houses — Charles Schwab, E*TRADE, and the like, because the elite banks provide ancillary services, such as research and analysis.

Now that commissions no longer are regulated and fixed, these new entrants have cut a large part of the profit out of an investment bank's brokerage functions, particularly when the traders are sophisticated institutions who can pick and chose their brokers to execute transactions. The investment banks, however, preserve some of their prior spreads by swapping the company research generated by their in-house analysts for commission income from major asset managers — mutual funds, insurance companies, and pension fund managers. The asset managers are paying for research with so-called *soft dollars,* commissions paid to the investment bank employing the analyst in question.

Investment banking houses also manage money themselves; they sponsor mutual funds and compete vigorously for private discretionary accounts, institutional and from high-net-worth individuals.

Managing buyout and venture capital funds

Finally, many of the investment banks, Donaldson Lufkin & Jenrette (which recently merged with Credit Suisse First Boston Corporation), for example, are affiliated with buyout and venture capital funds. Sprout Capital, for example, historically has been an arm of DLJ. Individual managers share the interests in profits from portfolio investments with DLJ but otherwise behave like the managers of freestanding venture capital funds. In some cases, the partnership capital for an affiliated VC fund is supplied entirely by the institution concerned — Chase Capital Partners, for example, from Chase Manhattan. In others, the affiliated institution supplies a large portion of the capital but admits other major investors as limited partners in the fund.

The short of the matter is that the investment banks today offer a full line of financial services. They can:

- ✔ Take a company public
- ✔ Act as agent in the private placement of debt and equity securities
- ✔ Supply advice (including fairness opinions) on corporate reorganizations
- ✔ Manage your money
- ✔ Invest their own capital in special situations and/or the capital of affiliated venture and buyout funds
- ✔ Act as the counterparty if you want to hedge against a particular market or currency move in the future.

And, with a gradual, and now almost complete erosion of the Glass-Steagall division between commercial and investment banks, investment banks are affiliated with commercial banks that accept deposits and make loans. The Glass Steagall Act — named for Senator Carter Glass and Congressman Henry Steagall — was a reaction to the stock market crash of 1929 and the subsequent bank failures. It separated the functions of commercial and investment banks, such as the House of Morgan into Morgan Guaranty (commercial) and J.P. Morgan (investment).

Like their European counterparts, Fleet (with Robertson Stephens), Chase Manhattan (with Hambrecht & Quist), Bankers Trust (with Alex Brown and now indeed part of Deutsche Bank), U.S. BanCorp (with Piper Jaffray), the investment banks are integrated agents and principals in the global capital markets.

Your Money Is Safe — Probably

Although money in the hands of an investment bank may not be quite as safe as if you kept it in your own personal bank vault, it's pretty close. Here are some of the safeguards in place at investment banks that ought to help you sleep a bit better at night.

- ✔ Investment banks are required to maintain certain amounts of capital (the equivalent of reserves) against the risks they take in underwriting securities.

- ✔ Investment banks are allowed to lend customers money, so-called margin debt, to purchase securities, but the loans are limited by the Federal Reserve to no more than 50 percent of the value of the securities purchased, which are held as collateral by the investment bank. If the price of the margined stock collapses, then the investment bank issues a margin call, which (if the customer is unable to respond with cash) is satisfied by the bank through selling the margin stock into the market and then repaying itself.

- ✔ The Securities Investor Protection Corporation (SIPC), a quasi-governmental agency, insures customer accounts at investment banks against insolvency and is roughly equivalent to the insurance of accounts at commercial banks and savings and loans. A cap, of course, is in place on the insurance — $500,000 for each customer (including a maximum of $100,000 for cash claims). What the insurance means in plain English is that if the investment bank has custody of your cash or securities (and most individual clients from time to time leave securities in the bank's custody) . . . *and* the bank goes broke . . . SIPC will get you the shares (or cash) back, up to $500,000.

Gaining Access to an Investment Bank

So how do you go about gaining the attention of a good investment bank — one that can raise private money for you or float your IPO? That truly is the $64,000 question (or perhaps the $64 million question). If you're new to this flavor of raising capital, a number of different approaches can help you achieve your financial goals.

The more you focus your efforts on utilizing these approaches, the greater your chances of having the I-bank of your dreams decide to take you on as a client.

Being a customer

Open an account at the investment bank that you're targeting and trade your portfolio with one of the brokers (assuming that the bank has a retail facility). They'll love you for the business. Then sit with your broker and ask for his or her advice. Will the bank take you on? If the broker is a big producer, he or she usually has clout with the corporate finance department. Further, if you have big personal bucks, let the bank manage your stock portfolio — assuming that they do a good job. That gives you additional clout. If the investment bank is owned by a commercial bank — well, you know where to put yours and your firm's checking accounts.

This is not a panacea. The separate departments — retail brokerage, corporate finance, and so forth — are often run independently. Sometimes the bank's people are more competitive than cooperative with each other. But the trick is getting in the door, and one good way is by giving business to get business.

Get bankers to call on you

The better way, but much more difficult to arrange, is inducing bankers to call on you. Energetic and ambitious investment bankers patrol the trade and financial press for ideas, and they go to events where companies formally present.

If you can get your story into the press (not a paid ad) and it has some sizzle, chances are you'll get a call. If you can get your firm on a program — one of the all-day affairs put on by commercial or nonprofit sponsors to present likely opportunities — the audience may include investment bankers. The sponsors are identified in *The Venture Capital Journal* and/or *The Private Equity Analyst* (plus a number of other print and online sources).

Work your connections

The last way to get acquainted is the good old-fashioned way: Know someone inside. Take him or her to lunch or breakfast (investment bankers do lunch a lot) and try out your idea, asking for the *order,* an introduction to corporate finance, as you pick up the check.

The criminal element

Despite the best efforts of regulators and prosecutors, a seemingly ineradicable group of unethical practitioners has popped up in the business. The dollars are too big, and the frauds, at least initially, are too easy to perpetrate to keep rogues out of the space entirely. Criminal prosecutions crop up all too frequently, from the mightiest, for example, Mike Milken, to a brokerage house playing *pump and dump* on the Internet — pumping and dumping is the practice of stock manipulation, when a broker or investor buys an obscure penny stock (any stock selling under $5 a share), circulates a rumor that the company just struck oil in Madagascar, and then sells into the resultant buying wave — the gullible flock to the shares on the basis of an old and should-by-now-be discredited theory . . . *buy on the rumor and sell on the news.* Nowadays the rumors often are traceable back to a manipulator rather than a *reliable source.*

Chapter 15

Initial Public Offering (IPO)

● ●

In This Chapter

▶ Exploring IPOs

▶ Deciding whether you want to go public

▶ Learning how to do an IPO

▶ Taking your show on the road

● ●

An initial public offering, or IPO — just the mere thought of those three little initials is enough to send even the most sober company owner, executive, shareholding employee, or investor into soaring flights of fancy and dreams of soon-to-come wealth that even last month's Powerball lottery jackpot can't hold a candle to. And why not? Although IPOs have been around for years — they're the traditional way that fledgling companies first sell shares of stock to the public to raise capital — the recent explosion of technology firms and dot-coms has brought IPOs into the public consciousness like never before. Even with the demise of those same offerings (and companies), the IPO still is viewed as the "big cash out" for company founders, owners, and investors. Certainly, significantly fewer are occurring now than just a few years ago, but the market has again regained some measure of sanity.

The initial offering of an issuer's securities to the public often is a watershed event — an achievement of a goal the founders have sought since the inception of the company, especially for founders who look at the IPO as an exit strategy, an event when they finally are able to convert their stake in the business into cash.

IPOs are a mixed blessing, however, because they may or may not be the best strategic alternative for your firm. As you'll soon see, you have a number of considerations to evaluate before taking the plunge. In this chapter, we examine the inner workings of the IPO — what it is, how to do it, when to do it, and whether it's a method of raising capital that makes sense for you and your company.

The ABCs of IPOs

So what exactly is an IPO? Gee — we thought you'd never ask!

An *IPO* is the act of moving a private company into the public arena where shares of its stock can be traded publicly — bought and sold through the stock markets (it is hoped) for profit (or loss). The IPO is a common financing device — almost every public company from General Electric to Hewlett-Packard to Amazon.com has had an IPO.

So, how is an IPO a financing device? When a company that is private opens ownership of the business through an IPO by selling shares of the stock to the public — and being listed on one of the major stock markets such as the New York Stock Exchange or NASDAQ — the company receives cash in exchange for the stock that it sells. In some cases, the cash generated by an IPO can be counted in the hundreds of millions or even billions of dollars. Now, that's raising capital!

Originally, IPOs were limited mostly to companies that had established themselves in the marketplace and had a clear track record of stability and profitability. Why else would anyone want to buy a company's stock? However, the maturity of companies offering securities to the public became less important during the late 1960s as new and unseasoned issuers tested the IPO waters. A new breed of underwriters — Charles Plohn was the 1960s paradigm — grew up selling shares of stock in early stage companies for public consumption. What made many of these offerings different from traditional IPOs is that they increasingly were made before the issuers had seen their first quarter of black ink — in other words, before they became profitable. See Chapter 14 for a complete description of the underwriting process.

Although many of the new breed of underwriters and their clients no longer are around, the phenomenon persists. A casual observation of the recent flood of dot-com IPOs reveals that fast-rising markets are fertile ground for IPOs. Not only that, but as investor excitement peaked, classic requirements of stability and profitability went right out the window. In fact, it seemed for a time that the less stable and profitable the firm and its markets, the more attractive the company's IPO became in the eyes of potential investors. Of course, this turned out to be nothing more than a mirage. The dot-coms that weren't stable and profitable at the end of the day are the dot-coms that are now out of business. Nevertheless, during down markets, the frequency of initial public offerings decreases, but never seems to completely stop.

One other factor has increased the frequency of IPOs in recent years. Access to the process for first-time issuers was simplified, first, with the adoption in 1979 of Form S-18 — available for offerings by nonpublic issuers in an amount of $7.5 million or less — and, more recently, by the Small Business Initiative, which, for firms with less than $25 million in revenues, substitutes Form SB-2 for S-18 (in the process discarding the $7.5 million cap), making life much easier for these firms. Not only that, but cumbersome post-IPO periodic reporting requirements also are relaxed — by substituting Regulation S-B standards for the more rigorous requirements of Regulations S-K.

Watch out, however, because small IPOs can be deadly! You get all the public company issues and costs but for far too little capital. Not only that, but you may end up as a *pink sheet company* — one that doesn't end up on investor radar screens. Long story short: IPOs of less than $25 million often are not a good thing. One more thing to keep in mind: IPO markets are fickle. You can't plan on when you can do an IPO. Your business can be perfectly positioned for an IPO but the market may suddenly become unfavorable to IPOs or the market may decide that your industry is one that should be avoided. Sometimes it can take years before the market is right for your IPO.

If this alphabet soup of forms and reporting requirements is beginning to make your eyes glaze over, don't worry. We take a close look at all this red tape — and attempt to make some sense of it — later in this chapter.

Deciding Whether an IPO Is Right for You

Almost any company now can consider an IPO — no matter how big or small it may be. The IPO is a viable option for almost all early stage companies. But before you rush out and file for an IPO to raise millions of dollars of good old-fashioned American cash, keep in mind that just because you can do it doesn't mean that you need to do it. An IPO isn't the best option in every case, but it *is* an option that requires your careful consideration.

Top ten largest IPOs of all time

Admittedly, one of the big attractions of the initial public offering is the promise of the ability to raise major funds in a relatively short period of time. Don't believe us? Then consider this list of the top ten largest IPOs of all time as of April 1, 2002:

1. Enel Spa	$16,496,062,500
2. AT&T Wireless	$10,620,000,000
3. Kraft Foods, Inc.	$8,680,000,000
4. Eircom	$5,516,550,000
5. United Parcel Service	$5,470,000,000
6. Infineon Technologies AG	$5,230,464,000
7. China Unicom Ltd.	$4,915,541,000
8. Conoco, Inc.	$4,403,197,821
9. Petroleo Brasileiro S.A.	$4,320,000,000
10. Travelers Property Casualty	$3,885,000,000

Having all sorts of questions about the IPO process is natural and expected. Chances are, that's one of the reasons you purchased this book. If you're even remotely thinking about an IPO, ask yourself the following fundamental questions:

✔ Are you big enough and can you grow fast enough to warrant interest in the public market? If not, your IPO won't sell and, if you go through with it, you'll probably end up on the pink sheets — the "walking dead."

✔ Will I be able to raise capital cheaply and more efficiently on the wings of an IPO than with any other method, taking into account the long-range consequences of becoming a public company?

✔ Will I be able to liquidate my sweat equity in the firm as a result of the IPO?

✔ Will the new IPO crash and burn, taking the reputation of my company along with it?

Each of these questions and more have to be considered in the process leading up to a decision to make initial public offering.

The good news about IPOs

On the plus side, IPOs have personally enriched many company founders and employees. Indeed, the home-run payoffs for celebrated founders usually are identified with a public stock sale. It's no coincidence that three of the world's richest people — Microsoft cofounder Bill Gates, Oracle founder Larry Ellison, and Microsoft cofounder Paul Allen — reached their lofty perches directly as a result of the public sale of their company's stock.

Of course, the ability of the world's richest people to stay at the top of the heap is subject to the whims of the stock market that put them there in the first place. For example, Bill Gates' personal fortune is largely determined based on Microsoft stock values, which dropped as a result of federal antitrust litigation and the bursting of the dot-com stock bubble.

Indeed, many founders and employees of dot-coms who saw their post-IPO fortunes crash into the ground learned the hard way that IPOs are not a panacea for building personal wealth.

In an IPO, to the extent that equity is being used to raise capital for corporate purposes, the price of obtaining the capital from the public usually will be cheaper, because any commodity that can be freely bought and sold is intrinsically more valuable than its illiquid private counterpart. Thus, a *public market* entails (although not for everybody) liquid securities, which present a classic exit strategy for founders and other shareholders who want to cash out their *private* stock holdings and perhaps start an early retirement or life of leisure, or simply start another business. But this may take time.

And collateral benefits of an IPO go well beyond simply being able to garner a higher price for your shares of stock and then being able to sell them readily through the public markets. These collateral benefits include:

- ✔ Customers and suppliers like the security of dealing with a firm in the public market. The perception is that the company is more stable and has lower risks that nonpublic companies. This premium also extends to employees, even when they don't possess their company's stock or stock options.

- ✔ A company's access to capital is increased. The same can be said of profile in the marketplace.

- ✔ A public company can do a broad national public-relations job; a well-prepared prospectus projects the company's image favorably from the start.

- ✔ A public market helps stockholders with their estate tax problems. It enables them to diversify and simplifies appraisal problems.

- ✔ The company is bestowed with so-called *Chinese Currency* with which to make additional acquisitions, meaning shares trading at a high multiple of earnings and, therefore, preferable to cash when buying other companies.

- ✔ With exceptions imposed by the stock exchanges, the regulatory issues that need to be addressed in the process of an IPO are about adequacy of disclosure; ostensibly, the SEC isn't authorized to delve into the merits of the offering.

And the bad news about IPOs

But although many pluses accompany an initial public offering, all is not sunshine and roses — minuses also are significant:

- ✔ **An IPO takes time.** The issuer and underwriter need 60 to 90 days to initially file the IPO and receive an SEC ruling, and the period between filing with the SEC and the effective date usually takes at least another three months or so. Many an issuer undergoes the time-consuming and expensive process only to see the process aborted at the last instant because — as a result of changing market conditions or other reasons — the IPO window has closed. If the issuer has counted on the proceeds of an IPO to keep the company afloat, the result can mean certain disaster and even bankruptcy for the issuer.

  If you really need the money, be sure you have a Plan B, because the window of opportunity may be closed for years. (The best Plan B may be to pursue what is known as a shelf registration. A shelf registration of a new issue can be prepared up to two years in advance, allowing the offering to be completed quickly when the market conditions are right. Details of shelf registrations are covered under SEC Rule 415.)

✔ **Transition costs are significant.** Underwriters can receive up to 15 percent (more or less) of the price of the offering (though 7 percent is usual) and legal, printing, and accounting expenses can bring the total costs up to 25 percent of the money raised. That means, for example, that in a $10 million public offering, as much as $2,500,000 is burned up before the company ever gets its hands on what's left. On the other hand, fees and expenses for private placements ordinarily run considerably less than 25 percent of the total amount raised — leaving much more of the capital available for the company to use to pay off debt or apply to expansion of its operations.

✔ **Public information.** For many entrepreneurs, the fact that their compensation and holdings, plus their pricing strategies and profits, are public for all to see is a very real turnoff to becoming a public company.

✔ **Lockups.** Too many founders think they can sell their stock with the IPO. Unfortunately, lockups (restrictions on the selling of stock by founders and other insiders from and after an IPO) typically prevent them from doing just that. Affected parties need to be aware of what fraction of their shares will be registered in the IPO, and what they'll have to do to make the balance of their shares tradable (and the restrictions they may still encounter even then).

✔ **New legal requirements.** Perhaps more frightening to a company that considers crossing the line from private to public ownership is that a number of new legal requirements are attached to the conduct of the business. These requirements alone are enough to scare off more than a few companies from conducting their own IPOs. Some of the more significant requirement are

- A public company must file periodic reports with the SEC (quarterly and annually) and *flash reports* when significant events occur. The thrust of these documents is financial. Letting the auction markets know how the company is doing on a short-term basis is in itself a potential problem for a management that is unconvinced that the market's avarice for short-term results is sensible business strategy.

- The annual meeting becomes a major event. Proxies are solicited with an expensive, printed information document complying with the SEC's proxy rules. This disclosure is heavily oriented toward exposing management's compensation packages in a manner that suggests key executive compensation is one of the principal clues for analysts to unravel in judging corporate performance (a curiously puritanical view because private analysts' reports seldom mention top-management compensation as a principal benchmark of a firm's prospects).

- Beyond the required reports, the public company must give daily consideration to current disclosure of important events. Regulation FD, adopted by the SEC in 2000, requires companies releasing public information to do so in a way that the general public receives it at the same time as analysts and institutional investors.

- A public company is exposed to strike suits, litigation initiated by underemployed lawyers ostensibly on behalf of a shareholder (usually with an insignificant stake) that is, in fact, designed to corral legal fees. The courts tolerate such claims, because they're thought to have therapeutic value, restraining management excesses in an era when the public shareholders otherwise are disenfranchised.

- A public company can be taken over by a raider in a hostile tender. Inserting so-called *shark-repellent* measures such as supermajority provisions, staggered-term boards, blank check preferred stock, and the like into the charter is easily done prior to an IPO, but underwriters may balk at some of these provisions.

And if all the factors listed in the previous paragraphs weren't bad enough news, a number of difficult rules also impact individuals associated with public companies: the directors, officers, and major shareholders. This group, for example, is subject to a curious rule that recaptures to the company any *short-swing profit* — profit that they realize on sales and purchases of the company's stock that match (offset one another) within a six-month period. The statute governing these transactions becomes hard to follow at the margin, but its consequences are severe.

One more thing: The threat that an insider will be deemed to have traded on inside information (a practice the federal government definitely doesn't approve of) means that insiders can safely trade only during specified *windows,* periods of time or fixed intervals in accordance with standard instructions — usually from a few days after a company discloses its earnings for the prior quarter until the end of the current quarter. In many ways, insiders are no more liquid after an IPO than they were before the IPO.

Will your IPO attract a crowd?

Have you ever given a party and nobody came? If so, you know that few other things can make you feel quite as lonely. So what if you threw an IPO, and nobody bought your securities? Actually, IPOs are canceled all the time when the underwriters sense that the market is going south and the offering will result in indifference (or perhaps even disdain) on the part of investors.

So, what can you do to boost your IPO's chances of attracting a crowd? Here are five suggestions:

- Clearly identify your market and prepare a polished sales pitch for potential investors.

- Have a proprietary product or process that sets your company apart in the marketplace.

- Have a strong management team in place with a track record of running profitable companies.

- Affiliate with a top-notch investment bank — the more experienced and the higher profile the better — to take you public.

- Take your company public when the time is right — not too early and not too late.

Opening up the private workings of a company to the public at large can be an extremely embarrassing event. When, for example, a particular family sold 1 million common shares of its company to the public, it was forced to disclose that the family had been using the company essentially as a private bank. When stock in a family owned breeding stable was sold to the public, a number of insider dealings between the family and the stable were revealed. Those not-quite-kosher practices apparently continued after the company became public. Litigation ensued, and the company was forced into liquidation.

Preparing for an IPO: A Step-by-Step Guide

Okay . . . so you've decided that you'd like to try an initial public offering, but you're wondering exactly how to do it. Well, the answer is not simple.

Ask anyone who's gone through the process if it was an easy and painless one, and chances are, they'll look at you like you've gone entirely nuts. Truth be told, the process of completing an initial public offering can be long, drawn out, extremely complex, and full of last-minute surprises — the kind that make your hair turn gray 10 or 20 years before it normally would. But despite these challenges, hundreds of companies get through the process each and every year and manage to survive just fine. And a lucky few of them do much better than survive; they actually earn huge gains in the value of their securities after the initial offering is made to the public.

By taking time to plan and to prepare, you're ensuring that your IPO flies and that it doesn't find itself stuck on the ground going nowhere fast. And when is the right time to file an IPO? The answer depends on your business and on the climate among potential investors. Before you launch your IPO, be sure that the market is ready for you and that you'll raise the greatest amount of capital possible. So, once you've decided that an IPO is for you, here's a step-by-step approach that can help guide your way:

Step 1: Assembling your team

Filing for an IPO is definitely not an easy process. You must assemble a team for taking your company public that is not just up for the challenge but that will ensure its success. Despite the efforts of the SEC to make the process less cumbersome — especially for small businesses — it's still a process best handled by people who are experts. That means assembling a team of people who are experienced and knowledgeable about each of the different pieces of information that feed into the IPO filing, including the registration form itself, the prospectus, financial statements, and other documents and data. In other words, don't try to do it by yourself with just this book for guidance.

Selecting the IPO team is most important. At a minimum, your IPO team needs to consist of representatives of:

- ✔ Top management, particularly your vice president of marketing, chief financial officer, and chief executive officer.

- ✔ Legal counsel that is experienced in taking companies public.

- ✔ An investment bank with a high profile, a track record of successful IPOs, and respected analysts that follow your industry.

- ✔ A financial public relations firm that specializes in publicizing companies that are going public. (Your current public relations firm may not have this specialized experience, but it may be able to recommend one.)

- ✔ A public accounting firm with substantial experience with public companies, preferably in your industry.

Selecting external members of your team — your investment banker, for example — requires taking the time to carefully research the experience and capability of a variety of firms to find one that offers the best fit with your company. While a successful track record of bringing IPOs to market certainly is important in choosing an investment banker, so is the firm's ability to work well with your business and the people within it. Keep in mind that you're going to have to live, eat, and breathe IPO with these folks for a minimum of four to five months — potentially much longer. Find people who are experienced and compatible with your organization's culture, values, and personality.

During the period of time that starts when you hire your investment banker until 25 days after the offering date, you enter into what's known as the quiet period. Mandated by the SEC, the *quiet period* restricts you and your employees from making any public comments about your IPO that are not contained in the prospectus. This restriction covers *any* release of information, including press releases, speeches, advertising — even talking to your spouse. If in doubt, it's far better to err on the side of not saying something than saying something that could put your offering in jeopardy.

Table 15-1 below summarizes the steps in the IPO process and gives a rough estimate of the time involved from beginning to end. What the table does not reflect is the initial team building and preplanning phase which takes a minimum of two to three months before the IPO process starts just to get all the people lined up and committed. Typically, people have to be "sold" on the idea that this is the time to do the IPO, and it may take some time to develop a consensus behind the IPO. The table also does not reflect the audit that needs to start about two months before the filing.

Table 15-1	The IPO Timeline
Event	*Week Number*
First organizational meeting	1
Drafting sessions/Due diligence	2–4
File registration statement	5
SEC review	6–9
Receive first round of comments from SEC	10
Response to first round of comments	10
Receive second round of comments	12
Response to second round of comments and print red herrings	13
Road shows	14–15
Pricing	16
Closing	17

Step 2: Completing registration forms

The next step in getting your IPO off the ground is filling out and submitting the proper registration form with the SEC. The good news is that your legal counsel will work out the details of the specific type of registration form and complete it with the assistance of the other members of your team.

The registration statement consists of two separate parts:

✔ **Part I: The prospectus.** This document contains a detailed description of the company's business operations, management, and financial condition. It serves as the selling document for the securities. The preliminary prospectus (called the *red herring*) must be widely distributed before the effective date of your offering (when it is cleared by the SEC) and made available to anyone who makes an offer to buy the securities and to anyone who actually executes a purchase.

✔ **Part II: Additional information.** Although the additional information in this part of the registration statement — including a breakdown of the expenses of the offering and a listing of exhibits filed with your registration statement (major contracts are one such item) — doesn't have to be delivered to investors, it is available to the public through the SEC Web site or by visiting an SEC public reference room.

You need to choose the registration form that is right for your company. The following subsections summarize the choices that are available and describe the kinds of businesses that can use them:

Form S-1

Any company, large or small, can elect to use the Form S-1 to register its securities offering. The S-1 is, however, the most complicated and time-consuming form of the ones that are available, so if your business and offering can be completed using one of the alternative forms, you may want to go that route. When filling out Form S-1, you'll be required to describe the following items in your prospectus:

- ✔ The nature of your business
- ✔ Your properties
- ✔ Your competition
- ✔ The names of officers and directors, and the compensation each receives
- ✔ Material transactions between the company and its officers and directors
- ✔ Material legal proceedings involving the company or its officers and directors
- ✔ The plan for distributing the securities to the public, and the intended use of the proceeds from the offering.

Specific direction on how to describe each of these items is prescribed in the SEC rules. Your legal counsel will be familiar with these descriptions.

You also need to submit a bit of supporting information along with the S-1. This information includes three years worth (less if your company hasn't been around that long) of audited financial statements in an SEC-acceptable format and any risk factors that investors need to be aware of when considering the purchase of your securities. These risk factors may include:

- ✔ Dependence on key personnel
- ✔ Adverse economic conditions in the company's industry
- ✔ The lack of an operating history.

If you are registering your securities with the SEC, you must enlist the aid of competent legal counsel and the services of an experienced accounting firm.

Form SB-1

Form SB-1 is an alternative to the basic registration Form S-1 that is designed specifically for small businesses and written in a question-and-answer format that is easier and less cumbersome to complete. To be considered a small business issuer, your company must meet two criteria:

✓ Have less than $25 million in revenues during the last recent fiscal year.

✓ A total of outstanding publicly held stock worth $25 million or less.

This form can be used by small business issuers offering no more than $10 million worth of securities during any 12-month period, and it must be accompanied by two years worth of audited financial statements using generally accepted accounting principles (GAAP).

Form SB-2

Form SB-2 also is an alternative registration form designated for use by small business issuers (less than $25 million revenues in previous fiscal year, and total outstanding publicly held stock worth $25 million or less). It can be used to register an unlimited dollar amount of securities during any 12-month period. The required text is less extensive than Form S-1, and submission requires two fiscal years worth of audited financial statements prepared using GAAP.

It is at this point where you (and your investment banker and professional advisors) make your first shot at pricing the IPO. The first step is deciding the overall amount of money to be raised based on the company's needs and the desires of the company's owners and management. Next, establish a price per share, usually between $10 and $20 each depending on market conditions and the stock prices of comparable companies. Of course, depending on the actual value of your company and the number of shares you have outstanding prior to the IPO, to arrive at the price for the shares in your IPO, you may have to do a reverse split of your company's existing capital stock. Given the total amount to be raised, and a target price per share, you can easily determine the total number of shares to be offered by simply dividing the former number by the latter.

When, for example, you want to raise $25 million, and the target price per share is $10, your initial offering would be for 2.5 million shares. Understand that this initial price exercise may be subject to considerable revision, especially during the final stages of the IPO process.

Again, all these different forms, regulations, exemptions, filing requirements, restrictions, and other conditions are extremely complex and potentially fraught with danger for you and your business. Before you embark on deciding which forms to complete and submit, enlist the help of an expert in securities filings for businesses of your size in your particular industry and competent legal counsel. Taking advantage of someone else's mistakes (and experiences) is better than making them yourself.

Step 3: Selecting accounting principles

Chances are, if you've already been in business for some time before you file for your IPO, you've probably decided on your approach to accounting for your company's financial transactions — one that is consistent with GAAP. Not only that, but you've probably had your financials audited by an independent CPA firm. That being the case, there's no reason to change your accounting approach in advance of an IPO. In fact, doing so at this point may send up red flags to potential investors who are curious to know exactly why you're making such a change.

However, if accountants are being hired to audit your company's financials for the first time in anticipation of an IPO, the present may prove to be just the occasion for taking the time to get your financial house in order by settling on accounting principles consistent with GAAP.

The company needs to have audited statements for either three years (S-1) or two years (other filings). That means you need to have had a CPA firm on board for two or three years *before* doing your IPO to avoid the time-consuming and expensive process of justifying and documenting your historical transactions to your newly appointed auditor. Besides, you don't want to change CPAs right before going public. So, if you think IPO is in your future, plan ahead!

When you've planned ahead, you probably won't have to address the issues raised in this section, because you will already have more financial disclosures prepared under GAAP rules than the SEC requires and, as a result, fewer decisions about your accounting policies will have to be made (mostly by your CFO and CPAs).

Step 4: Preparing the prospectus

The principal disclosure document in a public financing is the *prospectus*, that portion of the registration statement distributed to potential investors that offers the securities for sale. When you're requesting on a Form S-1, the guidebook for describing the company and the offering in the prospectus is Regulation S-K and the specific instructions contained in Form S-1. A simplified version of Regulation S-K, Regulation S-B governs the use of the prospectus by small business issuers using Form SB-2, but for purposes of simplicity, assume in this discussion that Regulation S-K governs. Detailed information on these regulations and forms is available at the Securities Exchange Commission Web site: www.sec.gov.

As mentioned in the previous paragraph, the instructions on the form that you use (S-1, SB-1, or SB-2) sometimes give fairly precise directions about the topics to be covered in the document (rather than a cross reference to Regulation S-K) and, in some cases, specific advice on how to cover them, such as:

✔ "Describe the general development of the business . . . during the past five years."

✔ "Describe the business done and intended to be done by the registrant and its subsidiaries, focusing upon the registrant's dominant industry segment."

The road map for drafting a prospectus is well defined; even an IPO novice need have little concern that anything has been totally overlooked, if he or she bothers to take the time to review the rules while looking at examples of other successful prospectuses.

Considering what exactly the SEC is trying to accomplish by putting you through the mild torture of drafting a prospectus is useful to you in doing the job properly. The intent of the rules on disclosure is to reduce the amount of *boilerplate* — the kinds of statements that are repeated again and again and that therefore lose their impact — that creeps into the document.

For example, one of the required disclosures is entitled "Management's Discussion and Analysis of Financial Condition and Results of Operations" (MD&A). It's the section in which the SEC tries to hold management's feet to the fire regarding the numbers set forth in financial statements and possible future events not reflected in those numbers. Disclosures in this Section require the candor that one would expect in a question-and-answer session between the issuer's chief financial officer and securities analysts. The regulation calls for mention of such matters as "trends . . . that are reasonably likely to result in the registrant's liquidity increasing or decreasing in any material way . . . [and] unusual or infrequent events . . . that materially affected reported income."

When considering how to phrase disclosure language, keep in mind that the SEC has confirmed and views as particularly important the fact that public disclosure documents should be decipherable by a nonexpert — a layman. Although it is true that most of the action in the public markets is the result of professionals trading with professionals, the SEC wants to make sure that Joe Q. and Mary Public aren't disadvantaged when *they* decide to join in the fun.

To that end, the SEC has passed the plain English rule, which dictates that disclosure documents, including prospectuses, be written in "plain English," meaning the simple declarative sentences recommended in the standard treatise, as outlined in *The Elements of Style* by Strunk & White.

Although prospectus writing is an art that doesn't require years of expertise to master, the more experience you have, the better. The SEC's Web site (specifically "EDGAR", or Electronic Data Gathering and Retrieval, section) is full of examples of previously submitted prospectuses, making it possible for you to capitalize on the successful work product of others. The real art is in anticipating the comments that the SEC staff is likely to make in its letters of comment to your firm. Addressing those staff comments means reworking your prospectus (assuming, as is always the case with an IPO, the prospectus is subject to full review) and thereby shortening the length of the letters of comment and — more important — the resultant comment period.

Getting your act together quickly

Market windows for IPOs come along only every now and then, and getting the issue out on the street before the window closes is up to the participants. Missing a window can result an issue that is substantially undervalued or an issue that is canceled altogether. Thus, *make sure every statement in your prospectus has a source to support it. Otherwise, you are risking unnecessary comments from the SEC and the attached delay.* For example when the first draft of the prospectus asserts that the issuer is the leading manufacturer of widgets in the country — without additional information to back up that assertion — the SEC staff routinely responds, "Prove it!" If you can't, then don't make such assertions in the first place.

Working the review board

Some information the SEC staff may zero in on can be confidential — the selling price of the issuer's products to major customers, for example — and the issuer may want to try persuading the staff that such information isn't necessary for a complete presentation. Formally requesting confidential treatment is open to the registrant, but that procedure takes time, and must be completed before your company can start its public offering.

Hence, informal persuasion is the preferred course. No amount of persuasion, however, is likely to eliminate certain sensitive disclosures that are mandated by the SEC.

No matter how carefully the prospectus is prepared, an IPO must await the SEC's letter of comment, and, other than making nagging telephone calls to Washington D.C., the issuer can do nothing but wait for it. Once a registration statement has been filed, within a couple of days (usually not more than four) a staff member will advise you whether it will be reviewed. IPOs are always subjected to review, and a first-time registrant can expect at least a 30-day period before receiving staff comments.

Prospectus, or not prospectus?

The term *prospectus* is used in Section 5 of the Securities Act of 1933, which makes it unlawful to sell securities unless they are accompanied or preceded by a prospectus that meets statutory requirements. Through the years, a number of issues have arisen concerning the nature of a prospectus; that is, exactly what is considered a prospectus. The formal document, as filed, obviously qualifies, but how about other attention-getting documents, such as tombstone ads, oral communications, road show materials, videotapes, research reports, and so on? Does one or more of these materials qualify as a prospectus as defined under Section 2(10) of the 1933 Act, which talks about "any . . . communication . . . written or by radio or television?" The answer is: Check with your attorney before showing any materials (other than your prospectus) publicly.

Once all comments are addressed to the satisfaction of the SEC (which, depending on the number of comments, can take several letters back and forth), the procedure then is to ask (two days in advance) for the issue to become effective at a particular date and time, a practice known for technical reasons as a *request for acceleration*. Acceleration is conditioned on a widespread circulation of the preliminary, or *red herring prospectus* (so called because a legend on the preliminary prospectus is printed in red ink) among the selling group.

Step 5: Presenting soft information

As most company owners and managers can well imagine, the business and financial *soft information* (predictions and opinions) that you develop and present to the public during the IPO process are important in developing investor interest in the issue. But, although it's hoped that projections created for an IPO are positive — and perhaps even a bit optimistic — a clear balance must be maintained between honest optimism and outright fraud.

Regulation S-K sets out the SEC policy on projections, which encourages the use in public reports of "management's projections of future economic performance that have a reasonable basis and are presented in an appropriate format." Rule 175 under the 1933 Act and Rule 3(b)-6 under the 1934 Act discuss the presentation of *forward-looking statements* — including projections — in periodic reports, and provide a *safe harbor* from liability unless the statements are shown (the burden of proof is on the plaintiff, the person filing the suit) to be without "reasonable basis" or not "in good faith."

Of course, check with your attorney before *any* use of such soft information.

Step 6: Embarking on your road show

A successful road show can quickly build strong support among investors for your issue — potentially driving up the demand for and the price of your securities. An unsuccessful road show, on the other hand, can cause potential investors to lose interest. In the worst case, the IPO may be canceled because of insufficient investor interest at a price that makes financial sense.

Federal securities regulations preclude you from disclosing financial forecasts about your business that are not contained within the four corners of your prospectus during these road-show meetings. Don't even think about doing it, regardless of the pressure to do so that may be brought to bear by certain members of your audience.

The reality road show

The traditional, good-old-fashioned *reality road show* is a time-honored part of the IPO process, and it's one that can put any IPO team, especially the company's top management, to the test. The road show is a barnstorming, city-to-city tour by top management and IPO investment bankers that is specifically designed to put you in front of as many decision makers as quickly as possible, generating interest in your new issue and, it is hoped, pushing its ultimate price upward in the process.

Once you become comfortable that SEC clearance is all but received, you'll be expected to be ready to hit the road and make your best pitch to institutional investors. This "dog-and-pony show" is a vital part of the IPO process and is the only forum that your company's management team has to really show its stuff to potential investors, analysts, brokers, and other interested parties. Not only will your team have to be sharp, but it also will have to exude an air of credibility and rock-solid industry knowledge. You and your team should know more about your business, your products, the competition, and the industry in which you play than anyone else in the room.

Two key parts to the road show described below are the presentation and the question and answer session.

- ✔ **Presentation:** The presentation is exactly what it says it is. It's your chance to pitch your opportunity, to explain where your company resides in its market, and to detail your business plan. You'll need to rehearse this presentation again and again with each member of your team present before you get anywhere near to taking it on the road.

- ✔ **Questions and answers:** This is the unrehearsed portion of the road show, where potential investors have the opportunity to ask (often pointed) questions about your company and about your opportunity. Expect to get pointed questions about details of your business plan, your industry, your competition, and historic financial data (including overall financial condition, revenue growth, market share, and so forth). You and your team will have to be especially on the ball during this portion of the road show. The better prepared you are, the better your team will look (and the better your issue will look).

Expect the road show to be a grueling experience. You and your team will travel from city to city, participating in meeting after meeting from early in the morning to late at night. You'll be grilled by many very smart people, and your patience and endurance will be pushed to their limits. But get through it, and the rewards can be many — a hugely successful issue that raises the capital necessary for your company to move to the next level in its development.

The virtual road show

The Internet has brought innovations to the time-honored traditions of the road show. Why spend thousands of dollars on air travel, hotels, restaurants, rental cars, and all the rest when you can do your road show virtually for far less money?

Yahoo! has gained permission from the SEC to create and deliver virtual road shows on the Web. Yahoo! accomplishes this task by using its NetRoadshow Web site (www.netroadshow.com) to deliver audio and video content and services to the investment banking community.

The advantages of the virtual Yahoo! NetRoadshow are many:

✔ Presentations can be viewed anywhere, anytime.

✔ An unlimited number of investors can view the road show.

✔ Viewers can skip directly to any part of the road-show presentation they desire.

✔ Virtual road shows are cost effective and can be implemented with only 24 hours notice.

✔ No special computer hardware or software is required.

Yahoo! must have something good going on here; clients include such top-notch investment banking firms as Lehman Brothers, J.P. Morgan, Goldman Sachs, Deutsche Bank, Bear Stearns, and many others.

Step 7: Pricing and closing

The last step of the IPO process — pricing and closing — is a step that is pretty much out of the control of the company's owners and management team. From here on out, the underwriter runs the show and the markets have the final say. But, all the hard work you have done thus far combined with no small amount of luck will result in the outcome you and your colleagues desire.

The price of each share of your company's stock and the total number of shares to be offered is not final until the effective date of the IPO (also known as the *offering date*) — the date that your stock first begins trading publicly.

Three business days after the IPO effective date, the IPO will close. After one last flurry of paperwork to finalize the IPO comes the event that everyone has anxiously awaited: disbursement of the official bank checks reflecting the proceeds from the IPO. For anyone who has gone through an IPO, this is indeed a very happy day — one that is the highlight of many business owners' lives.

The Road Show Never Ends

Finally, your IPO is complete. Your securities are in the hands of the public, and your company has the infusion of cash that will take it to the next level (or at least pay off the debts that are dragging it down). Think your job is complete? Wrong — you're just getting started.

The fact is that once your company goes public through an IPO, you must to stay closely involved with your securities, particularly with their _value_. Whenever the price of your stock starts to dip, you'll have to figure out why, and take immediate action to counteract the trend — before investors lose confidence in your company and in your securities, and start to turn a momentary downward trend into a panic sell-off.

Three key ways of supporting your stock after the IPO are

- **Establishing responsibilities for investor relations.** Now that your stock is being traded publicly, you must clearly establish responsibilities for investor relations, either with someone in your company or with an outside firm that specializes in investor relations. A good investor relations firm or individual accomplishes several goals: widely publicizing the news about your company and your stock, providing investors with a point of contact, and ensuring consistent communications with your investors.

- **Delivering strong financial results.** Nothing makes investors happier than strong financial results — and the promise of continued strong results in the future. Investors reward financial strength with strong stock prices. Management accomplishes financial strength by keeping costs under control and delivering steady revenue growth and profitability.

- **Enlisting the support of analysts.** Vigorous analyst support is worth its weight in gold because when analysts talk, investors listen. The best way to get analysts on board at the outset is to solicit the support of a quality investment-banking firm (or syndicate of firms) to underwrite your IPO. If you've selected an investment bank that routinely handles firms like yours, you'll increase the probability of getting analyst support. See Chapter 14 for more information about the role of investment banks.

And don't forget that the road show never ends.

Chapter 16

Mergers

*W*hen raising capital, the exit strategy is near and dear to the hearts of most business owners. The *exit strategy* means selling all or a portion of your business to compensate yourself for all the years of risk and hard work that have made the business a success.

An exit strategy generally means one of two things:

✔ The entrepreneur's company is sold and investors share in the proceeds.

✔ The company completes an initial public offering (IPO), the investors' shares become liquid, and they can cash in at their election.

This chapter covers everything you need to know about the first option. Chapter 15 provides an in-depth discussion of initial public offerings.

Defining What a Merger Is

A *merger* is a type of sale of one company to another in which the acquired company disappears into the acquiring company. Mergers are a particularly popular exit strategy for company owners, because they can raise substantial capital for owners and other investors in the business. In fact, far more entrepreneurs realize their wealth through mergers than through initial public offerings. Not only that, but mergers can be a key growth strategy.

Note: The idea of selling a company is simple: All the shareholders get together and decide to sell the company's assets, combine with the acquiring company, or transfer their interests to an acquiring company in exchange for cash, stock in the acquiring company, notes, or a combination thereof. When you're raising capital for your company, having a rough understanding of what happens when the trade-sale opportunity comes around is relevant.

A merger is not the only way to sell a company. A company sale, as it is sometimes called, can be achieved by stockbrokers getting together and selling 100 percent of their shares to the buyer, with the company that was sold becoming a 100-percent owned subsidiary. Or the target company can sell all its assets to the buyer and then liquidate, which sometimes is called a *practical merger*. Because the most common acquisition technique is a merger — also known as a *statutory merger* — we discuss that class of transaction in this chapter.

A merger is a handy device for selling a company. More important, a merger is a method for cramming the transaction down the throat of dissident shareholders subject, of course, to their appraisal rights, which are discussed in the section about "Exercising Appraisal Rights in Forced Merger" later in this chapter. Mergers also are creatures of state law — transactions authorized and governed by the general corporation law of the *domiciliary state* (state in which a company is incorporated) of the participants. Shareholders of the acquiring company and the company being acquired vote on the merger proposal, with the required favorable percentage (depending on the state) being, generally, either a simple majority or two-thirds of the outstanding shares. One corporate charter survives, and the other is merged into it. When a new corporation is organized and each constituent merges into it, the transaction technically is a *consolidation*.

If the target company is private, dissenting shareholders (who have no other option) are entitled to access a procedure that appraises the value of their shares (and provides payment therefor) in court — a supervised hearing. Dissenters in any merger also have the ability to appeal for judicial protection against unfairness — procedural and substantive — in the face of a merger that converts their target shares into something else.

Mergers are classified into a number of categories. Let's take a quick look at each:

- **A triangular merger** combines the target with a subsidiary of the acquiring company, hence a triangle; the consideration usually proceeds from the acquiring company rather than the subsidiary.

- **A forward merger** is one in which the target is combined with the acquiring company, and the acquiring company's *charter* (certificate of incorporation) survives.

- **A reverse merger** is, as you may expect, the reverse — the acquiring company combined with the target, with the target's charter surviving.

✔ **A reverse triangular merger** — perhaps the more common structure today — involves an acquiring company's subsidiary, a transitory subsidiary that is organized for the purpose of the merger, combining with the target, which ultimately becomes a subsidiary of the acquiring company.

As indicated earlier, the identities of the company making the acquisition and the one being acquired can become slippery, particularly when the pretransaction shareholders of one corporation overlap with the shareholders of the other. Think of the acquiring company as the *surviving entity,* meaning the firm whose shareholders wind up with more shares of the acquiring company than the shareholders of any other participant after the consummation of the transaction.

Taxable versus tax-postponed: Selling out and paying taxes later

Electing between a taxable versus a tax-postponed transaction turns on a multitude of factors. The principal feature driving the choice is the consideration (cash or other assets) to be paid either directly or ultimately to the selling shareholders. Unless that consideration consists principally of equity securities issued by the acquiring company, postponing indefinitely a seller's payment of tax on the gain it realizes is difficult. The question, then, is principally an economic issue: Are the sellers prepared, at least for some period of time, to own shares of the acquiring company as the lion's share of their profit from the transaction?

If the target is a public company and the shares are registered, then nonaffiliates of the acquiring and acquired companies are able to sell and diversify after the closing — sometimes subject to contractual holdbacks. However, the use of shares poses additional problems, including, in most cases, an extension of the time between the purchase and the execution of a reorganization plan and ultimately the closing.

Aside from the approval of the target company's shareholders, a vote of the acquiring company's shareholders also is required to issue shares when:

✔ The acquiring company lacks sufficient treasury, or authorized but unissued, shares.

✔ The transaction contemplates a merger and (in Delaware, the state of choice for most companies that incorporate) the stock to be issued represents in excess of 10 percent of the acquiring company's outstanding shares.

> ✔ The acquiring company's shares (or the shares of the parent of the acquiring company, in the case of a triangular merger) are listed on a stock exchange and the shares to be issued exceed (roughly) 20 percent of the outstanding shares.

If the target company's shareholders are a large, nonhomogenized group (including nonaccredited investors), issuance of the acquiring company's shares must be registered with the Securities Exchange Commission (SEC) under the Securities Act of 1933. Allow one or two months to prepare and contemplate that the SEC may take some time to review the transaction. Ultimately, however, preparation time depends on the status of your audits. If they're recent and done by a recognized firm, then the preparation and filing can be completed in 30 days; otherwise, it's likely to take much longer.

Many issuances, particularly the ones made by big companies with well-established track records with the government, are not reviewed by the SEC.

If the price of the acquiring company shares moves significantly in one direction or another, the deal can potentially fall apart. In other words, stock-for-stock transactions (stock-for-stock being the underlying fundamental of a tax-postponed transaction) pose the risks one can expect to attend on any transaction that stretches the time between agreement and closing.

One way to reduce this risk is using a *collar,* a common method by which publicly traded companies establish a means of averaging the acquirer's (and the target's) stock over a (negotiated) period of time with a *ceiling* and *floor* (high and low share prices negotiated in advance), with the right of either party to walk away or renegotiate when the other party's stock falls below the collar limits or the lucky party's stock price rises above the collar. This device helps mitigate price contingencies but not the other unforeseen problems that can arise while a transaction is in process — the little things like strikes, natural disasters, customer and employee issues, and the like.

Acquisitions not involving mergers: Asset versus stock purchase

Acquisitions other than statutory mergers may involve either stock or asset purchases, entailing differing consequences (tax and nontax). Planning opportunities and pitfalls are more sharply drawn when the choice is between a taxable asset purchase and a taxable stock purchase. The buyer offers cash or stock and the target sells its assets, or the target shareholders sell their stock, for the offered consideration. Taxable asset purchases were severely affected by the Tax Reform Act of 1986, when Congress curtailed the ability to step up the buyer's tax basis in the assets being acquired at the cost of a single tax.

Delaware: The corporate choice!

If a company has chosen to become a corporation, or is investigating a potential sale, one issue is determining where the corporation needs to be *domiciled,* or legally based. Ordinarily one can minimize expenses by incorporating the business in the state where business is being conducted, thereby saving the cost of appointing an agent in another state like Delaware, the most popular state for those seeking a flag of convenience.

Rarely is an income tax advantage to be gained by domiciling a business outside of its principal place of operations. The income of a business operated in Massachusetts generally is subjected to the same Massachusetts income tax regardless whether technically it's a Massachusetts or a Delaware corporation. Engaging a firm of professional representatives, such as the Corporation Trust Company, to serve as resident agent in Delaware entails a modest but not so trivial fee each year.

On the other hand, the Delaware corporate statute is well drafted and contains few of the anomalies you sometimes finds in the general corporation laws of certain other states. Moreover, the secretary of state's office in Delaware is well staffed and those Delaware bureaucrats process papers at a high rate of speed. Furthermore, Delaware maintains a separate court system — the *Court of Chancery* — to adjudicate, without the nuisance (for corporate practitioners, anyway) of jury trials, issues involving the structure and governance of domestic corporations. Moreover, a modern statute such as Delaware's is generally permissive, and the glitches that can frustrate counsel attempting to close on a financing already have been ironed out. For example:

✔ The Delaware statute expressly acknowledges the validity of agreements among stockholders, signed by fewer than all the stockholders, pursuant to which voting arrangements superseding the statutory scheme — one share, one vote — are explicitly authorized. In some jurisdictions, such agreements are suspect, in which event it is necessary to go to the trouble of creating a voting trust, segregating stock into special classes or wrestling with the murky principles of a proxy coupled with an interest.

✔ Delaware law expressly contemplates the merger of Delaware corporations into corporations organized under the laws of other jurisdictions, a curious omission for many years in states like Massachusetts.

✔ Delaware permits shareholder action without the necessity of a meeting upon the execution of signed consents by a majority of the shares outstanding.

✔ The Delaware statute sets out the criteria, extensively given gloss by Delaware courts, for validating or rescinding transactions when a majority of the board of directors is comprised of *interested parties* (individuals with a personal financial stake in the outcome of a transaction), a common occurrence when an early stage company does business with its own shareholders and directors.

✔ Responding to the explosion in so-called *strike suits* brought only for the purpose of rewarding plaintiff's counsel, Delaware recently adopted a state-of-the-art provision that protects directors from liability unless some egregious breach of duty, principally involving personal profit, is proven.

✔ Law firms around the country are willing to prepare opinions on matters that involve Delaware corporate law because of the general familiarity of the corporate bar with the Delaware statute and cases used to interpret it. The ability of counsel to offer opinions about an issue is no trivial matter.

(continued)

(continued)

Without the requisite opinion of counsel, no public stock offering or merger can go forward. Loan agreements routinely require comfort from the company's counsel in the form of opinions. Incorporating in Delaware gives the founder assurances that counsel will be able to render and/or appraise the necessary opinions for underwriters, lenders, merger partners, and others to enable business aims to be accomplished.

Delaware permits corporations to stagger the terms of their directors (only one third standing for election in any year, for example) and impose supermajorities, a routine antitakeover measure that some states — California is an example — do not fully recognize. Indeed, Delaware has adopted a useful antitakeover provision, a *control share statute* along the lines of an Indiana statute that was upheld by the United States Supreme Court.

The foregoing is not designed as an uncritical hymn of praise favoring incorporation in the state of Delaware. Other states conform to advanced notions of corporate practice, and some — Maryland, for one, in the area of franchise taxes — actually are preferred on some issues. However, Delaware is the rod against which other possibilities are measured.

The election to purchase a target's assets rather than its stock may, however, be driven by business rather than tax considerations. And, the more frequently encountered business factor is the desire to leave certain shaky or otherwise unwanted assets and/or liabilities behind. A stock purchase generally means that the corporate enterprise, *warts and all* (did you know that the phrase "warts and all" originated with Oliver Cromwell's answer to the inquiry as to how realistically detailed his portrait should be?), is inherited; an asset purchase, on the other hand, paves the way for selectivity to pick and choose — at least in theory.

Thus, for example, contingent liabilities, or unknown amounts that may result from underfunded pension plans, pending lawsuits, or the like, may pose risks that a buyer is unwilling to assume. Similarly, certain assets may be unassignable without first procuring difficult-to-obtain consents — for example, leases and stock in foreign subsidiaries. Consents from existing lenders may also be required. Thus, the consent factor may, indeed, cut both ways. If the assets can't be assigned either by direct sale or by a change in control of the corporate owner, then perhaps they must be carved out of the transaction in a selected asset sale. If a direct assignment is prohibited, but not a change in control, a stock purchase may be in order.

State transfer taxes also can be an issue in the equation — chargeable in the course of asset transactions, but not usually on stock sales. The law of the home state may attach different consequences and formalities to asset sales followed by liquidation versus stock sales followed by a merger.

Depending on circumstances, of course, the acquiring company may affirmatively desire to continue the target in business, warts and all, if the target owns a valuable franchise that won't withstand a transfer outside of corporate solution to the acquiring company.

The tax-postponed merger

A tax-postponed merger generally entails a so-called *carryover,* or *substituted,* basis under the Internal Revenue Code, meaning that the tax basis of the assets in the hands of the target business (or its shareholders) is the same as it is in the hands of the acquiring business (or its shareholders) — in other words, an even swap. Strictly speaking, these transactions are not tax free but they are, instead, tax-postponed. Gain is not recognized until a shareholder disposes of the stock received in the transaction, but gain is ultimately recognized, unless the seller holds the received stock until death. At that time, the basis is stepped up to fair market value.

The three principal avenues available for a tax-postponed mergers (*reorganizations*), the A-, B-, and C-type reorganizations, get their names based on their position in the Internal Revenue Code. They're commonly referred to as the *acquisitive reorganizations,* because they generally involve the coming together of separate corporations.

- ✔ **The A-type** contemplates generally a merger of two firms under state law authorizing firms to merge or consolidate, and it is the more flexible of the lot because it admits the largest amount of nonstock consideration during the course of the transaction. As much as 50 percent (and sometimes even more) of the consideration paid can be other-than-voting-stock of the acquiring company. The nonstock consideration, referred to as "boot" for some reason, is taxed as gain to the sellers.

- ✔ **The B-type** is a voting stock-for-stock exchange in which the acquirer obtains control of the target in the bargain.

- ✔ **The C-type** reorganization involves the *practical merger,* an exchange by the target of substantially all its assets for voting stock of the acquiring company.

Four other specified reorganizations are lettered D through G, and these seven instances (A through G) are the only categories eligible for tax-postponed treatment.

Please keep in mind that this discussion of the law and regulations is a summary of technical, intricate, and complex concepts and rules. The statements need to be read in that context — that they are merely summaries, that numerous exceptions and qualifications can be found to any summary statement in these complicated areas, and that the rules are often in the process of being changed by Congress, the various agencies involved, and by court interpretations. Thus, consulting experienced counsel is therefore vital when considering and acting on the basis of legal concepts and in the face of legal rules. Nothing stated herein should be construed as legal advice nor the opinion of Mr. Bartlett as counsel or his law firm, Morrison & Foerster.

A host of other differences exist, but most are of a technical nature from a tax standpoint. Table 16-1 highlights some of the basic differences.

Table 16-1	Three Basic Types of Reorganization (Mergers)	
Type of Reorganization	Pluses	Minuses
A Type	Safest (usually) if there is any nonstock consideration.	Statutory formalities required
B Type	Can be simple if there are only a few target shareholders, and all consent	100 percent for voting stock; no other consideration (or "boot") allowed
C Type	Useful if the parties want to leave some assets and liabilities (not a lot) behind.	Stricter IRC rules than for an A type.

Exercising Appraisal Rights in Forced Merger

As mentioned in several earlier sections in this chapter, one of the prominent features of a merger is that, if the requisite number of shareholders vote in favor, the minority shareholders are compelled to go along, absent fraud or overreaching that might lead a judge to intervene. Indeed, the label *squeeze out merger* lives up to its name. If the consideration is cash or notes, the minority shareholders are squeezed out as owners of the relevant entity.

Let's start with the basics. When you have only one class of stock (common) and no supermajority rules in your charter, 50.0001 percent is probably all that's required from shareholders to approve a merger. If you have anything else — preferred stock, for example — then read your charter carefully to understand special shareholder rights in merger transactions. Preferred shareholders almost certainly require special handling.

Just because you can get shareholder approval doesn't mean that it's the only thing that's required if the postmerger plan is to continue the business largely as before. Contracts with customers, vendors, and lenders generally have provisions about assignments and required consents in the face of changes of control that are important and, in some cases, critical to the successful transition of the business to new owners. A target company must highlight or provide warnings about this, because, when it discovers such issues, the acquiring company will be concerned about them. What can be challenging is figuring out how to assess the likelihood that no such problems will occur while you're still in a quiet evaluation and due diligence period under a nondisclosure agreement (NDA) with the acquirer. For example, you don't want to alarm your best customers, especially when you don't know for sure whether the deal is going to go through.

Shareholders dissenting from a merger or consolidation (and following the prescribed procedures) are often entitled to a judicially supervised appraisal of (and payment for) the interests being surrendered. The rights in question usually are referred to as *dissenters'* or *appraisal rights,* a nonexclusive right to be paid fair value as determined judicially and after the fact.

Some states, such as New York, provide appraisal rights in nonmerger combinations — sales of assets — and certain types of charter amendments. Under Delaware law, the prescribed procedure is for the corporation involved to send out notice to its shareholders at least 20 days prior to the meeting notifying them of their appraisal rights. The demand for appraisal is due prior to the date of the meeting, and a petition to enforce the rights is due in Chancery Court 120 days after the effective date.

However, in many states, including Delaware, appraisal rights aren't available in a stock-for-stock exchange, if the target's shares are liquid. Why clutter up the courts with proceedings to establish values for securities that already are appraised on a daily basis on an auction market? On the other hand, appraisal rights are an absolute right in the sense that a shareholder may assert these rights even though the offer is demonstrably in excess of the value of his shares. Valuation techniques in appraisal procedures have been liberalized; in various courts, the *old block method* (various elements of value weighted and then averaged) has given way to valuation through any techniques or methods that are generally considered acceptable in the financial community and otherwise admissible in court.

Selling Less than All the Assets: Do Shareholders Have a Vote?

When the acquiring company's goal is acquiring less than 100 percent of your business's assets, the question arises whether under the relevant provisions of state law the transaction involves a sale of all or substantially all your assets, which in turn requires a vote by your shareholders.

In close cases, finding the answer may be difficult because the term *substantially* covers a lot of ground. One line of authority suggests that any sale that can be deemed outside the "ordinary course of business" would be considered a *practical merger,* triggering the requirement of a vote. A more conventional test focuses on the percentage of assets being sold. The spectrum runs from uncertainty to certainty. According to some authorities, if 51 percent of the assets are being disposed of, the presumption is that the statute applies and a vote is required. A higher threshold is suggested by a federal district court opinion that indicates the package needs to be "quantitatively vital to the operation of the corporation . . ." and to strike "at the heart of the corporate existence and purposes." The latter sometimes is referred to as the *quantitative test.* The drafters of the Revised Model Business Corporation Act use a number of words to reach essentially the same conclusion.

According to the official commentary, the phrase "all or substantially all," chosen by the drafters of the Model Act, means what it says. The phrase "substantially all" is synonymous with "nearly all" and was added merely to make it clear that statutory requirements could not be avoided by retention of some minimal or nominal residue of the original assets. A sale of several distinct manufacturing lines, while retaining one or more lines, is normally not a sale of "all or substantially all" even though the lines being sold are substantial and include a significant fraction of the corporation's former business. Similarly, a sale of a plant but retention of operating assets (for example, machinery and equipment), accounts receivable, good will, and the like, with a view toward continuing the operation at another location, is not a sale of "all or substantially all" of the corporation's property.

Of course, before making any decision along these lines, you need to consult with an attorney familiar with the applicable corporate law.

Equitable Constraints in Corporate Reorganizations: Mergers

In mergers, particularly if public firms are involved, a number of issues must be addressed concerning the rights of outsiders in the process — the *little guys* who are not part of the negotiations (for example, the *mom-and-pop* investor who owns 150 shares of the company safely tucked away in a retirement account). Who speaks for them, particularly when top management of the target has a vested interest in the outcome? What legal constraints impinge on the insiders' ability to feather their own nests?

Let's find out what protections are in place to ensure that the little guy isn't injured — at least too badly — in the merger game.

The Revlon Rule

In *Revlon, Inc., versus McAndrews & Forbes Holdings, Inc.,* the board rejected Pantry Pride's initial unsolicited takeover bid and adopted various defensive measures — a maneuver that ultimately involved issuing securities that would substantially dilute the value of the company's stock. When Pantry Pride continued to press its bid, Revlon opened negotiations with Forstmann Little & Co., a *white knight* (a preferred suitor) that the board ultimately favored, even though

Pantry Pride indicated it would top *any* Forstmann offer. The Delaware Supreme Court concluded that Revlon's resorting to a white knight meant that the "breakup of the company was inevitable. Revlon board's authorization permitting management to negotiate a merger or buyout with a third party was a recognition that the company was for sale." 506 A.2d 173, 182 (Del. 1986).

Business judgment rule: The entire fairness standard and enhanced scrutiny

The Delaware Supreme Court's seminal opinion in *Weinberger* versus *UOP, Inc.,* introduced the *entire fairness standard* to the world of corporate sales. The *Weinberger* decision put into place a two-pronged test, against which *interested-party transactions* would be judged for fairness in a substantive sense, providing a fair price for the minority, and procedural fairness or fair dealing, meaning that the transaction must proceed in a fair manner. An inside transaction must pass both thresholds to admit the board to its desired *safe harbor* — the defense that its judgment is insulated from legal attack by the *business judgment rule,* which says that the decisions of the company's board should be given presumptive weight. Note that, in contested takeover cases, the desire of the controlling management to keep their jobs can color the transaction when management opposes the raider's bid.

Verbiage aside, the bulk of the case law since the *Weinberger* decision has involved the question of fair procedure, and yet quibbling over procedure often is a polite surrogate for a judge's displeasure with a given substantive result. The procedural breakpoints favored in the decisions (almost all emanating from Delaware) are considered separately.

The Revlon Rule: Duty to auction

If insiders propose a merger that involves eliminating the non-inside-target shareholders, the *Revlon Rule* (based on the decision in Revlon versus MacAndrews and Forbes, see "The Revlon Rule" sidebar) suggests that the target is *in play,* up for grabs, for sale, and the proper issue before the directors no longer is whether the company should be sold but how to obtain the best deal possible for the shareholders.

The Revlon Rule, in the Delaware Supreme Court's language, means that, once the duty attaches, "the directors' role changes from defenders of the corporate bastion to auctioneers charged with getting the best price for the stockholders at a sale of the company." In some states, the constituency to be consulted by the directors has been expanded to include other groups, including the employees (and creditors, in the case of financially troubled companies), but in Delaware, shareholders' interests remain paramount once the target company has put itself "in play," meaning up for bids. It goes without saying that the auction must itself be fairly conducted; tipping off one favored bidder to the strategy of its competitor(s), unless independently justified, is grounds for injunctive relief.

Various interpretations of Revlon have been rendered by the Delaware courts since 1986, involving nice questions around such things as the "just say 'no'" defense and the issue whether shark repellents ("poison pills") are justified as maximizers of shareholder value. However, the *Revlon* holding remains in essence the law.

Fairness opinions

It is the rare merger involving a public company or companies that dispenses with an expert *fairness opinion* — an expensive letter most often from a bank or investment bank providing an opinion that the transaction is *fair* to non-participating minority shareholders. The object of the exercise is to help the board fit inside the friendly cloak of the *business judgment rule,* a (generally) insurmountable obstacle to the ambitions of strike-suit plaintiffs. Fairness opinions are creating their own body of jurisprudence — the procedures required if the device is to work as programmed in a subsequent lawsuit.

Protecting directors with the disinterested directors committee

A grand strategy in the game of protecting directors ordinarily entails the organization of a special committee of *disinterested* directors to review potentially tainted transactions, ordinarily with the advice of *hired guns* — independent lawyers and investment advisors specializing in mergers and retained for their expertise. Suggestive language in the Delaware cases has caused this *special committee* device to become commonplace.

The SEC on fairness opinions

When fairness opinions are disclosed — and the Securities and Exchanges Commission says they must be — in public proxy statements, the SEC staff now insists on dramatically increased disclosure. As one commentary reports:

In recent cases, including several major bank mergers . . . the staff has even gone beyond the face of the line items, requiring expanded disclosure of any or all the following:

1. A description of each valuation procedure followed and the basis for selecting it

2. A description of each assumption made in rendering the opinion and the basis for selecting it

3. Quantified examples of each type of analysis or procedure conducted, including financial projections, discounted cash values, comparable acquisitions, comparable companies, and stock trading prices

Any information contained in investment bankers' blue books (and even books prepared only for internal purposes that aren't shared with the client) is, in the SEC staff's view, fair game for disclosure.

The establishment of the committee in the first place is an indication that promoters of the deal are prepared to honor requirements of procedural fairness. Moreover, the committee's proceedings, if thorough, are designed to satisfy for a reviewing court that the transaction, as a matter of substance, is fair. The assumption at this point is that, given special committee approval (with no other procedural flaws), the burden on the issue of fairness shifts to the complaining party.

However, the mere appointment of a special committee doesn't accomplish the job of completely varnishing the business judgment shield. A reviewing court may, for example, become unimpressed with the committee's deliberations if the committee undershoots the proper concept of its role, is manipulated by the board, or is too reticent and doesn't understand that it's charged with the duty of maximizing value, including on occasion soliciting additional offers to compete with management's offer.

In the case of *Mills Acquisition Co. v. MacMillan, Inc.*, 559 A.2d 1261 (Del. S. Ct. 1989), the Delaware Supreme Court thought that the committee had neither negotiated hard enough to improve management's bid nor inquired adequately whether competing bids could be raised. Furthermore, it is now clear that based on language in the cases, the committee itself, versus management, needs to select its own advisors — that is, counsel and investment bankers. Conducting multiple meetings also is helpful to the committee. In fact, it's viewed as a healthy sign by the courts if meetings are adjourned to provide directors more time to study the issues.

An essential condition: Hart-Scott-Rodino

The Hart-Scott-Rodino Antitrust Improvements Act of 1976 (HSR) mandates advance warning to the Federal Trade Commission (and the U.S. Justice Department) of proposed acquisitions of greater than a certain size, plus a *waiting period* while the agency chews over the antitrust implications of the transaction. The transaction must be flagged if it generally involves transaction consideration in excess of $50,000,000. If the tests are met (and if no exemptions apply), both parties must make elaborate filings. The waiting period generally is 30 days, unless it's shortened upon application or extended by the government.

Majority of the minority

One measure often recommended to preserve fairness is neutering the votes of the controlling shareholder(s) regarding the merger, especially in a *freeze-out merger*; the transaction is made conditional on approval by the minority, the thought being that, under Delaware law, shareholder approval sanitizes interested-party transactions.

In this connection, you need to note that this kind of approval process can be structured in more than one way. The controlling shareholders can cast their vote in proportion to the votes of the minority or the controlling parties vote all their shares in favor if a majority of the minority affirmatively votes in favor of the merger. If more than a majority of all outstanding shares is required to approve the transaction, the latter procedure, which can turn a simple majority into a high percentage of the outstanding shares, obviously is preferable.

Closing the Deal

Mergers are a fairly complicated method of raising capital for your business, so don't ever contemplate going through the process without a team of seasoned professionals at your side. That said, the following is a step-by-step guide to getting liquid through a merger. Although you may not become an expert at mergers, it is *your* business, and you need to guide the process if you want to achieve your goals.

1. **Pre-position your company for a merger through strategic partner relationships, being active in your market with an eye out for interested parties, sensing who'd value your company more, assessing what drives their valuation, and keeping close tabs, especially on the *timing* of the deal.**

Fact is, closing a merger can occur in good times and bad times, depending on the overall market conditions and specifics in your industry or company. Timing can significantly impact your chances of a good valuation.

2. **Put your team together and get the board of directors behind the goal.**

    To do this right, you need an experienced merger attorney, a good tax accountant who's grounded in mergers and acquisitions, an investment banker or equivalent *deal-maker,* and a couple of your more trusted staff members (one from finance, one from marketing/sales, and one from engineering/operations) to help with preparations and presentations.

3. **Build your plan to start the process:**

    - **Team kickoff:** Outline goals, a deal structure, known prospects, and initial assignments.

    - **Preparations:** Draft a business plan, conduct an internal audit to identify problem areas and key values, create an expanded prospect list, and draft an *elevator pitch,* three-page deal summary, initial nondisclosure agreement form, thumbnail presentation, initial follow-up materials, and valuation rationale backup sheet.

    - **Final reviews and your valuation:** See whether your materials support your valuation goal. Adjust and finalize all documents. Reconfirm that you're targeting the right companies that will see the greatest value in acquiring your firm. Remember that the best prospects aren't necessarily the first ones that come to mind.

4. **Make your initial contacts.**

    Contacting your prospect's CEO in person is best. We caution against writing letters or using your elevator pitch on the phone or at trade events. If a contact is interested, require that he or she sign your nondisclosure agreement (NDA — see special warning below) before sending out your initial materials; then schedule the next meeting.

At this point, you may receive an offer from the company that you've targeted. If you haven't taken the preceding steps, you'll have to do most of them quickly to ascertain whether the offer is reasonable. That it won't be reasonable is likely, but you'll need to explain why it's off the mark. You'll need to put your team together to address all the issues and to put your best foot forward during the rest of the process. More important: Although receiving an offer is flattering, having two or three interested parties is much better. If you're inclined to sell, get more than one bidder involved! In our experience, the first bidder's is not necessarily the best bid, but it inspires the target's CEO to go out and find a better deal.

5. **Narrow down the competition.**

    Having more than one prospect in your pipeline is best, but more than three can be hard to handle. Conduct follow-up meetings (usually two, or three at the most) with each prospect to pitch your opportunity and answer their questions. Listen for clues about the prospect's values and sensitivities. This step can be fun!

6. **Move to close.**

As you would in any other sales situation, find and answer their objections; push for a term sheet to proceed. Ask them to make an offer, but be prepared to tell them what you want — possibly discuss internally beforehand the pros and cons of asking high versus asking closer to your target. Don't be surprised if the prospect gives you a low-ball initial offer. Know your valuation inside and out and be able to argue for every aspect of it. Have good comparables (prices and terms of similar deals) for other recent transactions in your industry at your fingertips for ready reference.

7. **Negotiate the Letter of Intent (LOI).**

This is the defining outline of your deal. It is the basis for the *definitive agreement* and needs to include at a minimum:

- The names of the parties and what is being acquired.

- Price(s) and type(s) of consideration, earnouts if applicable (an *earnout* being a method of tying part of the sales price to the achievement of future milestones).

- Form of transaction and basic legal structures intended.

- Conditions to closing: listing of all the agreements that need to be negotiated, reviews that have to be made, and consents or approvals that have to be received for the deal to close.

- Confidentiality and publicity: generally, recognizing your current NDA as applicable and not authorizing public announcements without mutual consents.

- Termination of LOI: Generally, this is stated as a deadline by which the definitive agreement must be signed. The LOI is an interim agreement that leads to the definitive agreement, which is comprehensive and supersedes the LOI. Expect it to be 30 to 90 days after the LOI, depending on due diligence requirements and the complexity of the deal. If a definitive agreement isn't signed, the LOI terminates and the deal is off. Keep the period short! You can always extend it if the parties are really trying to close.

- Optional provisions: See Step 8. Add as many of these in the LOI as possible. If the topic has to be addressed sometime before the merger can close, we think it's best to get the general understandings settled at this stage and reflected in the LOI. That way, they can't be construed as changing the character of the deal and warranting a price change. Better to find out now what the sticking points are instead of going through all the work and then having to nix the deal.

The letter of intent

The letter of intent (LOI) contains all the terms and conditions of a merger. As such, you must be certain that you understand every single sentence that your LOI contains and the potential impact it can have on the merger and on the capital that you plan to receive. Be particularly on the lookout for the following terms and conditions, which can come back to haunt you if you're not careful.

- **No-shop, No-solicit agreements:** Agreements by the seller to negotiate only with the buyer for a given period — not an auction.

- **Break-up or topping fees:** These are liquidated damages which are triggered if the no-shop agreement is breached and a competitive bid is accepted; the seller would like a free hand to look elsewhere but buyers do not want their bid auctioned . . . and won't spend due diligence money without protection.

- **Collars:** It's better to cover collars early — in the LOI.

- **Holdbacks or escrow:** These may be required to back up the representations and warranties, but try to avoid payments contingent on future performance (earnouts), which can be an invitation to a deferred lawsuit.

- **Environmental issues:** A big topic, especially if any real estate is involved; special environmental auditors may need to be used to report on any potential or real environmental issues in the sale.

- **Due diligence:** It takes two to eight weeks to do and much of your staff's time. Be sure to make complete disclosures, because that makes things much easier in the long run.

- **Representations and warranties:** Keep these out of the LOI except to show what has been disclosed so far in the process. This needs to follow the due diligence. Sometimes the key staff must affirm with signatures that they have completely and accurately disclosed all. You can now obtain insurance for this purpose, and it is worth considering.

- **Nonproselytize:** You definitely don't want the buyer to review your operations in due diligence and then just steal your key staff, whom he's identified in the process! Actually this is good topic to cover in your NDA, because the buyers are exposed to your top people (those on your team) from the outset.

- **Key personnel:** Identify who these people are and any special deals for them, including their positions and compensation.

- **How to deal with existing stock options and with restricted stock.**

- **Employment agreements.**

- **Consulting agreements and noncompete agreements.**

- **How benefit programs will be handled:** You may be able to agree only in general terms at the point of the LOI signing, but these will be hot topics by the time you make employee announcements! Plan to spend time on these.

- **Operations and responsibilities:** Even if not covered in the LOI, you need to have answers about how future operations will be conducted to address your own, your employees', and your customers' questions.

8. **Due diligence commences. Hart-Scott filings prepared.**

9. **Definitive Agreement signed.**

   A public announcement (if either company is public) is made. Hart Scott filed.

10. **Prepare and file proxy materials (if the target is public).**

    Due diligence continues.

11. **Hart-Scott expires; other consents (in other words, targeting the landlord as consent to *changes in control*) are secured.**

12. **Shareholders of target (sometimes, also the acquirer) vote in favor.**

13. **Closing. New board takes over. Congratulations!**

Disclosing the deal to your staff and the public

Hardly anything can be as harmful to your business as for your employees, customers, competitors, vendors, or lenders to inadvertently find out that you're *shopping* the company before the deal is well in hand. All it takes is one person to start passing the rumor and you have a big problem on your hands. Pare the list of those in the know down to only your team and only those outsiders who sign your NDA.

Most NDAs are signed by an officer representing the buyer. That, however, is inadequate because others in the firm will hear of the potential deal without knowing of the NDA restrictions. That's where leaks can arise.

Structure your NDA so that it is personal and so that each person who has a need to know at the buyer's company is required to sign and return it to you. Apply the same rule to your internal staff. Include all signatures on the same page, and be sure that each person receives a copy of that page so that he or she knows who's cleared. Keep the cleared list to no more than five people on each side until the LOI is signed. Add to the list as necessary to enable the start of due diligence. Hold off on public announcements and lifting the NDA until the definitive agreement is signed. Allow one trusted person (perhaps your CFO) a little latitude to discuss it in private during due diligence with those outsiders who must consent to the deal (for example, the landlord and the bank), if you think that you may have a problem obtaining their consent.

When you're ready to disclose the deal to your staff, be prepared to answer all their questions. They're apt to panic. Have plans in place for dealing with the issues: What's going to happen to my job, my benefits, my pay, and so on?

Start the integration process with the acquirer as soon as possible by scheduling group and one-on-one meetings for your employees with their counterparts or supervisors at the acquirer's firm. Certain customers may require special handling, and of course, all those who have to consent to the deal must receive special treatment. Otherwise, limit your announcement to a mutually agreed-upon press release with one point of contact who has a well-prepared FAQ list as a guide to answering calls.

Part IV
The Part of Tens

The 5th Wave   By Rich Tennant

"The next time we get an additional round of funding, don't say anything. You're lucky I convinced them 'Ka-Ching, Ka-Ching!' was Swahili for Thank you, Thank you!"

In this part . . .

*E*very *For Dummies* book ends with top-ten lists —
this one is no different. Here, we present tips that will
help you to quickly locate and raise the capital that your
business needs to grow and to thrive.

Chapter 17

Ten Best Sources of Fast Cash

· ·

· ·

Money makes the world go 'round, and nowhere is this more the case than in the wide world of business. Cash is the high-octane fuel for making any business go — and the more cash you have, the better it's going to run. Cash pays for plenty, including:

✔ The office supplies you need to do your work

✔ The salaries of the people who help you do your work

✔ Your rent and utilities

✔ Almost anything else that you need to make your business a business.

To make a long story short: no cash — no business.

Although the purpose of this book is to present various ways of raising capital, the bad news is that many of them take time — often weeks, months, and sometimes even years. And, if you've been in business for any time at all, you know that when you really need cash to pay the bills, waiting weeks or months for financing is a going-out-of-business plan.

So, if you really need cash fast, what can you do?

The good news is that a number of options are available to you if you're looking for some fast cash. In fact, this chapter is all about a list of ten of the better options. Each has its own pluses and minuses, so be sure to carefully consider your financial situation before you settle on a particular approach.

Borrowing from Family and Friends

Many business owners — particularly owners of start-ups — first turn to family and friends for the capital they need to run a company once they've exhausted their own funds. This source of financing offers benefits to both parties. The business owner often gets a favorable interest rate and flexible payment terms with no need for credit checks or loan applications, and the lenders get an opportunity to become early investors in an enterprise that may pay off handsomely when it matures.

Keep in mind, however, that more than a few friendships and family relationships have been utterly ruined because of business disagreements or misunderstandings. Before accepting a dime from your family or friends, be sure that you put all these understandings, along with specific loan terms, such as the total amounts borrowed, interest rates, and loan terms (the number of months), into writing. If you're talking about a lot of money, you need to have your lawyer either draft this agreement or at least review it before you use it. Oh, and be sure to take a look at Chapter 3 where we cover this topic in quite some detail.

Utilizing Credit Cards

Credit cards offer one of the quicker and easier ways to raise capital for a business, and the histories of some of today's more famous companies are replete with stories of founders using their credit cards to fund their start-ups. Of course, all this quickness and easiness comes at a sometimes hefty price — interest rates that some may consider little better than what you can get from your friendly neighborhood loan shark, anywhere from 11 percent to 18 percent to 22 percent and sometimes more.

First, the good news about credit cards:

- ✔ They're supereasy to get. If you can sign your name, you probably qualify.
- ✔ If you've got a good credit history, you may qualify for a high line of credit, from $25,000 to $50,000, and even more.
- ✔ They're extremely flexible: Just about every store in the world accepts them, and you can use them for cash advances through a bank.

Of course, with the good comes the bad:

- ✔ They're supereasy to get. That means it's easier than ever to get into financial trouble when you fall behind in your ability to pay off your charge cards.
- ✔ Interest rates can be high, sometimes up to 20 percent and more.
- ✔ Membership fees, cash advance fees, and other fees can add additional costs to an already expensive approach to raising capital.

For short-term capital needs, credit cards provide a convenient and flexible way to raise the cash you need. However, if you don't pay them back quickly, the money you borrow with your credit cards can quickly become expensive, indeed.

Taking Out a Home-equity Loan

Need cash for your business? Own a house or other real estate? Have you got any equity? For many people who need cash fast — whether for their businesses or personal reasons (that trip to Tahiti sounds pretty nice!) — a home-equity loan is the best thing since sliced bread. Not only can you quickly raise a substantial amount of money, but your expenses and interest also may be tax deductible.

A home-equity loan is a loan from a financial institution such as a bank or savings and loan against the equity that you've established in your home. Say, for example, that you bought a home ten years ago for $75,000 and that you still owe $65,000 on it. Furthermore, assume that today that same home has appreciated in value and is now worth $125,000. The equity in your home is the difference between what your home is worth and the amount of money that you owe on it:

$125,000 – $65,000 = $60,000

So, as you can see in the example above, the home has built up $60,000 in equity during the ten years that you've owned it. Equity is great, but there's one problem with it: You can't get to it unless you sell your home. No ATM is built into the wall of your garage (at least not ours!) where you can withdraw your equity — $40 or $60 or $100 at a time — whenever you feel like doing so. That's where the home-equity loan comes in.

A home-equity loan is exactly that: a loan against the equity that you've built up in your home. How much money can you get? The answer to that question depends on a variety of factors, including:

- **The amount of your first mortgage:** Different lending programs — with different lending terms and conditions — are available for loans of less than $100,000, for example, and for loans of $100,000 and more.

- **Your credit history:** The better your credit history, the more money most lenders are willing to lend to you. As the quality of your credit history declines, so too does the amount of money you'll be able to raise from a home-equity loan.

- **Loan term:** The number of years of the term of your loan — five, ten, 15, 20, or whatever — also have an impact on the amount of money that you'll be able to raise. The longer the term of your loan, the smaller each monthly payment is. This may qualify you for a higher loan amount.

✔ **Loan-to-value (LTV) requirements:** Your lender usually is willing to loan an amount of money that equals only a certain percentage of the total value of your home when you combine the values of your first mortgage and your home-equity loan. If, for example, the total value of your home is $125,000, and your loan has an 80 percent *loan-to-value requirement,* that means the total of what you owe on your first mortgage and your home-equity loan cannot exceed $100,000 (80 percent of $125,000). So, if you still owe $65,000 on your home, you'd be qualified for a home-equity loan (assuming good credit history and sufficient income) of up to $35,000.

Obtaining a home-equity loan can be a fairly quick proposition. Some online lenders offer approval in mere seconds, but it's always better to anticipate your needs and give yourself several weeks to shop for the best deal, undergo the application and approval processes, and get that check in the mail. When you apply for a home-equity loan, you'll probably have the opportunity to decide whether you want your money all in one check or in the form of a line of credit against which you can write checks up to your credit ceiling. What's nice about the latter option is that you pay interest only on the money that you've taken against your line of credit.

Finally, don't forget that when you sign up for a home-equity loan, you're using your home as collateral in the event that you default in making loan payments. In other words, you can lose your home if you don't make payments on your home-equity loan. Be sure to keep this in mind before signing on the dotted line!

Considering an Uncollateralized Personal Loan

How's your credit? If it's good, and if you aren't already overextended on your credit cards or other unsecured loans, you may be a good candidate for an uncollateralized personal loan.

Every bank, credit union, savings and loan, and other financial institution offers *uncollateralized personal loans* — often known as signature loans — and they do so with an extremely wide variety of payment terms and rates of interest. Because the loan is unsecured — the bank has no right to your property in the event of a default — interest rates generally are higher than secured loans such as home-equity or automobile loans. Longer loan terms often result in lower interest rates — increasing the amount of financing for which you may be eligible.

Keep in mind that a longer loan term generally means that you're also going to end up paying more money in interest over the entire life of the loan, despite a slightly lower interest rate. Be sure to get all the details before you sign on the dotted line!

While your regular bank or financial institution is the first place to check for personal loans — if you have a long-standing relationship with a bank, your chances of securing a loan increase — the number of online loan providers has exploded. If you'd like to expand your loan options, give one or more of these online financial services a try:

- E-LOAN: www.eloan.com
- LendingTree.com: www.lendingtree.com

Refinancing a First Mortgage

Falling mortgage interest rates are good news if you own a home — especially if you're stuck with a high-interest-rate home loan. Falling rates also are good news if you need some (relatively) quick cash for your business. Lower interest rates offer you the opportunity to refinance your first mortgage. But, not only does the lower interest rate buy you a lower monthly payment, it may also enable you to take out some of the equity you've built in your home — especially if the value of your home has risen over time.

For example, if you currently owe $100,000 on your home and the value of your home now is actually $150,000, it's possible to refinance your home for more than you owe with a lender that requires a 90 percent loan-to-value ratio. That makes eligible for a loan of up to $135,000 (assuming your credit history is good and your income is sufficient). Thus, $100,000 of the new loan goes to pay off the holder of your original first mortgage, and you've freed up the remaining $35,000 to go right into your pocket for any purpose you want — including a much-needed capital infusion in your business, if that's what you want.

Remember, however, that when you refinance your first mortgage, your mortgage clock starts ticking all over again. So, if you originally had a 30-year mortgage, and you had only ten years to go until you paid off your home — and owned it free and clear — a new mortgage is going start at the beginning of a new 30- year payment term. If you long to own your own home free and clear, then taking this approach isn't going to get you closer to achieving that goal. In fact, doing so takes you farther away than ever — an outcome that may not be in your long-term interest.

Selling Some Assets

If you need some quick cash, you may be able to convert some of your assets into cash fairly quickly. Almost any asset can become cash: computers, office equipment, inventory, cars, trucks — the list goes on. Auctions always are popular places for businesses to sell assets, or simply placing an advertisement in the paper or networking with other businesspeople also may work.

Keep in mind, however, that you do need certain kinds of assets to operate your business. Be careful not to sell off critical assets, or to hobble your employees by not providing adequate equipment for them to do their jobs.

Borrowing Against a Life Insurance Policy

Depending on what kind of life insurance policy you have (assuming you have one in the first place!), you may be able to borrow money against it. For years, *cash value* life insurance policies, including such variants as whole life, variable life, universal life, and variable universal life, were touted as being terrific investment vehicles, and they were — mostly, however, for the salespeople who sold them and got to pocket fat commissions as a result. When you buy a cash value policy, you're not only buying a death benefit, you're also buying a savings component that grows as you pay your premiums. In most cases, you can borrow funds against this accumulated cash value at a favorable interest rate.

Term life insurance policies provide coverage for a specific period of time, often for up to 30 years, and are increasingly popular with more insurance buyers. However, unlike cash value policies, they have zero cash value unless you die. And for most of us, death is an event that makes the cash value of term policies quite frankly irrelevant.

If you're unsure what kind of policy you have, and what your financing options are, check with your insurance agent or call the company directly. If you have a cash value policy — and especially if you've had the policy for a number of years — you may be pleasantly surprised to find that you've got a pretty good-sized chunk of money to work with.

Factoring Your Receivables

If your business is like many, you probably have a lot of money tied up in your accounts receivable, the term accountants use for the money owed your company for products and services delivered to customers but not yet paid for by them. Whenever you sell something to a customer without requiring complete payment either in advance or as a condition of receiving your product or service (like those folks at McDonald's who make you pay before they give you

Factoring receivables: FleaTek Industries

Factoring receivables is a very commonly used source of capital for many businesses. Why? Because it's (relatively) quick and it's (relatively) easy. A typical factoring scenario works like this:

✔ FleaTek Industries needs cash to make its payroll next week, and needs it fast. FleaTek's CEO locates a *factor,* a person who factors receivables.

✔ The factor offers to buy FleaTek's receivables for 70 percent of their total due upfront, and then an additional 20 percent after the receivables are paid. The factor keeps 10 percent of the total for its troubles.

✔ FleaTek generates invoices for its products and services upon delivery, and sends them to the factor, who, in turn, forwards them to

FleaTek's customers for payment directly to the factor.

✔ The factor writes a check for 70 percent of the invoices and sends it to FleaTek within a few days after receipt.

✔ If FleaTek's customers pay later than 30 days, then the factor keeps more of the money collected — 13 percent for 31 to 60 days, and 15 percent for up to 90 days. Invoices unpaid after 90 days are sold back to FleaTek.

✔ As invoices are paid, the factor cuts another check to FleaTek for the remainder of its cut.

That's it!

your Quarter Pounder with cheese, French fries, and chocolate shake), you create a *receivable* — a promise to pay you later. How much later depends on the terms of your agreement with your customer, but often it's 30 days.

When you factor your receivables, you're essentially selling them for cash. However, the person buying your receivables purchases them at a discount. That discount determines how much money you'll get when you factor your receivables.

Factoring can put a lot of money into your pocket quickly and, although relatively expensive — you may pay the equivalent of a 20 or 30 percent interest rate or more for your money — if you need cash now (and who doesn't?), it's one of the better ways of providing you with it.

Borrowing Against 401 (k)

We'll guess that if you've worked for some time, you probably have quite a nice little nest egg built up in your 401(k) retirement plan. Not only have you had the opportunity to make regular tax-free contributions to your plan, but, if your company is like many others, you've also received corporate matching contributions. The net effect of all these contributions can really add up over time.

Of course, knowing that all that money is going to be waiting for you when you're ready to retire in ten or 20 years is nice, but what good can it do for you now — when you really need the capital for your business. If you simply withdraw money from your account, not only will you have to pay income taxes on it in the year you take it out, but you'll also likely have to pay additional penalties (generally 10 percent if you're 59½ years old or younger).

However, you *can* tap the power of your 401(k) by taking a 401(k) loan.

According to the Profit Sharing/401(k) Council of America (PSCA — We didn't make that up!), about 75 percent of all 401(k) plans allow employees to borrow against their accounts. How much can you borrow? The usual amount is up to half of your vested account balance, generally up to $50,000.

Here are some pluses to a 401(k) loan:

✔ Great interest rates — typically only 1 percent or 2 percent above prime.

✔ No credit check!

✔ Relatively long loan term of up to five years.

However, they also carry some pretty compelling negatives aspects:

✔ Not the fastest way to raise capital.

✔ You may be required to pay $200 to $400 in application fees.

✔ If you're laid off or quit your job, you may be required to pay off your loan quickly — within 30 to 90 days.

Although many financial professionals say that taking a 401(k) loan need only be done as a last resort, sometimes you gotta do what you gotta do. And if it that means the difference between a business that crashes and burns because of lack of capital to pay your bills, and one that takes off and flies, then a 401(k) loan may be just the ticket for you.

Playing the Lottery

Okay, we know it may sound a little kooky, but you just never know. Playing the lottery is far from a surefire way to raise capital for your business. In fact, depending on where you live and which game you play, you probably have a much better chance of getting hit twice by lightning than of hitting the jackpot. Yet people do still win the lottery every day of the week, and, if it's time for things to go your way, it just may be your lucky day!

Alternatively, you may consider purchasing a ticket to Las Vegas and a copy of *Gambling For Dummies* by our good friend Richard Harroch (and Lou Kreiger and Arthur Reber). We think that if you're going to seriously consider going this route, you may as well go all out.

Chapter 18

Ten Creative Ways to Raise Capital

. . . .

In This Chapter

▶ Getting advance payments from customers

▶ Swapping stock for payables

▶ Building strategic alliances

▶ Engaging a placement agent

▶ Finding an angel investor

. . . .

*O*kay. You've taken all the traditional routes to obtaining the capital you need to run your business — you've applied for loans, you've maxed out your credit cards, your friends and family hide when they see you coming — and you still need capital. What should you do next? Give up and start researching the differences between Chapter 7 and Chapter 11 bankruptcy?

No — not even close. The fight to obtain capital for your business has just begun. If you've reached the end of the road with your conventional arsenal of financing tools, here are ten of the best unconventional tools to get you the money that you need — when you need it. Of course, just because these ways of raising money are a bit off the beaten track doesn't mean that you can't put them to work for you *before* you exhaust your more conventional approaches to raising capital — in fact, you may just want to put them to work for you right *now*.

Getting Advance Payment from Customers

When it comes to financing your business, nothing is sweeter than getting your customers to pay you before you deliver the goods or services that they have agreed to purchase from you. If you're particularly astute at negotiating deals with your customers, you may be able to do just that. And if you can then turn around and convince your vendors to wait 30 days or more before you have to pay them for the materials and inventory that you buy from them, you'll end up really multiplying the positive impact on your cash.

Always ask your customers for a cash deposit of at least 10 percent of the total price before you start work. Whenever possible, try to get half or even complete payment in advance. If the work that you perform occurs over a relatively long period of time, then be sure to ask for progress payments — every week, month, or quarter — that will enable you to stay ahead of the financing game.

Extending Your Payables

In our discussions on improving cash flow (see Chapter 19), we talk about making sure that no invoice is paid before its time — the longer you keep your money in *your* bank account, the better your cash position is. Similarly, we suggest that you always pay your bills on time. In an ideal world, you would make your payments on the day that your bills come due — not a day before or a day after.

Another approach exists, however, and it's an approach that keeps cash in your hands for as long as possible, providing you with a ready source of cash when you need it most. "Extending your payables" may simply be a nicer way of saying, "Paying your bills late," but sometimes paying your bills late can give you the extra shot of capital that you need to stave off financial disaster and keep your business afloat.

Be upfront with your vendors about your payment extension plan, and use this option only when you have no other choice. By paying your bills late, you're breaking your agreement with your vendors — who likely think that they need their money as much as you need yours — and you're putting your future business relationships with them in no small amount of jeopardy. Be candid about the reasons why you need to extend your payables, and then schedule frequent but modest payments as evidence of good faith.

Swapping Stock for Payables

Picture this: Your firm owes its creditors a lot of money, and you don't have the cash in hand to pay your bills as they come due. What can you do to avoid defaulting on these transactions while digging your company out of the hole in which it finds itself? If you have a corporation with stock, why not turn your creditors into part-owners of your company by swapping some of your stock for the debt that you owe?

If your company has a pool of unissued stock available for distribution, offering stock in exchange for debt relief won't impact your cash reserves at all — a good thing when you're strapped for cash. And if your company's stock is attractive to your customers, such a swap can turn out to be beneficial for you and can remove the burden of debt from your shoulders.

Seeking Assistance from State, Regional, and Federal Programs

The government is your friend, and the government wants your business to succeed. The more companies that succeed, the fewer people who are out of work. And the fewer people out of work, the more people who pay taxes — something the government holds near and dear to its heart.

If you have a small business, start your search for capital with the Small Business Administration (www.sba.gov), and then check with your state and local governments to see what kinds of financial assistance programs they offer. If you have a large business, your state and local governments will be particularly interested in making sure that your business does well and that the furthest thought from your mind is moving your company to a different city or state. Cash grants, tax incentives and credits, and much more are available for the asking, so just ask.

Establishing Strategic Alliances

Is something about your company attractive enough to compel other companies to want to affiliate with you? Perhaps you have a Web site that gets a lot of traffic, or your products are highly visible in the industry — for example, a certain brand of tool among construction workers. In certain circumstances, strategic alliances offer an opportunity to generate cash or soft-dollar assistance in the form of services and products.

Say, for example, that your Web site plays host to 100,000 unique visitors a day, and the demographics of those visitors are attractive to companies that manufacture sports cars. One company in particular may be willing to pay you to appear on your site, or to provide you with financing to develop other mutual projects of interest.

Alternatively, this same company may be willing to include you in its marketing efforts or to keep you in the public eye or get you better distribution for some period of time. All these things can strengthen your business and hold the promise of future cash in the bank for you.

Exploring Investment Partnerships

It seems like lawyers, accountants, consultants, and other professionals always are on the lookout for a good investment. If your business is doing well, and the opportunities for growth look good, don't be surprised when professionals that you've hired to work with your firm approach you to see whether they can invest in your firm. When the professionals who work for you invest in your firm, everyone benefits: You get the cash that you need and, when your company performs well, your investors can get a nice return on their investment.

So the next time your professionals come looking in your neighborhood, be ready with a presentation about your business that you can pitch to them on a moment's notice.

Setting Your Sights Offshore

Capital markets are truly global nowadays. If your company is large enough and has a high enough profile, limiting your search for capital to local sources, or even to sources in the United States, isn't necessary. Just as American investors always are on the lookout for a good investment, investors in other countries also are on the lookout for lucrative places to park their money. This isn't an easy path, and it's definitely not fast, but it may be the option that you're looking for.

If you're interested in attracting foreign capital, you need to do a couple of things:

✔ Become an attractive investment for foreign investors. Target a specific group of potential investors and then be sure that your business is aligned in a way that will be appealing to this group.

✔ Get word to potential foreign investors that you have an opportunity in which they'll be interested, and then induce them to come and take a look. This tactic means networking like crazy with potential investors — and friends and associates of potential investors — and getting your company's name into the foreign press. If you're really serious about attracting foreign capital, it may be worth your while to hire someone to represent you in the countries you're targeting.

Finding the Right Placement Agent

Getting the right placement agent can be worth its weight in gold. A placement agent is someone hired to find prospective investors for a company.

Just as having a great salesperson selling your products and services can bring you more business than you know what to do with, a great placement agent can bring you more investors than you know what to do with. If you're looking for investors — not simply loans of cash to help you get through a tough spot in your operation — give a placement agent a shot at generating capital for your business.

For further information about placement agents, be sure to read all about them — who they are, how they work, and how much you can expect to pay — in Chapter 8.

Networking at Industry Conferences

Attending industry conferences is a great way of attracting people who may be willing to pump a bit of good old-fashioned cash into your operation. Here is just a sample of some of the nationwide industry conferences that are specifically designed to pull together companies looking for capital and investors looking for companies in which to invest their money and that provide companies with the information they need to more effectively raise capital. Every big city, and many smaller cities, offers conferences like these. Actively attend them and make a point of meeting as many people as you can while you're there. It takes only one — the right one — to get you the capital you need.

 ✔ Innovest (Cleveland, Ohio) http://www.innovest.org/
 ✔ Capital Venue (New England) http://www.capitalvenue.com/
 ✔ VentureNet (Irvine, California) http://www.venturenet.org/

Hooking Up with Angel Investors

For many companies, angel investors are made in heaven. An angel investor is an individual who has the financial wherewithal to invest directly in the companies of his or her choice. As the number of people who have earned true wealth increases, so do the number of opportunities for companies to hook up with these angel investors who want to put their wealth to work.

Because of the inefficiencies involved in pulling together companies that need capital with the people who have capital, a number of organizations have sprouted up to enable companies seeking capital to meet and network with angels. For an extensive discussion of matching services that pair up angel and other investors with companies looking for capital, be sure to check out Chapter 6. And for more information specifically about angel investors — and their advantages and disadvantages — be sure to take a look at Chapter 4.

Chapter 19

Ten Steps to Improve Your Cash Flow — Now!

. . . .

In This Chapter

▶ Requiring immediate payment

▶ Invoicing more often

▶ Budgeting your cash

▶ Staying on top of your accounts receivable

▶ Making sure that your invoices are right

. . . .

*W*hen you own your own business, or when you're involved in the management of one, you're probably well aware of the importance of cash flow — the difference between what comes in and what goes out. Cash is the lifeblood of every organization. It pays for your employees' salaries, their medical benefits, the chairs they sit in, and the computers they use to do their jobs. It pays your company's rent or mortgage payment, and it pays to keep the lights on and the water running. It pays your salespeople's expense accounts, and it pays for your outside accounting firm, your corporate lawyer, and your overnight delivery charges. Cash goes in and out of a business all the time.

Not all cash flows are created equal, however. There is the good kind of cash flow (*positive,* when you're bringing more money into your bank account than you're sending out of it) and the bad kind of cash flow (*negative,* when you're sending more money out of your bank account than you're bringing into it). Every business experiences positive and negative cash flows — it's a natural part of doing business. If your burn rate — the speed at which you spend your cash — is too high, and your cash isn't being constantly replenished fresh from the sales of products or services, you soon find yourself in financial trouble. Smart businesses manage their cash flows to maximize positive cash flows and minimize negative ones.

In this chapter, we take a close look at how to create more positive cash flow. Although you don't have to put all these recommendations into practice to have a positive and lasting effect on your cash, the more that you do implement, the greater the impact will be.

Requiring Payment Immediately (If Not Sooner!)

When was the last time you bought a pint of Ben & Jerry's at your local grocery store, a roll of stamps at the post office, or ordered a book from Amazon.com? Chances are, you've long taken something about these common transactions for granted: Before you can take your ice cream out of the store, put your stamps in your purse, or have that book shipped with just a click of your mouse, you have to pay for it. In advance.

So why do you give your clients or customers 30 or 60 days or more to pay *their* bills?

When you sell products and services to your clients and customers and then allow them to defer paying for those products and services, you're floating them a loan. Not only that, but you're floating them a loan for which you receive no interest. Payment terms such as these are not good for your cash flow; in fact, they can really put the hurt on it.

Looking for a quick way to jump-start your cash flow? Then you can require your clients to pay you when they receive your products or services. If you really want to improve your cash flow, require payment *in advance* of when you deliver your products or services, or at least get a deposit. Do that and, believe us, you'll have a cash flow made in heaven.

Don't Pay Bills Any Sooner than You Have To

Just as you want your clients to pay sooner rather than later, when you're looking to improve your cash flow, you want to avoid paying your bills for as long as you possibly can. The slower you pay, the better your cash flow, all other things being equal.

We're not suggesting that you sit on your net/30 bills for three or four months while your vendors frantically call to get you to pay. That just wouldn't be right. Not only that, but if you decide to do business that way, you'll soon find that your vendors aren't quite so happy to do business with you. What we *are* suggesting is that you drag out your payment until the very last moment. If your payment is due in 30 days, don't pay on day 10, and don't pay on day 20. Cut the check and stick it in the mail so that your vendor receives it on day 30.

Payment terms don't come out of thin air. Although your vendor may have a standard policy of requiring customers to pay immediately — or even in advance — everything in business is negotiable, even when the so-called "standard policy" says that it isn't.

So when you purchase a product or service from a vendor, ask for payment terms. When they say that they'll do net/10, ask for net/30. When they want you to pay right now, tell them instead that you want a 2 percent discount for making payment within 20 days. And when a vendor absolutely refuses to extend payment terms to you, then consider using a credit card to make payment. That way you'll still benefit from having the cash in your bank during the period of time that it takes for your credit card company to bill you for the transaction and then for you to pay the invoice. Remember: Every day that you delay payment for a product or service you've already received (and perhaps already resold to your own customers and collected payment on — now, that's *smart* cash management!) is a big plus for your cash flow.

Invoicing Frequently

Another great way of improving your cash flow is to send out invoices frequently. Here's an example of what we're talking about: Say that you're the owner of a management consulting firm with a six-month contract to complete a salary and compensation study for a small manufacturing company, and then to develop and recommend a new compensation and benefits plan. Which of the following two payment alternatives do you think will have a positive impact on your cash flow, and which one do you think will have a negative impact?

✔ You negotiate a fixed-price contract for $75,000 for the entire job, with payment to be made in full upon delivery of your final report six months after you start work.

✔ You negotiate a fixed-price contract for $75,000 for the entire job, with five equal payments to be made during the course of performance based on completion of the following milestones:

- Contract execution

- Delivery of salary comps

- Mid-project progress presentation to management

- Delivery of draft findings

- Delivery of final report and presentation to management

Clearly, the second alternative is the better one in terms of cash flow.

In the first example, you must wait a full six months before you can even invoice your client for the $75,000 owed to you under your contract. That means it's going to take a minimum of seven months from the time that you start the project until the time you're paid for it. During that time, you're performing work for your client — paying your employees' salaries and benefits, paying rent and utilities on your office space, and all the other expenses that go along with the way you do business. In other words, a lot of cash will be going out of your bank account with nothing coming in — definitely a recipe for bad cash flow.

In the second example, not only do you jump-start your cash flow by receiving a payment upon contract execution — *before* you start the project — but you also receive payments on a regular basis during the performance of your project. So, as you draw funds from your bank account to pay employees, overhead, and project expenses, periodic payments from your client are replenishing these funds. If you structure your contract payment schedule right, you may very well have a positive cash flow for the duration of the project.

Billing for your work or product delivery as often as you can always is going to be in your interest. Although billing this way may not really come into play when your project durations are short (for example, if you're delivering 100 widgets on one day and invoicing immediately), as the durations of your projects or deliveries become longer, it can play an increasingly important role in building and maintaining a strong positive cash flow.

Encouraging Fast Payment with Discounts

When you've decided to let your clients or customers pay you after you've delivered a product or service to them (instead of before), it may be in your interest to give them a bit of extra motivation to pay their bills more quickly. Faster payment by your customers improves cash flow for you.

One of the most common ways of motivating customers to pay more quickly is giving them a discount for prompt payment. This discount — typically from 0.5 percent to 2 percent for payment in 10 to 20 days — is negotiable and at your discretion. When you want to give it a try to see whether a prompt payment will improve your cash flow, start by offering the smallest possible percentage — say, 0.5 percent — for payment in 10 days. If this offer doesn't nudge your customers into making quicker payments, consider edging up your discount until they respond.

Try not to get carried away with prompt payment discounts. Is it going to be worth giving your clients 5 percent off their invoices when you can get your cash only a few days sooner? Probably not. Be sure to carefully analyze the impact of prompt-payment discounts on your financial position by calculating the equivalent interest rates for the discounts *before* you implement them, not after.

Budget Your Cash

Although cash flow can be predicted to some degree, an element of uncertainty always remains. A client may decide to pay late, your company may have a major unanticipated expense, or a key customer may go bankrupt and default on payments for a substantial order. In this uncertain world, creating a cash budget is a good idea, because you can use it to anticipate your cash flows into the future.

A cash budget is an estimate of a company's cash position for a particular period — a week, a month, or any period that you decide to track. Use your current cash position as the baseline for your report, and then project all cash in (payments from customers or other sources) and all cash out (payments to vendors, employees, and other entities), noted by date and amount.

Have a long-term cash budget of six to twelve months as a reference and overall guide. Manage your business, however, with a rolling four-to-eight week cash budget. Update your short-term budget at least monthly. After you lay out your cash flows during the period that you've selected, you can manage your cash much more easily, making intelligent decisions about when to make payments — and when to avoid making them — and other cash management issues.

Managing Your Expenses Rather than Letting Them Manage You

Given that cash flow can be represented by a simple equation — cash in − cash out = cash flow — it's obvious that there are three ways to create positive cash flow:

- Increase cash in
- Decrease cash out
- A combination of the two

In any business, cash out is represented by the business's expenses — things like payroll, rent, office supplies, utilities, computers, postage, benefits, and taxes. By managing your expenses — minimizing them wherever possible and avoiding them when they aren't truly necessary to doing business — you can help create a positive cash flow by decreasing the cash that goes out of your business.

Whenever possible, try deferring your expenses for as long as you can. Ask your vendors for payment terms that enable you to buy now and pay later at no additional charge, or consider renting or leasing the equipment you need rather than buying it. Or, if you need to purchase a new piece of equipment and you can live without it for a few more months, then by all means do so.

Keeping on Top of Your Accounts Receivable

Although managing your expenses — minimizing the cash going out of your business — is important, managing your receivables is equally important. *Accounts receivable* means all the money that your clients and customers owe you for the work that you do for them or the products that you deliver. When your clients aren't paying you for your work when you deliver it, you're creating a *receivable* — an obligation for them to pay you at some point in the future. The time set for payment generally is 30 days after delivery of an invoice, but that date can vary depending on the terms and conditions of your contract or agreement.

Unfortunately, getting all your clients to pay their obligations on time — in the full amounts they owe — can be likened to herding cats. The job is almost impossible, especially in large organizations with a wide variety and large number of clients and customers. But you need to do this job if you want to ensure that your cash flow stays on the positive side rather than the negative side.

Here are a few tips for managing your receivables:

✔ Create a system for tracking your receivables. This system needs to list all outstanding invoices, when and for how much each invoice was issued, and the date by which payment is due. If your company is large and you have many invoices, you may want to focus on invoices for more than a certain amount of money, say $10,000.

✔ Call your customers when invoices are issued to ensure that they are acceptable for payment and to determine the dates by which the customers will pay them.

✔ Call your customers a week before payments are due to ensure that they are on track for payment. If they aren't, you can address any problems before they threaten to delay your receipt of funds.

✔ When a payment is late — by even a day — call your customer to find out why and to determine what can be done to expedite payment.

Encouraging Your Customers to Use Credit Cards

If you're a retailer, you probably already take credit cards for payment and you're familiar with their benefits. While getting paid immediately with cash or a check generally is the best way to run your business, credit cards may be the next best thing, and encouraging your customers to use credit cards whenever possible is probably a good idea. Why? Here are a few reasons:

✔ **You get your money (fairly) fast.** Although cash is faster — you have it in your hand as soon as your customer takes it out of his or her wallet — credit cards aren't too far behind, and they're definitely much faster than those familiar net/30 payment terms. Most card companies will pay you within a couple of days. (If yours doesn't, find one that does!)

✔ **Anyone can do it.** You don't have to sell books or computers or auto parts or other goods to accept credit cards. Consultants accept credit cards, public speakers accept credit cards, and Web sites accept credit cards. Heck, by using a service such as PayPal (www.paypal.com), *anyone* can accept credit cards.

✔ **Customers using credit cards tend to spend more per transaction.** According to industry statistics, credit card users spend 34 percent more money per transaction than people paying with cash. The more your customers spend, the better your cash flow. And the better your cash flow, the better you'll sleep at night.

We have just one little bit of bad news about credit cards: You must pay a fee — typically between 2.5 percent and 5.0 percent of the total transaction amount — to the bank or credit card company that carries your merchant account. But considering the advantages of credit cards, they may be just the ticket for improving your cash flow. Before you settle on a company to handle your merchant account, however, be sure to shop around to get the best deal available. And then calculate the equivalent interest rate for the use of credit cards to be sure that they are creating a positive impact on your financial position rather than a negative one.

Making Sure That Your Invoices Are Right the First Time

You've done a great job for your client — perhaps the best job ever! You schedule your client's payment into your cash flow projections — great news, the cash is going to hit your books just when you need it. Any later and you may be in trouble. You send your invoice for $100,000 and wait. And wait. And wait some more. Finally, you get tired of waiting for the check to arrive. You call your client's accounting department to see whether you can pick up the check in person, because now you really need the money to avert a cash crunch.

There's just one little problem: Your client's accounts payable clerk tells you that your invoice contained a mistake, and payment can't be made until the invoice is corrected. "What?!?" you ask. "Why didn't you tell me that there was a problem?" "Sorry," says the clerk, "it's on my list of things to do, but my first priority is paying vendors whose invoices are correct. It's your job to ensure that your invoices are correct, not mine."

If your invoice is incorrect or contains a mistake or is not in the format that your client or customer requires, you're putting your cash flow at risk. And when you don't catch the mistake and correct it quickly, you may find that getting paid takes far longer than you had anticipated. If your cash flow is tight and you have little slack to allow for payments that arrive later than you anticipate them, take a couple of steps to ensure timely payment:

- ✔ Be sure that your invoices are correct and in the required format (including any required evidence of performance).

- ✔ When you submit your invoice, call the person who's going to handle it and ask him or her to look it over to make sure that it's all right — *before* a problem occurs, not after.

Always be as nice as possible when you're dealing with anyone who has *anything* to do with paying your invoices. Have your salespeople perform the follow up function. If they're on commission based on cash receipts, you can bet that they'll be sure the invoices are correct and that they get paid quickly.

When co-author Peter was the director of administration for a software development firm many years ago, he was in charge of a staff of 13 employees responsible for everything from negotiating contracts to accepting shipments of products to approving invoices for payment. Peter can't count how many times his staff paid the invoice of a vendor who was well liked early — or overlooked minor irregularities — and how many times his staff rewarded a vendor that disrespected the staff for its "attitude problem" by mysteriously losing its invoices or citing minor irregularities as reason for nonpayment.

If your firm's policies — or the policies of the firm with which you're doing business — don't prohibit the giving of gifts, an occasional, strategically placed box of chocolates or fruit basket can go a long way in improving your cash flow.

Invoicing upon Delivery

Unless you're collecting advance payments from your clients and customers for work that you have yet to perform or products that you have yet to deliver, the payment clock that determines when your clients or customers will pay you for performing work or delivering products doesn't start ticking until you deliver an invoice.

To get that clock ticking as soon as possible, be sure to include an invoice when you deliver goods or services to your clients or customers. When you're shipping or delivering a product, include your invoice in the box or packaging. When you're delivering a service, such as repairing a broken computer network or a summary report at the end of a consulting job, bring an invoice with you and hand it to your client right then and there.

If including an invoice along with the delivery of your services or products for some reason isn't practical, be sure to submit one as quickly as possible — make it a priority for your organization. Or, you can require collect on delivery (COD) payment or credit card payment on delivery. Don't forget: The sooner your customers receive your invoices, the sooner those invoices will be paid!

Bonus Step 11! Great Cash Flow Strategies

As if ten great cash flow strategies weren't enough, here are a bunch more! Put these into practice, and your cash flow soon will be the envy of your competitors. The strategies in this first list have a one-time impact.

- Banks have some good cash management systems that enable you to "float" your payments. These can yield up to 5 days of payables.

- Payroll pay dates can be extended to yield more cash — the exact delay can depend on state law. For example, a biweekly payroll can have a pay date as late as 7 days after the last day in the pay period. Many companies pay faster, but when you're tight on cash, extending payroll pay dates is a common legal way to wring out a few more days of cash. And don't allow electronic payment of paychecks — that gives you several more days of float.

✔ When your expenses or sales are seasonal, you sometimes can negotiate level payment plans that help manage cash more smoothly.

✔ Having your customers wire payments to you instead of using the mail can save days in receivables. Sometimes the use of regional lock boxes for collections also can save days.

The strategies that follow have long-term or permanent effects.

✔ Landlords and others often want a security or other type of deposit — money tied up and not available to you. Negotiate away from these by either having deposits refunded after you've established a good payment record or set up a *stand-by* letter of credit with your bank.

✔ Lease or rent equipment whenever you can. Outright purchasing can make a huge dent in your cash flow.

✔ Carefully review your federal tax elections with your CPA before you file your first return. Doing so directly affects how soon you must pay your income taxes. When you have *long-term* contracts or inventories or significant capital equipment, these basic elections can delay the taxes you must pay for years.

✔ Use stock or warrants to pay for some critical items with key suppliers.

Glossary

• •

The business of raising capital is loaded with jargon, inside references, and obscure phraseology. This guide is intended to help you find your way through this thicket of words.

accredited investor: An investor wealthy enough (in terms of specific amounts of assets and/or income) to absorb the high risk of investing in securities that cannot be readily bought and sold on the open market.

after the money: The value of a company *after* it receives a venture capitalist's cash investment.

angel investor: A high-net-worth individual who's willing to make a private-equity investment in an emerging growth company.

barter: The exchange of a product or service for another product or service rather than a cash payment.

before the money: The value of a company *before* it receives a venture capitalist's cash investment.

blue-sky statutes: State laws controlling the sale of securities.

bootstrapping: Finding money and resources by any means possible, including begging, borrowing, bartering, sharing, and leasing everything a company needs

closed-end lease: In a closed-end lease, you owe nothing at the end of the lease term — you can simply walk away, assuming that you've returned the equipment and that it has suffered no damage beyond normal wear and tear.

common stock: Basic form of stock, which conveys a fractional ownership in the company that issued it.

convertible debt: Debt that can be converted into stock at the option of the holder or the issuer.

debt financing: Borrowing money for a fee.

dilution: The lessening of ownership stakes as more stock is issued and sold in later offerings.

due diligence: Checking behind and around statements that someone with an investment opportunity makes to see whether they're accurate. The process by which potential investors fully investigate an investment opportunity before committing resources to buy into it.

EBIDTA: Earnings before interest, depreciation, taxes and amortization, and it specifically excludes capital purchases (plant and equipment) and working capital requirements.

elevator pitch: A brief explanation of an entrepreneur's business plan, presented to potential investors and short enough to be completed in a minute or less. Also known as an *elevator summary*.

equity financing: Selling a piece of a business in exchange for an investment of cash.

exit strategy: Strategy for selling all or a portion of your business, or the stock therein, to compensate yourself for all the years of risk and hard work that have made the business a success.

fair market value: The price at which an interest would change hands between a willing buyer and willing seller, who are adequately informed of the relevant facts and not under any compulsion to buy or sell.

illiquid securities: Stock and other securities that cannot be readily sold and converted into cash.

initial public offering (IPO): The initial offering of an issuer's securities to the public.

investment bank: A securities firm, financial company, or brokerage house that helps companies take new issues to market.

issuer: The company offering its securities for sale.

lease: A contractual arrangement whereby an individual or company that owns specific business equipment or property (the *lessor*) allows another business (the *lessee*) to possess and use the equipment or property in exchange for cash payments or other agreed-upon compensation.

letter of intent (LOI): A nonbinding agreement on the terms and conditions for a merger.

market capitalization: The value of a company on the stock market, *market cap* for short.

merger: The consolidation of one company into another.

net present value: The present value of an investment's future net cash flows, less the amount of the initial investment.

nondisclosure agreement (NDA): An agreement not to disclose confidential company information to unauthorized parties.

open-end lease: In an open-end lease, you pay the difference between the fair market value of the equipment and the residual value established in your lease agreement (only if the fair market value is less than the residual value) if you decide to return the equipment to the lessor at the end of the lease term.

pink sheets: Daily listings of buy and sell prices for over-the-counter stocks not listed on NASDAQ or other major exchanges.

placement agent: A person who raises funds for a company that's in the market for capital.

placement memorandum: The document that details the agreed-to terms and conditions of a private-placement financing.

preferred stock: Stock that gives its owners priority in the payment of dividends or in the event of liquidation of the company.

primary (issuer) transactions: Offerings made directly by the issuer, with proceeds going to the issuer.

prime rate: The interest rate charged by banks to their better and creditworthier customers.

private equity offering: Selling ownership stakes in your business — securities — directly to a small number of individuals or organizations but not to the general public.

prospectus: The selling document for a company's securities in a public offering. This document contains a detailed description of the company's business operations, management, and financial condition.

public shell: A company that went public at some point in the past (usually through the IPO process) but currently exists with few assets and liabilities.

rated debt: Debt that has been judged by an independent rating firm as to its quality, that is, the likelihood that it will be repaid in full and on time.

receivables financing: A short-term loan made against a company's accounts receivable.

registration statement: Form filed with the SEC to request approval for sale of securities to the public.

Regulation D: The regulation that allows exceptions from SEC registration for private equity offerings that meet certain conditions.

Regulation FD (for *fair disclosure*): Regulation requiring the release of important nonpublic information to the public at the same time it is released to securities analysts.

retail brokerage: A brokerage that sells securities primarily in small amounts to individual investors rather than large, institutional investors.

road show: A barnstorming, city-to-city tour by top management and IPO investment bankers that is specifically designed to put you in front of as many decision makers as quickly as possible, generating interest in your new issue.

SEC: The Securities and Exchange Commission — charged with regulating securities transactions in the United States.

secured loan: A loan for which the borrower has pledged collateral. Generally considered less risky than an unsecured loan.

seed investment: The capital required to prove that the concept works — in other words, capital invested prior to the production of a working model or prototype. A preseed investment occurs at an even earlier stage.

trade credit: A common form of financing where vendors provide products or services and allow their customers to pay for them later.

underwriter: An intermediary between an issuer of a security and the investing public, usually an investment bank.

unsecured loan: A loan for which no collateral is pledged. Generally considered riskier than a secured loan, with higher interest rates as a result.

valuation: Assigning a fair market value for a company.

venture capital: Money made available to growing firms by funds (*venture capitalists*) that take a major stake in the company's ownership (and often management) in exchange for their cash.

Index

• •

VC EXPERTS

Expertise and Opportunity in Venture Capital

www.vcexperts.com

This is a special invitation to become a member of the <u>VC Experts</u> community. <u>VC Experts</u> offers a full suite of tools for those interested in Venture Capital, by combining distance learning and reference materials with current industry news from the US and Europe, including weekly commentary on the VC industry from Joe Bartlett and other experts in the field.

"Raising Capital For Dummies" readers receive 20% off!
Save up to $100

Purchase online at <u>invitation.vcexperts.com</u>
(Enter *Promotional Code* "ForDummies")

VC Encyclopedia

The VC Encyclopedia is a complete reference manual on all aspects of venture capital. The online system includes standardized forms and annotations, as well as polls and message boards, which encourage an open dialogue on venture capital. As the community grows, you can find out the latest trends, standard contract terms and the best deal terms for early-stage financing negotiations.

VC University

The VC University offers HTML-formatted classes on the terminology and basics of the term sheet, executive employment agreement, stock purchase agreements, and early-stage company valuation.

Plus, the VC University also contains ten videos covering all aspects of the venture capital field, from the embryo to the IPO. These sessions are delivered via Real Video and Windows Media Player, so they are accessible from any computer on the Internet. The sessions are led by Joe Bartlett and other experienced VC professionals.

Whether you are an Entrepreneur or a practicing VC, these are "must-have" materials. Don't be left behind. Capitalize on our Expertise. Visit <u>www.vcexperts.com</u> today.

Purchase online at <u>invitation.vcexperts.com</u>
(Enter *Promotional Code* "ForDummies")
